HISTORY

OF

TENNESSEE

FROM THE EARLIEST TIME TO THE PRESENT; TOGETHER WITH AN HISTORICAL
AND A BIOGRAPHICAL SKETCH OF CARROLL, HENRY AND
BENTON COUNTIES, BESIDES A VALUABLE FUND
OF NOTES, ORIGINAL OBSERVATIONS,
REMINISCENCES, ETC., ETC.

ILLUSTRATED.

NASHVILLE:
THE GOODSPEED PUBLISHING CO.,
1887.

This volume was reproduced from
An 1887 edition located in the
private Library of Margaret U. Sykes,
Paris, Tennessee

All rights reserved. No part of this publication
may be reproduced, stored in a retrieval system,
transmitted in any form, posted on to the web
in any form or by any means without the
prior written permission of the publisher.

Please direct all correspondence and orders to:

www.southernhistoricalpress.com
or
SOUTHERN HISTORICAL PRESS, Inc.
PO BOX 1267
375 West Broad Street
Greenville, SC   29601
southernhistoricalpress@gmail.com

Originally published: Nashville, 1887
Reprinted with New Material by:
Southern Historical Press, Inc.
New Material Copyright 1978 by
The Rev. Silas Emmett Lucas, Jr.
Easley, SC
ISBN #0-89308-098-5
All rights Reserved.
Printed in the United States of America

CONTENTS.

HISTORY OF TENNESSEE.

CHAPTER I.

	PAGE.
GEOLOGY OF TENNESSEE	13
Area and Boundary of the State	13
Ages, The Geologic	15
Canadian Period, The	17
Coals, The	27
Carboniferous Age, The	22
Crab Orchard Section, The	31
Cretaceous Period, The	22
Cross Mountain Section, The	33
Champlain Period, The	23
Coal of Raccoon District	30
Divisions, The Eight Natural	15
Eastern Iron Region, The	34
Elevations, The Principal	40
Fossils, The Characteristic	36
Glacial Period, The	23
Hamilton Age, The	21
Iron Ore, The	34
Lower Helderberg Period, The	21
Lignitic Period, The	22
Marble Beds, The	39
Metals, The Principal	37
Niagara Period, The	20
Primordial Period, The	16
Recent Period, The	23
Subcarboniferous Period, The	21
Soils, The Various	23
Temperature of the State, The	39
Trenton Period, The	18
Thirteen Tennessee Periods, The	16
Western Iron Region, The	35

CHAPTER II.

THE MOUND-BUILDERS	42
Age of the Mounds	56
Arguments of Judge Haywood	45
Classification of Earthworks	50
Contents of the Mounds, The	53
Carthage Cave, The	54
Evidences of Prehistoric Occupation	42
Fortifications, Etc	51
Location of the Earthworks	49
Mounds of Tennessee, The	51 to 57
Natchez, The	48
Opinion of Bancroft, The	42
Peruvians, The	45
"Stone Fort," The Old	55
Sun Worshipers, The	47
Tribal Resemblances	46
View of Hildreth	44

CHAPTER III.

THE INDIAN TRIBES	57
Avery Treaty, The	77
Battle of Chickasaw Old Field	69
Beloved Town, The	69
Battle of Long Island Flats	73
Battle of Boyd Creek	80
Boundary Established, A New	82
Battle of French Lick	89
Christian's Expediton	76
Chickamaugas, The	79
Chickasaw Treaty of 1786, The	85
Coldwater Expedition, The	90
Cession Treaties, Numerous	95 to 108
Cherokees, The	57
Campaign of Williamson	75
Chickasaws, The	59
Destruction of Indian Towns	65
Expeditions of Sevier	86, 87
Encounter of Untoola and Hubbard	83
Expeditions of Rains	91
English Supremacy and Intrigue	64
Expedition of Col. Grant	68
Earliest Indian Occupation	57
French Trading Stations	62

	PAGE.
"Great Grant" and "Path Deed"	70
Holston Treaty, The	93
Incidents and Anecdotes	74
Killing of the Cavetts, The	94
Massacre of Fort Loudon	63, 66
Massacres upon the Cumberland	89
Nickajack Expedition, The	97
Point Pleasant, Battle of	70
"Pocahontas of the West," The	73
Rutherford's Campaign	75
Shawanees, The	58
Shelby's Campaign against the Lower Towns	80
Sevier's Destructive Campaigns	81
Spanish Influence	90
Traditions of a Former Race	58
Tennessee Soil, First Cession of	61
Treaty of Hopewell, The	84

CHAPTER IV.

SETTLEMENT OF TENNESSEE	108
Brown's Settlement	124
Chisca, The Indian Village	110
Charleville's Trading Station	112
Carter's Valley, Settlement of	124
Daniel Boone	116
Donelson's Journal	129 to 134
Expedition of De Soto	108
French and English Designs	112
Fort Assumption	113
Findley's Excursion	117
French Lick, First Appearance of	123
Fort Loudon, Construction of	114
Henderson's Treaty	124
Hunting Parties, Sundry	116, 117
"Long Hunters," The	121
La Salle and Marquette	111
Results of the Treaty of 1763	118
Regulators and the Scovilites, The	122
Stations on the Cumberland, The	127
Spottswood's Expedition	112
Traders, The French	115
Wood's Tour of Discovery	111
Walker's Expedition	115
Watauga Settlement, The	121
Washington District, Watauga Settlement	125
Washington County, N. C.	126

CHAPTER V.

SETTLEMENT CONCLUDED	135
Affairs on the Cumberland	141
Brown's Disastrous Voyage	144, 145
Continental Land Warrants	139
Clinch-Cumberland Road, The	142, 143
Catalogue of Land Grants	151
Chickasaw Bluffs, The	152
Greene's Reservation	139
Land Companies, The	147 to 150
Military Reservations, The	140
Nashborough	137
Perils on the Cumberland	136
Provisions, How Obtained, Etc	143
Settlers of West Tennessee	154 to 163
Territorial Government, The	146
Transylvania	136
West Tennessee, Settlement of	151
Western Purchase, The	153

CHAPTER VI.

ORGANIZATION	164
Cumberland Compact, The	184 to 188
European Charters, The	164 to 167
Eastern Boundary, The	182
Government of the Notables, The	183
Northern Boundary Question, The	168 to 180
State of Franklin, The	189 to 198
Southern Boundary Question, The	181 to 182
Watauga Association, The	183

CONTENTS.

CHAPTER VII.

	PAGE.
ORGANIZATION CONCLUDED	199
Administration of Gov. Blount	205
Acts of the Convention of 1796	213
Acceptance of the Tennessee Cession	202
Census of Tennessee, The First	211
Constitutional Provisions	224 to 228
Constitutional Convention of 1834, The	223
Cession Act of North Carolina, The	199
Constitutional Convention of 1796, The	212
Cession Deed, The	202
Constitutional Convention of 1870, The	227, 228
General Assembly of the State, The First	219
Legislature of the Territory, The	207 to 210
Pioneer Legislation	221
State Governor, The First	220
State Constitution, The First	214 to 218
Tennessee Admitted to the Union	218
Territorial Government Established, The	203
Territorial Officers, The	203

CHAPTER VIII.

GROWTH AND DEVELOPMENT	229
Agricultural Methods, The Early	229
Census Reports, The	252
Corn Crop, The	233
Cotton Gin, The Purchase of	240
Cotton Culture	239
Fruit Crops, The	233, 251
Fertilizers, The Use of	245
Farmers of Middle Tennessee, The	232
Farmers of East Tennessee, The	230
Hay and the Grasses	242
Hemp, Flax, Sorghum, Etc	244
Live Stock	246
Maple Sugar	245
"Money Crops," The	236
Methods of Agriculture Compared	230
Poultry, Butter, Cheese, Honey, Etc	249
Peanuts, The Growth of	241
Potatoes, Sweet and Irish	235
Rye, Barley, Oats, Buckwheat, Etc	235
Tobacco Crop, The	237
Wheat Crop, The	234

CHAPTER IX.

GROWTH AND DEVELOPMENT CONCLUDED	253
Bureau of Agriculture, Etc	279
Coal Productions, The	265 to 267
Copper Ore, The Mining of	270
Cotton Seed Oil	278
Cotton Goods, The Manufacture of	273
Flour-Milling Industry, The	271
Gunpowder	275
Iron Industries, The	260 to 264
Industrial Development	272
Leather, Boots and Shoes, Etc	276
Lumber Productions and Traffic, The	259
Marble Quarries, The	267 to 270
Paper, The Production of	275
Timber of the State, The	253 to 258
Whisky Products, The Enormous	277, 278
Woolen Goods, The Manufacture of	274

CHAPTER X.

STATE INSTITUTIONS	280
Ancient Order of United Workmen	320
Bureau of Agriculture, Mines, Etc	308
East Tennessee Insane Asylum	293
Grand Army of the Republic	322
Institutions for the Blind	289
Insane Hospital at Nashville, The	291
Jackson's Equestrian Statue	284
Knights of Honor, Grand Lodge	315
Knights of Pythias, Grand Lodge	318
Knights and Ladies of Honor	316
Legion of Honor, Grand Council	320
Masonic Grand Lodge, The	309
Odd Fellows Grand Lodge, The	314
Royal Arcanum, Grand Council	321
State Capitol Located, The	280
State Library, The	286
State House, Construction of the	281 to 284
State Penitentiary, The	294
State Historical Society, The	298
State Medical Society, The	302

	PAGE.
State Board of Health, The	305
Tennessee Deaf and Dumb School, The	287
Tennessee Agricultural and Horticultural Society	307
West Tennessee Insane Asylum	294

CHAPTER XI.

STATE INSTITUTIONS CONCLUDED	323
Counties, The Formation of	361, 362
Commercial Highways	335
Funding of the Debt, The	328 to 330
Gubernatorial Election Returns	356
Internal Improvement Systems, The	337
Presidential Election Returns	358, 359
Population of the State, Aggregate	360, 361
Receipts and Expenditures, The Early	323
Railroads, The Sale of	339
Receipts and Expenses, Catalogue of	340
Repudiation, The Question of	329
Railway Enterprises	340 to 348
Railway Commission, The	348
State Indebtedness, The First	326
Steam-boat Navigation	348
State Bonds, Total Issue of	357
State Officers, Catalogue of	350 to 356
State Banks, The	331 to 335
State Debt Proper, The	327 to 329
Treasury of the State, The	324

CHAPTER XII.

BENCH AND BAR OF TENNESSEE	363
Courts of the Watauga Settlement	363
Courts on the Cumberland	367
Circuit Courts, The	376
Courts of the Constitution of 1796	368
Courts of the Constitution of 1834	375
Courts of the Constitution of 1870	378
Impeachment, Cases of	372
Professional Character of Distinguished Members of the Bench and Bar of Tennessee	382 to 412
Territorial Courts, The	368
United States Courts, The	380
Washington and Sullivan County Courts	364

CHAPTER XIII.

EDUCATIONAL HISTORY	413
Colleges Chartered	416
County Academies, The	420
Constitutional Educational Provisions	426
Common School Convention, The	428
Colored Education	434
Common Schools, The	435
Cumberland College	442
Endowment Funds, The	415
Educational Systems Compared	420
East Tennessee College	447
Educational Tax, The First	422
Educational Statistics	441
Graded Schools, The	430
Gigantic Problem of 1865, The	431
Provincial Schools, The	413
Public Schools Established	426
Peabody Fund, The	433
State Colleges Founded	418
School Lands, Disposal of the	423
Superintendents of Public Instruction	428
School Officers, Duties of	438
State Normal School, The	445
Special School Funds	439
State Board of Education	447
School Funds, Creation of the	424
Schools in Tennessee, The First	415
Tennessee Industrial College	451
West Tennessee College	453

CHAPTER XIV.

THE EARLY WARS	454
British, Battles with the	456
Charleston, The Capture of	460
Creeks, The War with the	461
Entochopco, Battle of	464
Jackson's First Battle	462
Jackson, Activity of	470
King's Mountain, Battle of	458
Mexican War, The	473

CONTENTS

	PAGE.
New Orleans, The Movement upon	467
New Orleans, Jackson's Victory at	468
Seminole War, The	469
Tories of East Tennessee, The	454
Talladega, Battle of	463
Tohopeka, Battle of	465
Texas-Mexican War, The	472
Tennessee Troops Sent to Mexico	474 to 476
War of 1812, The	461
Wahoo Swamp, Battle of	472

CHAPTER XV.

FEDERAL MILITARY HISTORY	477
Burnside's Occupation of East Tennessee	490
Bridge Burners Ordered Hanged	488
Campbell's Station, Battle of	491
Confederate Movements	486
Fishing Creek, Battle of	488
Federal Troops Furnished, Total	497
General Movements	489
Greenville Union Convention, The	481
Issue Joined, The	483
Knoxville Union Convention, The	479
Knoxville, Siege of	492
Longstreet vs. Burnside	491
Loyalty of East Tennessee	477
Morgan, The Killing of	495
Regimental Sketches	497 to 512
Skirmishes, The Concluding	496
Union Leaders, The	478
Union Regiments Organized	484

CHAPTER XVI.

CONFEDERATE MILITARY HISTORY	513
Army Bill, The	522
Arms, Condition and Quantity	515
Aid Societies	539
Advance to Columbus, The	543
Army Rolls	595 to 617
Belmont, Battle of	545
Burnside in East Tennessee	558
Call to Arms, The	518
Confederate Government, The	535
Chickamauga, Battle of	556
Confederate Line, Danger to the	547
Confederate Forces, Aggregate	546
Defensive Measures, Extent of	536 to 539
Election Returns of June 8	532 to 534
Evacuation of Middle Tennessee	550
February Convention, The	514
Fishing Creek, Battle of	547
Fort Henry, Fall of	548
Franklin, Battle of	560
Fort Donelson, Fall of	548
Georgia Campaign, The	559
Legislature Convened, The	518
Militia, Reorganization of the	515
Military League, The	528
Militia Transferred to the Confederacy	540
Memphis, Surrender of	553
Military Appointments	530
Murfreesboro, Battle of	555
Missionary Ridge, Battle of	557
Neutrality Question, The	544
Nashville, Federal Occupation of	549
Nashville, Battle of	560
Ordinance of Secession, The	520
Ordnance, The Manufacture of	541
Perryville, Battle of	554
Position of the General Assembly	516
Reserve Corps, The	542
Rock Castle Hills, Battle of	544
Regimental Sketches	561 to 595
State Sovereignty and Secession	513
Shiloh, Battle of	550
Secession Overwhelmingly Favored	517
Tennessee Admitted to the Confederacy	535
Troops, Call for and Refusal to Furnish	517

CHAPTER XVII.

TENNESSEE LITERATURE	617
Brownlow	622
Bright	628
Brunner	625
Baskerville	625
Baldwin	625
Brown	628
Chattanooga Press, The	631

	PAGE.
Crockett	623
Carr	625
Cross	629
Fitzgerald	625
French	627
Geological Authors	623
Guild	624
Graves (Joseph C.)	624
Graves (Adelia C.)	627
Gilchrist	629
Harrison	624
Haywood	618
Journalism	629
Ketchum	627
Knoxville Press, The	629
Law	628
Lindsley (Phillip)	624
Lindsley (J. Berrien)	619
Legal Authors	626
Murfree	626
Memphis Press, The	637
McAdoo	629
McAnally	621
McFerrin	621
Martin	622
McTyeire	622
Medical Authors	622
Maury	623
Nelson	621, 623
Nashville Press, The	632
Putnam	619
Pearson	621
Ramsey	618
Redford	624
Ryan	622
Rivers	622
Summers	625
Tannehill	620

CHAPTER XVIII.

RELIGIOUS HISTORY	638
Arminianism, The Creed of	648
Buildings Erected, The first	646
Baptist Church, The	687
Church and State, Union of	640
Camp-Meeting, The first	650
Creeds, Formation of the	658
Cumberland Presbyterian Church, The	658
Christian Church, The	700
Catholic Church, The	704
Colored Churches, The	708
Episcopal Church, The	694
Irreligion Punished	641
Jerks, The	651 to 655
Jerks, The Cause of the	655 to 657
Jewish Church, The	706
Lutheran Church, The	705
Methodist Church, The	662
Methodist Church South	676
Methodist Statistics	676 to 679
Methodist Book Concern, The	679
Preaching in Tennessee, The first	645
Presbyterian Church, The	680
Revival, The Great	649 to 654
Religious Intolerance	639
Separation of Church and State	644
Slavery Divides the Church	667 to 676
University of the South, The	699

CHAPTER XIX.

BIOGRAPHICAL CHAPTER	708
Blount, Gov. William	716
Bell, Hon. John	733
Brownlow, Gov. William G	740
Carroll, Gov. William	719
Crockett, Col. David	728
Forrest, Gen. N. B	742
Grundy, Hon. Felix	729
Haywood, Judge John	714
Houston, Gov. Sam	724
Jackson, President Andrew	720
Johnson, President Andrew	745
Johnson, Hon. Cave	735
Polk, President James K	738
Robertson, Gen. James	712
Sevier, Gov. John	708
White, Hon. Hugh L	732
Zollicoffer, Gen. Felix K	747

CONTENTS.

CHAPTER XX.

	PAGE.
POLITICAL HISTORY	749
Administrations of Gov. Sevier	751
Abolitionism, Growth of	758
Abolishment of Imprisonment for Debt	764
"Arnell Bill," The	780
Bill of 1831	756
"Brownlow's Legislature"	780
Campaigns of 1844 and 1848	771–772
Campaigns of 1872 and 1876	789–791
Dresser's Arrest and Punishment	757
Elections	765–767
Free Negroes	755
Franchise Measures	782–786
Free Negro Bill of 1859–60	758
Houston's Governorship	761
Impeachment of Senator Blount	750, 751
Industrial Depression and Revival	753
Important Political Events	769–771
"Instructing Resolutions," The	768
Jackson's Official Career	760
Ku Klux Klans	785
Later Political Events	789–796
Nullification	762–763
New Constitution, The	787
Politics of the "Fifties"	773
Pro-Slavery Movements	757
Public Polity, Questions of	759
Restoration of Tennessee	781
Resumption of Federal Authority	777
Resignation of Senators Foster and White	768
Spanish Controversy, The	749–750
Slavery Question, The	754
Slave Legislation, Early	755
Secession	773–777
State Debt, The	793
War of 1812, The	752

CARROLL COUNTY.

	PAGE.
CARROLL COUNTY	797
Bench and Bar	804–806
Churches	812–813
County Court	800
County Officers	802–803
Huntingdon	808–809
Industries, The Early	798
Land Warrants	798
Military Record	806–808
McKenzie	809–810
Organization of the County	799
Productions	799
Public Buildings	801
Paupers	802
Railroads	802
Smaller Towns	810
Settlement	797
Streams, Timber	797
Schools	811
Taxation	803

HENRY COUNTY.

	PAGE.
HENRY COUNTY	813
Attorneys and Judges	824
Boundary, Area, etc	813
Buildings, etc	819
Creation of the County	817
County Seat Located	818–819
Courts, The	821–825
County Officers	820–821
County Court, The	817
Education	830
Entries of Land	816
Mills, Stores, etc., Early	815
Prehistoric Earthworks	814
Productions, Statistics, etc	816–817
Paris	826–829
Rattlesnakes	815
Railroads	820
Religion	830–832
Smaller Towns	829
Settlement	814–816
Streams, Soil, etc	814
War Record	825–826

BENTON COUNTY.

	PAGE.
BENTON COUNTY	832
Bench and Bar	840–841
Big Sandy	839–840
Boundary, Area, etc	832
County Court, The	834–835
Courthouses and Jails	835
County Seat Established	837
Churches	845–846
Camden	837–838
Drainage, Timber, etc	833
Formation of the County	834
Milling Enterprises, Early	834
Military Account	842–844
Officers of the County	835–836
Settlers, etc	833–834
Schools and Teachers	844–845

BIOGRAPHICAL APPENDIX.

	PAGE.
Benton County	935
Carroll County	847
Henry County	888

PORTRAITS, MAPS AND VIEWS.

		PAGE.
Aboriginal Map	...Frontispiece	
Blind Asylum	between	124, 125
Bell, John	"	732, 733
Blount, William	"	716, 717
Brownlow, W. G.	"	508, 509
Chapel, University of the South	"	348, 349
Chickamauga	"	556, 557
Crockett, David	"	156, 157
Donelson	"	476, 477
Deaf and Dumb Asylum	"	268, 269
Franklin	"	588, 589
Grundy, Felix	"	380, 381
Insane Asylum, West Tenn	"	140, 141
Insane Asylum, East Tenn	"	92, 93
Jackson's Statue	"	284, 285
Jackson, Andrew	"	460, 461
Johnson, Andrew	"	636, 637
Johnson Cave	"	668, 669
Murfreesboro	"	572, 573
Missionary Ridge	"	492, 493
Nashville	"	604, 605
Normal School	"	428, 429
Polk, James K	"	396, 397
Robertson, James	"	76, 77
Shiloh	"	540, 541
State Capitol	"	28, 29
Sevier, John	"	220, 221
Thompson Hall, University of the South	"	316, 317
Tennessee University	"	444, 445
University of the South	"	700, 701
View on Emery River	"	44, 45
View on Falls Creek	"	188, 189

CARROLL COUNTY.

CARROLL COUNTY lies on the dividing ridge between the Tennessee and Mississippi Rivers. It is bounded north by Weakley and Henry Counties, east by Benton and Decatur, south by Henderson and Madison, west by Gibson, and has an area of about 650 square miles. The eastern portion is drained by the Big Sandy River and its numerous tributaries. This river flows through the county in a northerly direction, and thence to its junction with the Tennessee. The central and western portions are drained by the Obion River (which flows to the Mississippi) and its tributaries, Beaver Creek, Crooked Creek and Rutherford Fork. In the western and northwestern portions of the county the surface of the country is gently undulating, while in the eastern and southeastern portions it is somewhat broken and hilly. The soil is generally a clay loam mixed with sand, and the subsoil is a reddish clay. With proper cultivation the land produces well. The timbers are the oak in its varieties, hickory, poplar, gum, beech etc. There are numerous springs, but for family use the people generally depend upon wells and cisterns.

The first settlements in the county were made at McLemoresville and Buena Vista about the year 1820. R. E. C. Dougherty, at whose house the county was organized, held the land office for West Tennessee at McLemoresville as early as 1820. The first entry of land at this office, was made December 6, 1820, by David Gillespie. Other early settlers in the western part of the county were Dr. S. Y. Bigham, Rev. William Bigham, David Marshall, Robert Gilbert who cleared the site of McLemoresville, Rev. Abner Cooper, Rev. Reuben Burrow, Revs. James and Robert Hurt, Reddick Hillsman, William Harris, Lewis Demoss and Nathan Fox. James Hampton, Wm. Horton, Moses Roberts, W. A. Crider and son R. H. Crider (who is still living), and Nathan Nesbit and son Wilson (the latter still living), and Samuel Rogers were among the first settlers in the vicinity of Buena Vista, and elsewhere in the eastern part of the county. The first settlers in the vicinity of Huntingdon were Samuel Ingram, John Crockett (father of W. G. Crockett now of Huntingdon), James H. Gee, Wm. A. Thompson Thomas Ross, John Gwin, Robert Murray and others. Among the early settlers in the vicinity of McKenzie were J. M. Gilbert (the present mayor of that town, who is now over eighty-six years of age), Ambrose Dudley, Thomas and Wm. Hamilton, Elam Cashon, Green Bethel, Wm. Rogers and John

Green. Later came James and Richard Cole, Stephen Pate, John McKenzie and others. As the organization of the county took place almost immediately after the first settlements were made, it should be borne in mind that every person hereinafter named in connection with the organization of the county and of the courts were early settlers, Large tracts of the most valuable lands of the county were entered by the location of North Carolina military land warrants, and owned by non-residents. Mimucan Hunt & Co. held such warrants for twenty tracts of land, each containing 5,000 acres. In September, 1794, Mr. Hunt conveyed to Isaac Roberts five of said tracts, 25,000 acres, all lying on Beaver Creek in Carroll County, for Mr. Roberts' share for locating the land warrants, and obtaining the grants from the State for the aforesaid twenty 5,000-acre tracts. These lands were all located west of the Tennessee River and largely in Carroll County. In January, 1821, Dr. Thomas Hunt, executor of the will of Mimucan Hunt, then deceased, conveyed to Thomas H., Jesse, Samuel and Nathan Benton, the interest in said lands belonging to their father, Jesse Benton of North Carolina, all of which appears of record in the register's office at Huntingdon. The Indians left the county about the time the settlers appeared. But the unbroken forest was then infested with bears, wolves, panthers, deer, wildcats, the smaller wild animals, and snakes. It is said that the reputation this country then had in North Carolina, was "fifty bushels of frogs to the acre, and snakes enough to fence the land." The wild animals destroyed many of the domestic animals of the early settlers, but they were hunted and subdued until all of the more destructive ones have become extinct. The first bridge built in the county was McKee's bridge on the Big Sandy. In 1822, and prior thereto, there were no mills in the county, and the first settlers had to go to Humphreys County to get their milling done, and family supplies, such as salt, coffee, etc, were then brought from Reynoldsburg on the Tennessee River. The first gristmill in West Tennessee, was built in Carroll County by Isaac Blount on Blount Creek, on the site of the mill since owned by Joshua Butler. In March, 1824, Wm. Harris and Reddick Hillsman obtained leave of the county court to build a mill on Reedy Creek, and John Stockard was granted leave to build one on the same creek. Prior to this the same privilege had been granted to one Green, on Hollow Rock Creek. About the same time R. E. C. Dougherty built a mill on Clear Creek. James Shields erected the first cotton-gin in the county, on a place near Buena Vista. The first will probated in the county was that of David Clark, deceased, probated in June, 1824. Andrew Neely was the first infant ward and John S. Neely the first guardian. Wm. Roberts, called

Bit Nose Bill, was the first man married in the county. About 1831 the Huntingdon turnpike leading to Jackson was constructed. For the years 1821 and 1822 the counties of Gibson and Dyer were territorially attached to Carroll, and for 1823 Gibson alone,

The raising of cotton was begun by the early settlers, and it has always been the staple production of the farmers. Grains and vegetables have been raised for home consumption, while cotton has been raised for the market. Tobacco to some extent has always been, and continues to be raised, in the northern part of the county. The people are industrious and generous, primitive in their habits, and manufacture and wear a great deal of home-made clothing. The United States census report for 1880 gives the agricultural products of the county as follows: Indian corn, 1,018,415 bushels; oats, 37,694 bushels; wheat, 88,396 bushels; hay, 1,131 tons; cotton, 10,505 bales; Irish potatoes, 9,377 bushels; sweet potatoes, 25,099 bushels; tobacco, 69,167 pounds. And the live stock was enumerated as follows: horses and mules, 7,428; cattle, 10,754; sheep, 7,166; hogs, 35,398. In 1860 the population of Carroll County was white, 13,339; colored, 4,098. In 1880 the population was white, 16,524; colored, 5,579, the increase of the white population for the twenty years being 3,185, and of the colored 1,481, the per centum of increase of the former being nearly twenty-four, and of the latter a little over thirty-six.

The county of Carroll was organized by an act of the General Assembly of the State of Tennessee, passed November 7, 1821, which provided that a new county, to be called Carroll, should be established within the following bounds, to-wit: "Beginning on the west boundary of Humphreys County,* at the southeast corner of Henry; running thence west with the south boundary of said county to the southwest corner of Henry County; thence south parallel with the range line to a point two and a half miles south of the line dividing the Ninth and Twelfth Districts; thence east parallel with the sectional line in the Ninth District; thence north to the northeast corner of Range 2, Section 11, in said Ninth District; thence east with the district line to the west boundary of Perry County;† thence northwardly with the west boundary of Perry and Humphreys Counties, to the beginning." The act also provided that the court of pleas and quarter sessions should be held on the second Mondays of March, June, September and December of each year, at the house of R. E. C. Dougherty at McLemoresville until otherwise provided by law. By a subsequent act passed November 21, 1821, Sterling Brewer of Dickson County, James Fentress of Montgomery County, and Abram

---
*Now the west line of Benton County.
†Now the west line of Decatur County.

Maury of Williamson County, were appointed commissioners to fix on a place as near the center of the county as an eligible site could be procured, within three miles of the center thereof, for the seat of justice. In accordance with said act the first bench of justices of the peace consisting: of John Gwin, Edward Gwin, Senator Mark R. Roberts, Samuel Ingram, John Stockard, Thomas Hamilton, Samuel A. McClary, Banks W. Burrow, Daniel Barecroft, and John Bone, commissioned as such by Gov. Carroll, met on the 11th of March, 1822, at the house of R. E. C. Dougherty at McLemoresville, and organized the first county court, then known as the court of pleas and quarter sessions, by electing John Gwin as chairman. The first entry on the minutes of the court following the caption, read as follows: "Ordered that the county tax be equal to the State tax, except on white and black polls. That each white poll be taxed equal to one hundred acres of land, and black polls equal to two hundred acres of land. And that James A. McClary take a list of the taxable property south of Rutherford Fork of the Obion River, and Thomas Hamilton a list of all north of the South Fork of the said river; John Stockard a list of all west of the dividing ridge dividing the waters of Sandy and Obion Rivers and between the South Fork and Rutherford Fork of the Obion; John Brown a list of all east of said ridge and north of Sandy Bridge, and Samuel Ingram a list of the property south of said bridge and east of said ridge." On the second day of the term the following county officers were elected: Sion Rogers, sheriff; Littleton W. White, register; Wm. Adams, ranger; Banks W. Burrow, trustee; John S. Neely, coroner, and John McKee, George Sevier and Wm. Barecroft, constables. And thus the organization of the county was completed.

At the June term, 1822, Banks W. Burrow, Thomas A. Thompson John Stockard, Samuel Ingram and Mark R. Roberts were appointed commissioners to lay out the county seat and superintend the sale of the lots and the erection of the public buildings. Nathan Nesbit was subsequently added to said committee. Then came Sterling Brewer and James Fentress, two of the commissioners appointed by the General Assembly, and reported that they had chosen for the site of the seat of justice, a tract of land belonging to the heirs of Mimucan Hunt, and lying on the north bank of Beaver Creek. The title of this tract, consisting of fifty acres, was not obtained until July 21, 1823, when it was obtained by said commissioners from Thomas Hunt, executor of the will of Mimucan Hunt, of North Carolina. The first courthouse, built in 1822, was a small log cabin, without a floor, erected where the present one now tands, and Nathan Nesbit, chairman of the court of pleas and quarter sessions, blazed his way through the forest from his residence, five miles east of Huntingdon, to the county seat, carrying with him his cross-cut saw, with which he sawed the door out of the new court house, and entered therein and opened the first court held at Huntingdon, December 9, 1822. At this term the jurors of the court brought their provisions with them and camped out. The town of Huntingdon was surveyed and platted by James H. Gee, under the supervision of the commissioners appointed to lay out the town. And at the March term, 1824, of the court the following allowances were made to the surveyor and commissioners, to-wit: "James H. Gee, for 5 days' services, at four dollars per day, $20; two chain-carriers, for five days' services, $1.50 per day, $15; for making 480 posts for the lots, $12; for whiskey and paper at the sale of lots, $10; Nathan Nesbit, 24 days as commissioner, $72; John Stockard, 18 days as commissioner, $54; Samuel Ingram, 24 days as commissioner, $72; Thomas A. Thompson, 20 days as commissioner, $60; Banks W. Burrow, 4 days as commissioner, $12." At the December term, 1823, the name of the county seat, which up to that time had been called Huntsville, was changed to Huntingdon. They were anxious to retain the first syllable, and thereupon James H. Gee, who was a musician as well as a surveyor, and who was fond of the old tune Huntingdon, suggested that name and it was adopted. The sale of the lots, the date of which the records do not show, must have taken place prior to March 10, 1823, as evidenced by the record of a deed of that date from the commissioners of Huntingdon to John Crockett for Lot 16. There were 117 lots and the public square in the original plat of the town. At the March term, 1824, of the court of pleas and quarter sessions commissioners were appointed to let the job of clearing the public square, and Jack Aspy was awarded the contract.

The first courthouse, heretofore described, was sold in 1824 to John Crockett who moved it away and used it for a kitchen. It was replaced that year by a frame house 20x24 feet, This stood until about 1830, when the third court house, 30x50 feet, was built of brick. John Parker and Jacob Bledsoe built the foundation, and George and John Simmons were the brick masons, and Joel R. Smith the carpenter. The fourth and present courthouse was completed in 1844. Joel R. Smith and Thomas Banks were the contractors. The rock for the foundation was hauled from Benton County. The brick work was sub-contracted to Wm. S. New for one cent per brick actual count. Mr. New in fulfilling his part of the contract lost heavily. The house cost about $12,000. It is a two-story brick structure, with two offices and a court room on each floor.

The second courthouse was sold to Robert Murray and moved to his lot east of the public square and used as a warehouse. The first jail, erected in 1824, stood nearly opposite from the present one. It was a small hewed-log cabin, from which the prisoners frequently escaped. The second jail was built by Samuel Ingram, in the west part of town. It is now used for a residence. The present jail and jailor's residence combined was erected in 1875, under the supervision of J. P. Wilson, W. B. Grizzard, G. W. Humble, A. R. Hall, W. E. Mebane, Alfred Bryant and L. A. Williams. It is a commodious two-story brick building, containing five cells for prisoners, and altogether cost $11,000. The poor farm, consisting of 134 acres, was purchased in 1852 from Thomas Butler. The buildings were improved in 1877 and later, by removing the old log cabins and erecting in their stead neat frame cottages. The farm was enlarged in 1886, by the purchase from W. O. Davis of 104 acres of timber land adjoining it. The inmates of the poor asylum average about thirty in number, and appropriations are made by the county court for the support of about forty poor persons who reside with their friends throughout the county. The poor of Carroll County are well cared for.

The Nashville, Chattanooga, & St., Louis Railroad was completed through the county soon after the close of the civil war. It has stations within the county at Hollow Rock, Huntingdon and McKenzie. The Memphis & Louisville Railroad was completed through the county in 1860. It has stations within the county at McKenzie, Trezevant and Atwood. The following is a list of county officers with dates of service: County court clerks—Edward Gwin, 1822–36; George Hern, 1836–40; Young W. Allen, 1840–52; Wm. H. Graves, 1852–68; Cyrus Wilson, 1868–70; W. H. Eason, 1870–78; Elijah Falkner, 1878–86; J. C. R. McCall, 1886. Sheriffs: Sion Rodgers, 1822–24; Thomas A. Thompson, 1824–25 (died before close of his term); Sion Rodgers, 1825–30; James Latimer, 1830–32; Thomas Banks, 1832–36; Andrew Neely, 1836–38; John Norman, 1838–44; Jeremiah T. Rust, 1844–48; John H. Boyd, 1848–52; Geo. W. Holaday, 1852–58; Alfred Bryant, 1858–62; John Norman, 1862–64; Joseph A. Johnson, 1864–66; James M. Neely, 1866–70; Alfred Bryant, 1870–74; E. W. Williams, 1874–78; J. F. Leach, 1878–82; E. E. Pate, 1882–84; F. C. Sanders, 1884–86 and re-elected. Registers: Littleberry W. White, 1822–27; H. H. Brown, 1827–32; Thomas A. Hawkins, 1832–40; John R. Clark, 1840–44; Martin Dill, 1844–48; Nathan Williams, 1848–52; Benj. F. Harrison, 1852–56; George L. Harris, 1856–63; J. H. Noell, 1863–68; Joseph McCracken, 1868–74; J. W. Walters, 1874–78; E. G. Ridgeley, 1878–82; J. W. Walters, 1882–86; S. A. Brown, 1886. Trustees; Banks W. Burrow, 1822–

28, and perhaps to 1836; Mathews Bigham, 1836–42; China Wilder, 1842–52; Thomas Gray, 1852–54; Pleasant G. Wright, 1854–58; James N. Gardner, 1858–62, Wm. Harrison, 1862–70; James S. Ramsey, 1870–78; J. F. Rogers, 1878–86; A. E. Hastings, 1886. Circuit court clerks: Benjamin B. McCampbell, 1822–40; James M. Henderson, January to August, 1840; Joel R. Smith, 1840–44; John Norman, 1844–56; B. F. Harrison, 1856–70; W. R. Grizzard, 1870–82; C. P. Priestley, 1882–84; A. E. Hastings, 1884–86; A. W. Hawkins, 1886. State senators: Henry H. Brown, 1823; James R. McMeans, 1826; John D. Love, 1829; Robert Murray, 1831; James L. Totton, 1835; Robert E. C. Dougherty, 1837; Valentine Sevier, 1839; Isaac J. Roach, 1847; Beverly S. Allen, 1849; M. R. Hill, 1851; A. Benton, 1853; Isaac J. Roach, 1857; V. S. Allen, 1859; John Norman, 1865; Wm. H. Hall, 1869; J. M. Coulter, 1873; M. D. L. Jordan, 1875; A. G. Hawkins, 1877; L. M. Beckerdite, 1879; S. F. Rankin, 1881; James P. Wilson, 1883; John H. Farmer, 1885. Representatives in lower house of the Legislature: David Crockett, 1823; Duncan McIver, 1826; Joel R. Smith, 1833; A. M. Cardwell, 1837; Yancey Bledsoe, 1839; A. P. Hall, 1845; Beverly S. Allen, 1847; Granville C. Hurt, 1851; J. W. Wilson, 1855; J. B. Algee, 1857; J. D. Porter, Jr., 1859; J. M. Martin, 1867; B. A. Enloe, 1869; T. B. Brooks, 1873; L. L. Hawkins, 1877; J. R. McKinney, 1885.

The aggregate amount of county taxes charged upon the duplicate of Carroll County for the year 1825, three years after the organization, was as follows: "196,932 acres of land, at $64\frac{3}{4}$ cents per each hundred acres, $1,353.87; 60 town lots, at $62\frac{1}{2}$ cents each, $37.50; 421 free polls, at $12\frac{1}{2}$ cents each, $52.62; 245 black polls, at 25 cents each, $61.25; 9 stud horses, $21.50. Total, $1,526.75." The State taxes charged in 1824 amounted to $266.07. Presuming that a like sum for State purposes was charged on the duplicate of 1825, and added to the $1,526.75 of county taxes for that year, the amount for both State and county would be $1,792.82. It will be interesting to compare the foregoing with the recapitulation of the duplicate of the county for the year 1886, which is as follows:

Number of town lots, 610; valued at	$ 346,064
Number of acres of land,—; valued at	2,172,067
Personal property, valued at	91,716
Other property, valued at	4,935
Total taxable property	$ 2,614,782

The taxes charged on the total value of taxable property and on 3,456 polls are as follows, to wit: State tax, $7,844.34; county tax, $9,992.95; school tax, $13,448.95; road tax, $1,876.08. Total tax, $33,162.32.

At the second term of the court of pleas and quarter sessions, held in June, 1822, William Arnold, Robert Hughes, Will Stoddart, Archibald C. Hall and Thomas Taylor were admitted and sworn as attorneys to practice in said court. At the same time William Arnold produced his commission from the governor and was sworn as solicitor general of the Thirteenth Solicitorial District. At the next term of said court, September, 1822, John C. Bowen, John McBride, Peter Honnell, David Crockett, the famous hunter, and Hezekiah McVale appeared, and each made oath to the killing of a certain number of wolves, and were allowed the usual bounty for destroying those destructive animals.

Then came Nathan Nesbit, John Stockard, Samuel Ingram, Robert Jamison and Enoch Enochs, commissioners previously appointed to divide an estate of 5,000 acres belonging to the heirs of Isaac Roberts, deceased, and submitted their report in full, which was confirmed, and each was allowed $4 per day for nine days' services, and James H. Gee, the surveyor, was allowed $6.50 per day for ten days' services, all to be paid by said heirs in proportion to their respective interests. The names of the men composing the first grand jury in this court were Samuel Woods, Robert Algee, Joseph Dixon, John Kelough, Lewis Demoss, Stephen Warren, William Patton, Thomas Finley, John Martin, Abram White, Henry Rogers and Peter Honnell. They were sworn and charged at the September term, 1822, and after deliberation they returned into court a "bill of indictment against William Robinson and Hawkins Wormack for an affray," and a presentment against Edward Gwin, the clerk of the court, for an assault and battery "on the body of a woman slave, the property of Samuel McCorkle." At the June term, 1823, David Crockett was indicted for an assault, and upon being tried he made his own defense and the verdict of the jury was "not guilty." At the same term the fare at taverns was established as follows: "Breakfast, 25 cents; dinner, $37\frac{1}{2}$ cents; supper, 25 cents; lodging, $12\frac{1}{2}$ cents; whiskey, per half pint, $12\frac{1}{2}$ cents; per pint, 25 cents; per quart, $37\frac{1}{2}$ cents; feeding horse, 25 cents; keeping horse per night, 50 cents; night and day, 75 cents; man and horse per day, $1.50."

William Anderson, James H. Russell, James R. McMeans, James K. Chalmers, John L. Allen and M. A. Q. McKenzie were all admitted in 1823 as attorneys to practice law. The last term of the court of pleas and quarter sessions was held in March, 1836, and the first term of the county court under the constitution of 1834, was held in May, 1836. This court was composed of thirty-four justices of the peace, elected by the people, and was organized by appointing Samuel Ingram as chairman. From that year the county court continued to hold its regular sessions until December, 1863, when it suspended business, on account of the war, until July 3, 1865, when it was reorganized under Gov. Brownlow's administration. It now consists of fifty-three justices of the peace, with Judge G. W. Humble, who has been the presiding officer as judge ever since 1872, and prior to that date he presided over the court for many years as chairman thereof.

The first term of the circuit court was held at the house of R. E. C. Dougherty, at McLemoresville, beginning on Monday, April 1, 1822, with Hon. Joshua Haskell, judge, presiding. Benjamin B. McCampbell was appointed clerk, and Edward Gwin, Samuel Woods, John Gwin, Samuel McCorkle, Enoch Enochs, David Moore, Jonathan Dawson, Lewis Demoss, Edward Busey, John Stockard, Levi Woods, James H. Gee and John Komez were sworn and charged as grand jurors. This was the first grand jury empaneled in the county. Then came John W. Cook, Robert Hughes and Alex B. Bradford and were admitted and sworn as attorneys to practice in said court. At the September term, 1823, John Montgomery was prosecuted by the State for an "affray," whereupon Howell Ward, Julius Webb, Walter Connell, Wilson Lightfoot, Mathis Brigham, David Robison, Edward Busey, Theophilus Morgan, Jesse Walker, Nathan Nesbit, and Elijah Wheelis were empaneled and sworn to try the prisoner, which they did upon the law and the evidence, and returned a verdict of "not guilty." This was the first petit jury empaneled in the county, and the trial was the first criminal prosecution in the circuit court. During the war period this court suspended business from April 1862, until August, 1865, when it was reorganized, with Hon. L. L. Hawkins as judge thereof.

Only two persons have been hanged for the crime of murder in Carroll County. The first was Frank Oliver, colored, for the murder of a widow lady by the name of Rumley. After trial and conviction he was executed on the gallows in May, 1847, in the presence of 10,000 spectators. The other was Charley Phillips, colored, for the murder of Frank Prince, colored. After trial and conviction he was executed on the gallows in July, 1884. This execution was private, as provided by late statute.

The chancery court was established at Huntingdon about the year 1835, for all of West Tennessee. The records thereof having been destroyed during the civil war, the exact date is not given. As fast as chancery courts were established in other counties, the territory over which this court held jurisdiction grew less until finally it was limited to that of Carroll County. Pleasant M. Miller, of Jackson, Tenn., is said to have been the first chancellor. He was succeeded by George W.

Gibbs, Milton Brown of Jackson, Andrew McCampbell of Paris, Calvin Jones of Somerville, and Stephen C. Pavatt of Camden, Tenn., the latter being chancellor at the beginning of the civil war. This court suspended business from 1862 until February, 1866, when it was reorganized, with Robert H. Rose as chancellor, and S. W. Hawkins, clerk and master. Chancellor Rose was succeeded by James W. Dougherty, and he by John Somers, who was succeeded in 1886 by A. G. Hawkins, the present chancellor. Joel R. Smith was the first clerk and master, and the following gentlemen have been his successors in that office, in the order here named: Henry Strange, Napoleon Priest, who died during his term; J. P. Priestley, who held the office when the war began; S. W. Hawkins and J. P. Priestley, the present incumbent, who has held the office ever since 1870. Among the distinguished early resident attorneys of Carroll County were Chancellor Milton Brown, Thomas Jennings and Berry Gillespie. Later came John McKernan, Benjamin C. Totton, Chancellor Stephen C. Pavatt, William and J. W. Dougherty, Josiah Hubbard, N. B. Burrow, V. S. and B. S. Allen, none of whom now remain. Then came the Hawkinses, all of whom still remain except Col. Isaac R. Hawkins, who has since died. The present resident attorneys are ex-Gov. Alvin Hawkins and his son Alonzo, Capt. A. W. Hawkins, the present clerk of the circuit court, who is also a physician and minister, and a survivor of the Mexican and civil wars; Joseph R. Hawkins, L. L. Hawkins, S. W. Hawkins and Albert G. Hawkins, the present chancellor; L. W. Beckerdite, H. C. Townes, the present State Senator elect; W. W. Murray, H. C. Brewer, the present postmaster; G. W. McCall and J. P. Wilson; also Commillis Hawkins, B. P. Gilbert and George H. Ralstone, the latter three being residents of McKenzie, and also I. M. L. Barker, who resides in the Nineteenth Civil District.

The people of Carroll County are patriotic, and whenever the alarm of war has been sounded and the call to arms made, they have responded with gallantry. A company of volunteers, commanded by Capt. B. C. Totton was raised in the county for the Florida war. They went as far as Fayetteville, and not being needed, were not mustered into the service. In 1846 the county furnished a company for the Mexican war. Its officers were Capt. H. F. Murray, Lieutenants Isaac R. Hawkins, J. Richardson, N. B. Burrow; Sergeants J. C. Hawkins, James Ingram, B. F. Harrison and R. P. McCracken; Corporals John W. Myrick, Jesse Wiley, Ashton W. Hawkins and J. F. Townes; privates, seventy-four in number. The company served through the Mexican war as Company B, Second Tennessee Infantry, commanded by Col. Wm. T. Haskell. At this date, 1886, only twenty of these veterans are living, and of that number Dr. A. W. Hawkins, J. F. Townes, H. T. Bridges, M. Bunn, W. G. Crockett, A. R. B. Churchwell, Joseph Hamilton, Wright Mebane, E. D. Shoffner and Ephraim Williams are citizens of Carroll County. In February, 1861, a mass-meeting of the citizens of Carroll County was held in the courthouse, and Isaac R. Hawkins, Alvin Hawkins, B. M. Gains, L. M. Jones, A. P. Hall and Dr. Seth W. Bell were appointed a committee to draft resolutions expressive of the sense of the meeting. The majority report of this committee, signed by Isaac R. Hawkins, Alvin Hawkins, Dr. Bell and A. B. Hall, was adopted. It read as follows: "That we are in favor of the seceding States being restored to their allegiance to the Government of the United States, peaceably if possible, but forcibly if necessary." The territory being first within the lines of the Confederate armies, the first company of soldiers raised in the county was known as the "Carroll Invincibles," commanded by Capt. E. P. Hall. The next were the companies of Capts. W. A. Marshall and — Shoffner. These three companies were mustered into the Twenty-second Tennessee Confederate Infantry at Trenton, Tenn.; in June 1861. The next were Companies C and H of the Fifty-fifth Tennessee Confederate Infantry, the former commanded by Capt. L. W. Clark and the latter by Capt. Alfred Bryant. These companies joined their regiment at Trenton in October, 1861. In the spring of 1863, Company B, of the Nineteenth and Twentieth consolidated regiments of Tennessee Confederate Cavalry, was raised in this county. The company was commanded by Capt. W. H. Hawkins. During the latter part of the war Capt. Rufus Thomas commanded a company in a Kentucky Confederate regiment, which was composed mostly of citizens of Carroll County. Parts of other companies from this county, also served in the Confederate armies. The following commands all served in the Federal armies: Five companies commanded respectively by Capts. A. W. Hawkins, J. M. Martin, P. K. Parsons, John A. Miller and Thomas Belew, were raised in Carroll County and mustered into the Seventh Tennessee Cavalry at Trenton, in September, 1862. The companies of Capt. Hawkins and Capt. Belew, were mustered for twelve months only, and were mustered out at the end of their term, and many of the men re-enlisted in another company which was raised in Carroll County, in the fall of 1863, by Capt. Clinton King and mustered into the same regiment. Another company raised in the county and commanded by Capt. John Neely was mustered into the First West Tennessee Infantry in the fall of 1862. The following year this regiment was consolidated with the Sixth Tennessee Cavalry. Company M of the latter regiment was also raised in this county by Capt. John W. Harwood and Lieut. H. L. Neely. During the early period of the war, while Carroll County was subject to the control of the Confederate armies, many of her citizens remained loyal to the United States, fled to the armies of the government for protection, and enlisted in regiments from other States. The guerrillas and bushwhackers were a terror to the people of the county, who suffered much more from their depredations than from the armies of the contending parties. These roving bands of outlaws committed several most brutal and fiendish murders within the county. Since the war the people have become reconciled to the results thereof, and with manifest forgiveness for past offenses, are now peaceable, happy and prosperous. The records of the chancery court were nearly all destroyed during the war, while all the other county records were well preserved.

Samuel Ingram and John Gwin each built a dwelling house on the site of Huntingdon before it became the seat of justice for the county, and John Crockett, the first merchant of the place, built his storehouse on what is now the public square, before the town was surveyed. Other early merchants of Huntingdon were Robert Murray, Ennis Ury and Armer Lake & Co. The first physicians were Jacob White, Robert Nicholson, Gabriel Norman and Dr. Hogg. Thomas Ross located the first tanyard in the town. The merchants during the thirties were those already named, and Clark & Morrison, Everett & Bullard, Edmund Grizzard, G. W. Grizzard and others. After 1840 Thomas K. Wiley and Thomas Hall became merchants of the place, and they and some of those already named continued in business until the beginning of the civil war, when all mercantile business was suspended and remained so until the war closed. When peace was restored, A. R. Hall, Allen & Dougherty, Joseph McCracken and A. C. McNeal & Co. were the first merchants to resume business. The present business and business men of the town are as follows: Dry goods, Joseph McCracken, S. N. Williams, Priest & Son, J. C. McNeal and Carter & Priest; family groceries, Lee Brothers, E. G. Ridgeley, J. Finley, Frank Johnson and W. T. Warren; drugs, C. P. Priestley and Dr. John Threadgill; hardware, Samuel Hendricks. In addition to the above there is the milliner store of Mrs. Mollie Grizzard, two jewelry stores, two livery stables, two undertaker's shops, one tin shop, one meat shop, one wagon and other mechanics' shops, and three drinking saloons. The hotels are the Easen House, Ownsby House and Brown House. There is a grist-mill, sawmill, planing-mill, stave factory and shingle-mill all combined, and the proprietors, Wilder & Dalton, do an extensive business. There is also the steam cotton-gin of J. F. Leach & Co. which gins and puts up from ten to twelve bales of cotton per day. The benevolent societies are the

Masonic Fraternity, K. of H. and Golden Cross. The religious denominations are Southern Methodist, Cumberland Presbyterian and Christian. The latter has no church edifice. The colored people have three churches: Methodist, Cumberland Presbyterian and Baptist. The first newspaper published in Carroll County, was the *Huntingdon Advertiser*, the first number of which was published at Huntingdon, July 8, 1839, by W. W. Gates, who advocated the principles of the Whig party. After the suspension of this paper another one, known as the *Courier*, was established about the year 1849 by C. R. P. Byers. A few years later the *Carroll Patriot*, was established by Wm. H. Hawkins, and published until the beginning of the civil war. In 1868 *The West Tennesseean* was established by Dr. A. W. Hawkins, and afterward merged into the *Huntingdon Courier*, and published about two years. The *Tennessee Republican*, was established in March, 1870, by E. G. Ridgeley, and its publication is still continued. About the same time or a little later *The Vindicator* was established by Grizzard & Algee, who published it about two years, and then T. H. Baker published *The Democrat* for a short time. Huntingdon was incorporated November 14, 1823, re-incorporated January 2, 1850, and the charter was so amended in March, 1883 as to require the mayor and marshal to be elected by a popular vote instead of by the aldermen as was the former custom. Hon. George T. McCall is the present mayor. The town has a pleasant and healthy location on high rolling ground, and its population is about 800.

McKenzie is situated at the crossing of the Nashville & Northwestern and the Louisville & Memphis Railroads. It was surveyed and platted in 1865 on lands belonging to James M. McKenzie, and buildings began at once to be erected, and the foundation for a prosperous town was at once established. A. G. Gilbert was the first merchant, and the next McKenzie & McClintoch and Mebane, Elbow & Covington. The town now contains four dry goods stores, six family groceries, two drug stores, one hardware store, three drinking saloons, two railroad depots, four steam cotton-gins, one planing-mill, one flouring-mill, two saw-mills, a livery stable, wagon and carriage shop, other mechanic shops, two hotels, the McKenzie House and Briant House; one weekly newspaper, the *Tri-County News*, established in 1882 and published by H. C. Lawhon; two colleges, two public schools, white and colored, and three churches; Methodist, Cumberland Presbyterian and Baptist; also two colored churches, Cumberland Presbyterian and Baptist. The population of McKenzie is about 1,000. Being located, as it was, on uncleared land, many of the forest trees have been preserved for shade, and altogether the town has a very attractive appearance. Trezevant on the Louisville

& Memphis Railroad, ten miles southwest of McKenzie, was established in 1859 on lands belonging to L. B. White and W. A. Marshall. The first merchants were A. White and R. H. Algee. The former was the first postmaster. The business of the town now consists of five dry goods stores, two family groceries, one drug store, one grist-mill and three cotton-gins. The churches are the Cumberland Presbyterian, established in 1862; Baptist Mission, 1866; Southern Methodist, 1870, and Christian, 1875. The population of the place is about 400. Hollow Rock which took its name from a natural curiosity, being a large hollow rock located there, is nine miles east of Huntingdon on the Nashville & Northwestern Railroad. It was established soon after the close of the war, and its first merchants were Aaron Lipe and John G. Martin. It now has three general stores, one drug store, a good academy and four churches in its vicinity, viz.: Missionary Baptist, Primitive Baptist, Methodist and Southern Methodist.

McLemoresville, nine miles west of Huntingdon and the place where the county was organized, is now only a post hamlet, containing two stores, a steam cotton-gin, and a good school, the Methodist Institute, and it has a population of about 150. In the early history of the county, and before railroads were established through it, McLemoresville was a place of considerable business importance. Clarksburg, nine miles south of Huntingdon, is a post village which was established about the year 1850 on lands of Peter Wood. Kelly Clark was its first merchant. It has three general stores, a drug store, grist-mill, cotton-gin and about 100 inhabitants. Buena Vista, about eight miles east of Huntingdon, was established about the year 1850 on lands of Thomas A. Pasture. W. P. Chambers, its first merchant, is still in the business there. It has two general stores, a cotton-gin, a Baptist Church and a good academy. Atwood, four miles southwest of Trezevant and on the same railroad, was established in 1872 on lands owned by J. H. W. Cage. The first merchants of the place were W. H. Scalloin and J. J. Clark. The postoffice was established the same year, and J. H. W. Cage was the first postmaster. The town now contains four general stores, a cotton-gin, grist-mill and saw-mill, and two churches, Methodist and Baptist, the former having been established in 1859, and the latter in 1874. The village has 118 nhabitants. The Shiloh Cotton Factory was established about the year 1850, in the Ninth Civil District, by Prince, Carson & Co., who prior to the war manufactured cotton yarns. Since the war the property passed into the hands of Messrs. Cheek, Ethridge & Co. who for a number of years manufactured carpet warp. They have recently changed the business and now manufacture woolen goods entirely.

Among the pioneer school teachers of the county were Soloman Perry, Wm. H. Province, Henry M. Bunch and Samuel Winn. In early times there were but few schools in the county, and they were supported by the subscription of the parents patronizing them, and were all of a primary character. Later as the population increased, academies were established at the villages throughout the county, and more competent teachers were employed. But all children residing at too great distance to attend such academies, and whose parents were not able to send them away to school, had but meager opportunities for obtaining an education before the inauguration of the free school system adopted since the civil war. Some statistics from the report of S. E. Tucker, the county school superintendent, for the last school year, 1886, will show the progress being made under this system. The items copied are as follows: "Scholastic population: White—male, 3,190; female, 3,129; total, 6,319. Colored—male, 1,008; female, 1,017; total, 2,025. Pupils enrolled in the schools during the year: White—male, 2,414; female, 2,214; total, 4,628. Colored—male, 648; female, 660; total, 1,308." From the foregoing it will be seen that of the scholastic population 1,791 white children, more than one-fourth of the whole number, and 717 of the colored children, nearly one-third of the whole number, were not enrolled in the public schools. This proves that the free school system is not as yet well sustained in this county. This is probably due to the fact that there were seventeen private schools sustained in the county during the same year. Several of the small villages each sustained a good academy. Huntingdon has a high school which employs a principal and two assistant teachers. This school is run five months in the year under the free school system, and five months as a private school. The county of Carroll is fortunate in having two good colleges, both located at the town of McKenzie, viz.: Bethel College and McTyeire Institute. The former was founded at McLemoresville in 1847, and became a chartered school in 1850. Its presidents before the civil war, named in succession, were Rev. B. N. Roach, Rev. C. J. Brady, Rev. A. Freeman, D. D., and Rev. Felix Johnson, D. D. The school was suspended during the continuance of the civil war, after which Rev. B. W. McDonald, D. D., Rev. J. S. Howard, A. M., and Rev. M. Liles, were presidents until 1871, when the school was moved to McKenzie, and Rev. W. W. Hendricks, then conducting the Hendricks High School, was chosen president. He superintended the construction of the main building, consisting of eight rooms, at a cost of $7,000. Two additional rooms were joined to the main building in 1886. The whole is constructed of brick, and finished in modern architectural style. Dr. Hendricks served as president until 1882, when he was succeeded by W. B. Sherrill, who served until June 1886, when Rev. John L. Dickens was unanimously chosen to fill that office. The college has an excellent faculty, a thorough course of study, and about 200 students in attendance.

The history of the McTyeire Institute as published with the minutes of the Paris District Conference of the Methodist Episcopal Church, is as follows: "This school was founded September, 1867, by Capt. H. C. Irby, A. M., and called the McKenzie Male and Female Institute. In 1871 he associated with himself E. H. Randle, A. M., and chartered it as McKenzie College. They continued joint principals until the retirement of Capt. Irby, in 1874, when Mr. Randle became sole president, remaining until the close of the spring term of 1877. The Rev. Preston A. Miller, A. M., of Georgia, was then elected president, and remained one year; he was followed in 1878 by L. W. Galbreath, A. M., who likewise retired at the close of one session. Dr. A. P. Waterfield, who had owned the college property for some years, secured the services of the Rev. Edwin B. Chappell, B. A. (Vanderbilt), and W. D. Vandiver, Ph. B. (Central), as joint principals. He also produced some change in the character of the college, advertising it as a fitting, rather than a finishing school—a classical training school, auxiliary to the Vanderbilt and other higher educational institutions. Mr. Vandiver's health failing, he returned to Missouri in 1880, and Granville Goodloe, M. A., another Vanderbilt graduate, was associated with brother Chappell; they continued in charge of the school two years. During this time the college was sold to the Rev. H. M. Sears, as a boarding-house for young ladies, and the trustees of the Methodist Church built a fine brick academy, which was so far completed as to be occupied by the school in the spring of 1882. The trustees named this new building McTyeire Institute, in honor of our present beloved senior bishop. The same year brother Chappell, believing that he ought to enter the regular work of the ministry, provided for his retirement by the election of E. R. Williams, A. M., principal," who, with Mr. Goodloe, continued in charge of the school until September, 1886, when the latter resigned and was succeeded by Rev. J. H. Harrison, A. B. (Vanderbilt). It is accepted as the authorized school of the Methodist Church by the Paris, Union City, Dyersburg and Bolivar Districts. In 1882 the church came in possession of the property, as well as the school.

The pioneer churches of Carroll County were the Baptists, Presbyterians, Cumberland Presbyterians and Methodists, and among the pioneer ministers were Rev. Willis Bridges, Rev. Benjamin Peeples, Rev. Robert Baker, Parson Wear, Rev. Johnson, Rev. Allen T. Graves, Rev.

Samuel McNutt, Revs. James and Robert Hurt, Rev. Wm. Bigham, Rev. Reuben Burrow and Rev. Abner Cooper. These ministers were all among the early settlers of the county, and they and other pious men and women led the way into the wilderness and established religious societies in various parts of the county, as soon as enough persons could be assembled together for that purpose. And the above named religious denominations have always been the leading churches in the county, and now have church edifices in all of the towns and villages, as well as in all parts of the county, so that the people are fully and conveniently supplied with opportunities for public worship. The Christian, and other churches, have also been established within the county. The first camp-meeting was held, in a very early day at the Shiloh Camp-ground in the northern part of the county, by the Cumberland Presbyterians. And the next camp-meeting was held by the Methodists at Carter's Chapel. Afterward, camp-meetings were held at Black's Camp-ground in the southwestern part of the county, and at William's Camp-ground in the eastern part of the county. And later the Christian Church established a camp-ground about twelve miles south of Huntingdon, where they held annual meetings. No services have been held at any of these camp-ground for many years. But the Methodists continued to keep their camp-ground at Chapel Hill in the northeastern part of the county, in order, and to hold their annual meetings there.

Acknowledgments are hereby made to ex-Gov. Alvin Hawkins, Dr. A. W. Hawkins, W. G. Crockett and Judge G. W. Humble, and others, for valuable information pertaining to the history of Carroll County. Mr. Crockett is the only survivor of the first settlers of Huntingdon, being a lad when his father, John Crockett, settled there and opened the first store.

HENRY COUNTY.

HENRY COUNTY, named after Patrick Henry, lies on the dividing ridge between the Tennessee and Mississippi Rivers. It is bounded north by the State of Kentucky, east by Stewart and Benton Counties, south by Carroll, and west by Weakley, and has an area of 600 square miles. The central and southeastern portion is drained principally by the Big Sandy River and its tributaries—the West Sandy being the largest of the latter. The Holly Fork and Bailey Fork, which drains the central portion of the county, flow southwardly and empty into the West Sandy.

The northeastern portion of the county below the mouth of Big Sandy is drained by the Tennessee River and tributaries, of which the principal one is Blood River. The northwestern portion of the county is drained by the North Fork of the Obion River and its tributaries; the southwestern portion by the Middle Fork of the Obion and its tributaries. The North Fork of the Obion rises in the north central part of the county, and the Middle Fork about one mile south of Paris. The natural drainage of the county is excellent. In general the surface of the county is gently undulating, with the eastern portion broken and hilly in places, and the northwestern mostly level. The soil of the bottom lands is alluvial, while that of the uplands is composed of a mixture of clay and sand, supported by a red clay subsoil. By constant farming without a rotation of crops, and without any application of fertilizing matter, a large percentage of the lands has been worn out and abandoned. It is thought, however, that with proper cultivation these lands could all be restored to fertility. Originally, the timber on the level lands was very heavy, consisting of the several kinds of oak, hickory, sassafras, dogwood, etc. The bottom lands were covered with beach, gum, cypress and oak, and the high, rolling and hilly lands with a light growth of scrubby oak. The latter were almost like a prairie when the county was first settled, there being no underbrush. On the North Fork of the Obion are remarkable earth-works consisting of two large mounds about seventy and seventy-five feet in height, respectively, together with some smaller ones, and all surrounded with an earthen wall one mile in circumference from the point where it leaves the river to the place where it returns to it, only a short distance from the point of departure. When the county was first settled, this wall was from three to four feet in height, with elevated points at regular intervals about 100 feet apart, and between the two large mounds was a well which the early settlers called Jacob's Well. In an early day Andrew Hartsfield, while plowing near these mounds, found a stone image representing a human being. The whole is, without doubt, the work of the Mound Builders.

The settlement of Henry County began in 1819. Joel and Willis T. Hagler (both living at the present writing), James Williams, Wm. Wyatt, Rev. Benj. Peeples, Rev. John Manly, Richard and Hamilton F. Manly, John Stoddart, Abraham and Wm. Waters, Cullen Bryant, Wm. Jones, James Hicks, Thomas T. Lilly, Johanan Smith, Henry Wall, the Randles, Reuben Bomar, Wm. Porter, and his son (now known as Maj. John Porter, who lives about three miles from Paris, and from whom the writer has obtained much valuable information pertaining to the history of the county), all settled in the southeastern part about the year 1820. Crawford Bradford, Araby Brown, Wm. Deloach, Thomas Gray and Hardy Mizell were among the first settlers in the northeastern part of the county. John B. House came in 1819, and settled on the Obion near the famous mounds, and raised five acres of corn that year, and the following year returned and brought his family from Montgomery County. Amos Milliken settled on the same river in 1820. These men were followed in the northwestern part of the county by John Lawrence, who settled in the extreme corner, and Josiah Cavitt, who settled on Terrapin Creek, and Jesse Kuykendall and Jesse Paschall, the latter of whom has left a numerous progeny in the Twenth-first District, and Col. R. D. Caldwell and his father, James Caldwell, and Samuel Rogers, all of whom were prominent early settlers. Adam Rowe settled on the head waters of the North Fork of the Obion before the county was organized, and was the first man married in the territory composing it. The territory then belonged to Stewart County, and Mr. Rowe had to go to Dover to get his marriage license. David Lemonds, father of the present county court clerk, settled on Town Creek, and afterward moved to Paris, where he worked at blacksmithing in 1827. John Maxwell, Daniel Ary, Henry Humphreys, Wm. Webb and Dr. Jacob Braswell, were also early settlers. The latter settled at the place known as Naples, and built his cabin so that a rock embedded in the earth formed the hearth to his fireplace. After making a fire and heating the rock, the rattlesnakes harboring beneath it commenced coming out, until a dozen or more were killed by Mr. Braswell and his family. The pioneer settlers, it should be remembered, built their houses with dirt floors. Lewis and Samuel McCorkle settled in 1822, about seven miles southwest of Paris. James Greer, Alex. Harman, Col. Richard Porter, Hugh W. Dunlap, Daniel Culp, John Brown and John Young, were among the early settlers at Paris. In August, 1822, David Searcy Greer and his father, James Greer, came from Robertson County, bringing with them a stock of goods which they put up in a log cabin on the Middle Fork of the Obion. They made counters out of the store boxes and shelves of common lumber, and there being but little money then in the country, they exchanged the goods for furs, venison, hams, hides, beeswax, tallow, etc. This was the pioneer store of Henry County, and, probably of all of West Tennessee. In this connection the names of only a few of the most prominent early settlers have been given. There were many others equally as prominent, some of whose names will appear hereafter in connection with the organization of the county. The county was settled so rapidly that it is impossible to learn and make mention of more than a small percentage of the settlers. Some correct idea of the great influx of settlers can be obtained from the fact that in 1830, only ten years after the settlement of the county was fully begun, its population was 12,249. In 1835 the Indian lands of northern Mississippi came into market, and many of the early settlers were thus induced to emigrate to that State.

The first and most extensive land entries were made by locating land warrants granted by North Carolina to her soldiers for their services in the Revolutionary and Indian wars. These warrants were bought up by speculators, who obtained large tracts of the best lands of the county, and afterward sold them to actual settlers. John G. and Thomas Blount at one time located land warrants covering 21,000 acres of the best lands of the county. Landon Carter, of North Carolina, and the trustees of the University of North Carolina also obtained large tracts of land in the same manner. Many of the actual settlers also purchased land warrants before coming to the county, and thus obtained their lands. But very few, if any, of the soldiers to whom said warrants were issued, ever obtained a home in Henry County, by locating them. The next land entries were known as the "occupant entries," or entries of lands belonging to the Federal Government, and of these lands Morgan Bricken, Daniel Campbell, Jos. Castlione, Philip Babb, James Howard, Littleton Allen, and Michael Embry made the first entries in the order here named. The first water power grist-mill in Henry County, one mile northeast of Paris, was erected about the year 1823 by Charles Crutchfield, and the next one was erected on Town Creek by a Mr. Lyons. About the year 1824, Jesse Kuykendall built a saw and grist-mill on the North Fork of the Obion. The following anecdote is related of him: When he first put his saw-mill in motion, he looked at it with anxiety, and observing that it was complete and in good running order, exclaimed "Lands and niggers; when the saw comes down it says lands, and when it goes up it says niggers." He obtained wealth rapidly, but met with trouble further on; his mill-dam caused an overflow of about three square miles, and when the timber died and began to decay, it became very unhealthy in that neighborhood. Accordingly the citizens thereof petitioned court to have the pond declared a nuisance, and the dam removed. After much continued litigation it was finally decided in favor of the petitioners about the year 1848, and the dam was cut down. Josiah Cavitt and sons, about the year 1835, built a grist-mill on Terrapin Creek. These early mills have been replaced with new ones, and the county is now well supplied.

The cultivation of cotton commenced with the settlement of the county, and cotton-gins soon became numerous. Some cotton was ginned in 1824 at the place where Dinwiddie's factory now stands.

The first tobacco was raised in the county by Wm. Waters, about the year 1826. Cotton, tobacco, the cereals and vegetables, have always been the productions of Henry County, and the amount produced in 1879, as given by the census of 1880, is as follows: Indian corn, 1,128,660 bushels; oats, 35,407 bushels.; rye, 961 bushels; wheat, 124,537 bushels; hay, 1,898 tons; cotton, 5,516 bales; Irish potatoes, 11,443 bushels; sweet potatoes, 28,254 bushels; tobacco, 1,902,979 pounds. The Chickasaw Cotton Mill, two miles east of Paris, was established about the year 1830 by Currier, Mann & Peters. It is now owned by Mrs. Maria Currier and son, and consumes about 900,000 pounds of seed cotton per year in the manufacture of yarns and carpet warp. About forty hands are employed, and the mill has both steam and water power attached. The Dinwiddie Cotton Factory, located about twelve miles southwest of Paris, was established since the civil war. The proprietors manufacture yarn and cloth, and employ about thirty hands. Both of the foregoing factories have been run very successfully. Oakley, White & Co. established a cotton factory near Paris about the year 1835, and did a successful business for many years; after which it changed hands, and since 1884 has not been operated. Col. R. D. Caldwell established his tobacco factory, fourteen miles northwest of Paris, in 1846. This factory has always had a successful career, and from forty to fifty hands are constantly employed. The tobacco is principally manufactured into plug.

The county of Henry was created by an act of the General Assembly of the State of Tennessee, passed November 7, 1821, which provided that a new county, to be called Henry, be established within the following bounds, to wit: "Beginning on the west bank of the Tennessee River, where the north boundary of the State leaves the same, running thence with the said boundary west to the second range line in the twelfth surveyor's district; thence south to a point two miles and a half south of the sixth sectional line in said district; thence east parallel with the said sectional line, to the west boundary of Humphreys County; thence with said county line northwardly to the Tennessee River; thence down the said river with its various meanders to the beginning." In 1835 all that portion of Henry County as above described, lying east of Big Sandy River, was cut off and became a part of Benton County, which was then created from portions of Henry and Humphreys Counties. Since that date Big Sandy and the Tennessee Rivers have formed the eastern boundary of Henry County. The aforesaid act also provided that the court of pleas and quarter sessions for Henry County should be held at the house of Henry Wall on the first Mondays of December, March, June and September of each year until otherwise provided by law. By a subsequent act, passed November 16, 1821, Sterling Brewer, James Fentress and Abram Maury were appointed commissioners for the county of Henry, to fix on a place as near the center of the county as an eligible site could be procured, within three miles of the center thereof, for the seat of justice, and to procure a deed for not less than fifty acres of land thus selected, either by purchase or donation. And the same act further provided that the court of pleas and quarter sessions should appoint five commissioners "to lay off the town, and superintend the sale of the lots, and the erection of the public buildings and stocks."

In accordance with the foregoing the first bench of justices of the peace met, on the first Monday of December, 1821, at the house of Henry Wall, now known as the place where Peyton Randle lives, and organized the court of pleas and quarter sessions by electing John Marberry, Esq., as chairman thereof. The court then elected the following county officers, viz.: James G. Swisher, register; Thomas Gray, sheriff; Henry Wall, ranger; Samuel McGowan, trustee; Peter Liggin, coroner. Constables were then appointed for each captain's militia company as follows: Amos H. Lacy, in Capt. Lacy's company, and Alsey Elkins in Capt. Grace's company, and thus the organization of the county was completed. Henry Wall then obtained a license from the court to keep an ordinary at his house, and gave bonds in the sum of £1,000, conditioned "to constantly find and keep in his said ordinary, good, clean and wholesome diet, and lodging for travelers, and stables, fodder, corn and pasture for their horses." Abner Johnson was permitted to keep a public ferry across Sandy River where he then resided, and gave bonds accordingly. At the next term of the court (March, 1822,) John House was appointed administrator of the personal estate of George House, deceased. He was the first administrator appointed in the county. At the June term, 1822, John Atkins was appointed constable in Capt. Brewer's company, and Timothy Dalton constable in Capt. Reed's company. In December, 1822, the said court appointed Abner Pearce, James Leeper, John H. Randle, John Stoddart and James T. Williams commissioners to lay off and sell the lots in the town to be established as the seat of justice in the county of Henry, and to superintend the building of a courthouse, prison, and stocks in said town. At the same time James Jones, Dudley S. Jennings and Amos Milliken were appointed commissioners for the ensuing four years, to settle annually with the trustee and tax collector.

The commissioners appointed by the General Assembly to locate the seat of justice for the county, selected fifty acres where the town of Paris now stands—thirty-seven and one-half acres belonged to the estate of

Joseph Blythe, and the balance to a tract entered by Peter Ruff. Title to the fifty acres was afterward obtained. The tract was then covered with wild pea vines, and most of the timber was poplar. The town of Paris was laid out by the commissioners appointed for that purpose, early in 1823. It contained, according to the original plat, 104 lots, the public square, and streets and alleys. The record of the sales of lots seems to have been lost, but David Searcy Greer, heretofore mentioned as the pioneer merchant of the county, and who died at his late home near Memphis, February 17, 1881, says in a letter to Hon. W. A. Dunlap, dated January 9, 1880, "that 104 lots were sold at the sale on the 14th and 15th of April, 1823.* There was a large number of persons on the ground considering the newness of the county—not less than 200 to 300 * * * and they were intelligent, enterprising men, well dressed and quite sober, and about one-fourth of them bought lots." Prominent among the purchasers of lots were James Greer (father of David S.), Samuel Hankins, Rev. Samuel McGowan, J. W. Looney, John Manly, Samuel McCorkle, Daniel Kulp and others.

The first courthouse, which was erected in 1823, was a small cabin made out of poplar logs. A year or two later a brick courthouse was erected which stood until about 1850, when the present one was erected by Calvin Sweeny at a cost of about $42,000. The first jail, erected in 1823, consisted of two rooms, the prisoner's room, and debtor's room. The whole was made of logs. This stood until after the close of the civil war when it was replaced with a brick jail with patent iron cells. The latter was soon condemned on account of its insufficiency to the prisoners, and was torn down and the present jail erected in its stead. The latter cost about $7,000. About the year 1837 the county purchased of Robert Aycock a farm of 160 acres for a home for paupers. It was located six miles northeast of Paris, and was used as such home until 1873, when it was sold to R. D. Collins for $1,000. On the 12th day of March, 1873, the county purchased of James D. Porter, Jr., a farm of 243 acres, lying in the Seventeenth District, for $4,000. This has been fitted up as an asylum for the poor. It has comfortable buildings for about thirty inmates. The average number of the inmates is about fifteen. The county also provides annually for about twenty-five poor persons by farming them out to citizens. Altogether the dependent poor of Henry County are well cared for. In 1836 the county was subdivided into seventeen civil districts by commissioners W. S. Patterson, Constantine Frazier, Crawford Bradford, James C. Gainer and Michael Brooks, who were appointed for that purpose. And in 1850 the districts

---
*Maj. John Porter, of Henry County, says the lots were sold March 22 and 23, 1823.

were reorganized and increased to twenty, and in 1870 to twenty-five, the present number. In 1857 the county subscribed $100,000 toward the building of a railroad now known as the Memphis division of the Louisville & Nashville Railroad. The money was raised by issuing bonds in the sum of $1,000 each. The certificates of stock were afterward traded to the Louisville & Nashville Railroad Company for $25,000 of stock, which has since been doubled in value. It cost the county about $287,000 to redeem the original bonds for the $100,000, the last one of which was canceled in 1880. The railroad was completed through the county in 1860, and has stations at Springville, Paris and Henry. In 1827 the taxable property of Henry County, as shown by the duplicate of that date, and the taxes charged thereon were as follows: 138,345 acres of land, 909 free polls, 797 slaves, 93 town lots, 6 stores, 3 taverns, 18 stud horses, 4 four-wheeled carriages, 2 two-wheeled carriages—the amount of taxes charged thereon, $2,597.58. The rates were, "on each 100 acres $1, on each free poll $37\frac{1}{2}$ cents, on each slave 75 cents, on each town lot $1, each tavern $3, each store $3, each stud horse two seasons." It will be interesting to compare this with the aggregate of the tax duplicate of the county for 1886, which is as follows: "Town lots 483 valued at $300,640; 360,347 acres valued at $2,152,913; personal property valued at $193,830, total $2,647,383, polls 3,184 in number." Amount of taxes charged, $30,079.73

The following is a list of county and other officers, with date of service from the organization of the county to the year 1886. Sheriffs: Thomas Gray, 1821–24; Edward H. Tarrant, 1824–26; Spearman Holland, 1826–29; R. S. Holland, 1829–32; James C. Gainer, 1832–35; John H. Randle, 1835–36; James C. Gainer, 1836–40; John H. Warren, 1840–44; John C. Porter, 1844–48; John H. Williams, 1848–52; George W. Moore, 1852–56; Elijah Ethridge, 1856–58; Preston G. Haynes, 1858–60; Elijah Ethridge, 1860, to September, 1861; John C. Porter, June, 1865–71; George W. Moore, 1871–76; T. O. Barbee, 1876–80; M. H. Freeman, 1880–86; R. M. Blakemore, 1886, elected. Trustees: Samuel McGowan, 1821–30; John Woodfin, 1830–32; Benj. C. Brown, 1832–34; Sterling Organ, 1834–42; Matthew C. Bowles, 1842–48; Robert J. Hamby, 1848–54; H. G. Norton, 1854–60; O. F. Braswell, 1860–65; James C. Guthrie, 1865–66; S. C. Love, 1866–68; Joseph Hill, 1868–70; J. J. Madison, 1870, one month and died; W. C. Diggs, 1870–72; J. L. Lemonds, 1872–76; W. C. Diggs, 1876–78; James T. Russell, 1878–80; James Bomar, 1880–84; John Hicks, 1884–86; R. P. Diggs, 1886, elected. Registers: James G. Swisher, 1821–24; James Leeper, 1824–40; Constantine Frazier, 1840–44; Edward J. McFarland, 1844–52; S.

S. Broach, 1852–54; B. B. Bunch, 1854–60; Peter Poyner, 1860–65; Thomas Nutt, 1865–66; Peter Poyner, 1866–70; Edward J. McFarland, 1870–78; J. R. Crosswell, 1878–86; S. W. Puckett, 1886, elected. County court clerks: James Hicks, 1821–29; Thomas K. Porter, 1829–39; Wm. Porter, 1839–41; Constantine Frazier, 1841–52; Robt. Lemonds, 1852–55; James Bond, 1855–56; James W. Ray, 1856–65; James Worthen, 1865–66; James W. Ray, 1866–78; J. L. Lemonds, 1878–86, and re-elected. Circuit court clerks: James Jones, 1822–35; Benj. C. Brown, 1835–48; Calvin C. Venable, 1848–56; Thomas H. Conway, 1856 to September, 1861. John Anderson, 1865–70; George S. Russell, 1870–86; W. T. Landis, 1886, elected. Representatives in Congress: Adam R. Alexander, 1823–27; Col. David Crockett, 1827–31; Wm. Fitzgerald, 1831–33; Col. David Crockett, 1833–35; Adam Huntsman, 1835–37; John W. Crockett, 1837–41; Milton Brown, 1841–43; Cave Johnson, 1843–45; L. B. Chase, 1845–49; Isham G. Harris, 1849–53; Emerson Etheridge, 1853–57; J. D. C. Atkins, 1857–59; Emerson Etheridge, 1859–61; Isaac R. Hawkins, 1865–70; R. P. Caldwell, 1870–72; J. D. C. Atkins, 1872–82; John M. Taylor, 1882–86; B. A. Enlow, 1886, elected. State senators: Henry M. Brown, 1823; James R. McMeans, 1826; John D. Love, 1829; Robert Murray, 1831; John D. Love, 1835; Wm. H. Johnson, 1837; Thomas Love, 1839; John A. Gardner, 1841; Isham G. Harris, 1847; J. D. C. Atkins, 1849; James T. Dunlap, 1851; W. E. Travis, 1857; B. L. Stovall, 1859; C. Underwood, 1867; Emerson Etheridge, 1869; J. A. McCall, 1873; Clinton Aden, 1875; George W. Martin, 1877; Thomas R. Shearon, 1879; D. D. Bell, 1881; S. A. Champion, 1883; George W. Martin, 1885. Representatives in Lower House of the Legislature: Abner Pearce, 1823; * * Julian Frazier, 1833–41; Solomon Copeland, 1841–43; Owen H. Edwards, 1843; James T. Dunlap, 1847; J. C. D. Atkins, 1849; W. E. Travis, 1855; J. J. Lamb, 1857; J. D. Porter, 1859; Thomas Crutchfield, 1865; W. J. Hurst, 1867; J. S. Longacre, 1869; J. H. McCampbell, 1873; W. P. Smallwood, 1875; W. E. Travis, 1877; S. C. Hearn, 1879; W. M. Janes, 1881; J. N. Thomason, 1883; J. W. Lewis, 1885.

The organization of the court of pleas and quarter sessions has already been given and in addition to the first officers named, William Arnold was the first solicitor general. This court held its sessions at the house of Henry Wall until the latter part of 1823, when it moved to Paris. The records fail to give the names of all of the first justices of the peace composing the court, but the following are those who composed it in 1824, viz.: Jacob Hoover, Samuel Wynn, Spearman Holland, John H. Crutcher, Peter Liggin, John Horton, John Stoddart, Kenneth Reddick, John A

Newland, Rev. Benj. Peeples, Wm. Ward and Bryan Bunch. This court had jurisdiction of both civil and criminal cases, and while it was holding its sessions at the house of Henry Wall, a colored man was arraigned before it charged with the crime of rape committed on a white woman. He was tried on Monday and Tuesday, and hanged on Friday of the same week. Before the execution he made full confession of his guilt. This was the first man hanged in the county. The first will probated was that of Thomas Wilson, deceased, in June, 1823. In March, 1823, James Boyd obtained license to keep an ordinary in the town of Paris, and William Massey and Joel Robertson were granted the same privilege, and in December, 1824, Wm. Wyatt obtained license "to keep a public ferry across Sandy River at his landing above Wyatt's mill," and Wm. Holt to build a dam across the Middle Fork of the Obion River, and at the next term of the court David Davis obtained license to keep a ferry across Sandy River at his landing, and James B. Quigley and Jesse C. Gainer each obtained permission to keep an ordinary at his residence. At the March term, 1825, the following named persons were sworn as a grand jury "to inquire for the body of the county" etc., viz.: Willis G. Williamson, Everett House, Samuel Swearengen, John Marberry, Wm. Palmer, Peter Meeheny, Stephen Parker, Wm. Newland, Alex Scarborough, Aaron Pearce, Aaron Cary and John Barnett. This was not the first grand jury, but the first one of which the record has been preserved. In 1826 Obediah B. Smith and Hugh W. Dunlap each obtained permission to keep an ordinary at his house in the town of Paris. The last term of the court of pleas and quarter sessions was held in March, 1836, and the first term of the county court, which consisted of the justices of the peace and other officers elected by the people under the constitution of 1834, was held in May, 1836, when, as shown by the record, thirty-three justices of the peace were present. The county court was presided over by a chairman elected annually by the several justices, until 1856, when under a new law Rev. Benj. Peeples was elected by the people as county judge. He served one year, and then said law was repealed, and Constantine Frazier was elected chairman for the year 1858. After the civil war, this court was reorganized in June, 1865, when the new county officers filed their bonds and qualified for the performance of their duties. From 1858 to 1868 the court was presided over by a chairman chosen by its own body. Then, under the present law, W. J. Hurt was elected, and served as judge up to 1870. He was succeeded by John W. Harris, who served from 1870 to 1878, when John L. Booth was elected his successor. The latter has served ever since, and in 1886 was elected for another term of eight years.

The first term of the circuit court of Henry County was held at the house of Henry Wall, in October, 1822, with Hon. Joshua Haskell judge presiding, and the October term of said court for the following year was held in Paris. One of the most noted cases ever tried in this court, and upon which a famous decision was rendered by the supreme court, was that of the State *vs.* Grainger. John Grainger, the defendant, was indicted for the murder of Berry Broach. It appeared from the evidence that Grainger and Broach, on the night of July 9, 1829, were riding together on horseback, on a highway; that Broach inflicted a blow upon Grainger, whereupon the latter alighted from his horse and retreated to a house near by, and called to the inmates to let him in, but was refused admittance. Being closely pursued by Broach, and not being able to obtain admission into the house, he raised his gun and shot and killed his assailant. He was tried in court, found guilty of murder, and sentenced to be hanged. The defendant took an appeal to the supreme court, where the decision was reversed, and the case remanded for a new trial, with the following important decision: "If a timid, cowardly man, much alarmed, in imminent danger of a violent and instant assault, and cut off from the chances of probable assistance, as a result of fear kill the man from whom the danger is apprehended, and the jury believe that the defendant was in danger of great bodily harm from the deceased, or thought himself so, then the killing would be self defense, and if the defendant thought the deceased intended to commit a battery upon him less violent, to prevent which he killed him, the killing would be manslaughter." (13th Tennessee Report, page 459). Upon second trial the defendant was found guilty of manslaughter, and was branded with M. S. on his hand, as the law then provided, and set at liberty. This was the first trial for murder in the county, and Broach was the first man known to have been killed. In 1845 a colored man by the name of Skelt, belonging to Bird Greer, killed, with a hatchet, a traveling tailor by the name of Dupree, on the Huntingdon road about four miles south of Paris. He was tried in this court, and for his crime suffered the penalty of death upon the gallows, April 15, 1846. Also, in 1845, a colored man by the name of Gilbert killed his master, Mr. Forrest, in his barn, then burned the barn together with the body of the slain and several thousand pounds of tobacco. This occurred about five miles south of Paris. The murderer was tried in the circuit court then presided over by the Hon. William Fitzgerald, found guilty and suffered the death penalty by hanging in 1847. Both of the foregoing criminals made full confession of their guilt before being executed. The circuit court suspended business during the war period from September, 1861, to September, 1865. On December 1, 1882, Shim Forrest, of Henry County, killed his grandfather, David Cruise, and his own mother, Mrs. Jane Forrest. He was first tried in the circuit court at the May term, 1883, and sentenced to be hanged August 3, following. He took an appeal to the supreme court, where the decision of the lower court was affirmed; on July 11, 1884, he suffered the death penalty in the manner aforesaid. The judges of the circuit court have been, Joshua Haskell, 1822–24; John C. Hamilton, 1824–32; John W. Cook, 1832–36; Wm. R. Harris, 1836–46; William Fitzgerald, 1846 to September, 1861; Lucien L. Hawkins, 1865–70; James D. Porter, 1870–74; Joseph R. Hawkins, 1874–78; Samuel B. Ayers, 1878–79; Clinton Aden, 1879–86; W. H. Swiggart, 1886, elected. Of the foregoing, Hamilton, Harris, Fitzgerald, Porter and Aden were residents of Paris.

The first term of the chancery court of Henry County was held in the courthouse at Paris, beginning on the first Monday of June, 1846, with Andrew McCampbell, chancellor presiding, and Eldridge G. Atkins, clerk and master. The business of this court was suspended on account of the civil war, from January, 1862, to September, 1866. The chancellors of this court have been as follows: Andrew McCampbell, 1846–47; Calvin Jones, 1847–54; Isaac B. Williams, 1854–60; William M. Smith, 1860–62; John Somers, 1866–86; Albert G. Hawkins, 1886, elected. Clerks and masters: Eldridge G. Atkins, 1846–48; Aquilla P. Greer, 1848–53; Benjamin C. Brown, 1853–59; Isaac M. Hudson, 1859–86, and still holding the office. The Paris bench and bar has included many eminent men. Andrew McCampbell, the first chancellor, was an able jurist, and universally respected. He declined a position on the supreme bench of the State, and a position on the supreme bench of the United States, the latter being tendered him by President Johnson. Chancellor Isaac B. Williams was also an able and conscientious jurist, and much respected by the people, and the same may be said of Judges John C. Hamilton, William R. Harris, William Fitzgerald, and many others. The members of the bar in 1824 were William Fitzgerald, B. Gillespie, Hugh W. Dunlap, M. A. Martin, J. W. Cooke and William Arnold. They were followed by Chancellors McCampbell and Williams, and Judges Hamilton and Harris, and Attorneys John H., James T. and Will C. Dunlap, Benjamin F. and J. J. Lamb, Sol C. Braswell, Edwin Fitzgerald, James S. and B. C. Brown and W. D. Lannom, all of whom have quit the forum and passed away. Other prominent members who have discontinued their connection with the bar, are Senator Isham G. Harris, Ex-Gov. James D. Porter, Lewis D. McKissick and J. B. Brown. Those composing the present bar are A. P. Greer, J. N. Thomason, Clinton Aden, S. A. Champion, R. P. Cole,

John C. Sweeney, R. K. Ward, T. M. Thompson, S. J. Taylor, James Skelton, T. C. Fryer, T. L. Fryer, W. L. Carter, William A. Dunlap, W. M. Janes, J. W. Lewis, present State senator, J. L. S. Travis, present representative in the Legislature, and W. W. Farabough.

The people of Henry County have always vied with their brethren of the State in military prowess. The first settlers inherited the patriotism of their ancestors, and imparted it to their children. And under the laws of the State militia, companies were organized, before the organization of the county was fully completed. The first action of the court of pleas and quarter sessions, after electing county officers, was to appoint constables for certain captains' militia companies. David S. Greer, heretofore quoted, says in regard to the early militia of the county, that "J. W. Cooke and H. W. Dunlap were candidates for brigadier-general; the former was elected and Maj. J. L. Hagler and E. H. Tarrant were candidates for colonel; the latter was elected. Gen. Cooke and Col. Tarrant appointed a time to hold a military encampment, which they did on Spring Creek near Caledonia. It lasted three days and was attended by about 100 to 150 men. * * * I was there as a spectator. Tarrant acted as an Indian warrior, and attacked the encampment in the night in Indian style, using the war whoop, and finally guns, and the assailed party flew to arms with the rattle of drums, and the shrill, sharp call of the fife, which made everything lively and all enjoyed the excitement." He did not give the exact date of this occurrence, but related it with other matters which took place in 1823 and 1824. During the Florida war, Capt. Wm. N. Porter raised a company of soldiers in Henry County and took them as far as Fayetteville, Tenn., where he learned that their services were not needed, and then returned home. This was undoubtedly the first company organized in the county intended for actual service. At the outbreak of the Mexican war, Capt. Preston G. Haynes raised a company in Henry County which joined the United States Army and served through that war.

At the approach of the civil war between the States a strong sentiment prevailed in Henry County against secession. But as time passed, and actual war began, the sentiment of the people changed, so that at the election in June, 1861, on the question of separation from the Federal Union, the votes cast show that the people were overwhelmingly in favor of that measure. The votes cast at that election are given elsewhere in this work. The first company raised in Henry County for the Confederate Army was that of Capt. Edward Fitzgerald, which was raised in April, 1861, and joined the One Hundred and Fifty-fourth Tennessee Regiment, organized at Memphis. The next companies were those of Capts. B. B. Bunch, M. Long, T. H. Conway, J. D. Dumas, J. H. Porter, J. E. Fowler, W. D. Hallum, H. W. Ballard and A. W. Cardwell, which were mustered into the Fifth Confederate Infantry May 20, 1861. This regiment contained three other companies—two from Benton County commanded respectively by Capts. S. Corbett and Jack Winfrey, and one from Obion and Ballard Counties, Ky., commanded by Capt. Lauderdale. The Forty-sixth Tennessee Confederate Infantry, consisting of ten companies, was all raised in Henry County excepting a few individuals from adjoining counties. There were also four cavalry companies raised in the county, commanded respectively by Capts. J. G. Stocks, T. H. Tayloe, M. H. Freeman and Cardwell Wilson, all of which served under Gen. Forrest. This makes twenty-four companies which the county furnished for the Confederate Army—in all about 2,160 men. After the Federal Army got possession of the territory, Capt. Edward Arbuckle raised a company in Henry County, which served in the Federal Army. In the spring of 1862, Col. King occupied Paris with a force of from 400 to 500 Confederate soldiers, when Capt. Croff with a force of from 300 to 400 Federal soldiers and a battery of artillery came out from Fort Hyman and attacked Col. King's command and drove it from its camp and then returned to the fort from whence he came. In this short engagement two Confederate and three Federal soldiers were killed and two Federals wounded. On this occasion John Farris, of Paris, piloted Capt. Croff through the town toward the Confederate camp, and for this offense he was afterward captured and hanged by the Confederates. Guerrillas and bushwhackers preyed upon the people during the war and committed many depredations and murders. During the absence of the Federal or Confederate Armies, the people lived in constant fear of the roving bands of outlaws. All business was then suspended and it is remarkable how the people have recovered from the devastations of internecine war.

The origin of the town of Paris has been given with the organization of the county. David S. Greer, in his historical sketch to Hon. Wm. A. Dunlap, says, pertaining to Paris and the sale of the town lots, that "the first one was struck off to Daniel Culp. It was the same one on which Mr. T. Cooney afterward did business so long. Culp built a log house immediately, and soon had a stock of dry goods opened. James Hicks, then the county court clerk, bought and immediately commenced building a frame house designed for a hotel, which he opened and kept two or three years, and then sold it to Squire Dunlap. John C. McLemore bought two or three lots on the north side of the square, and sold one or two of them to Arman & Lake, who immediately commenced building a log store-house, and by fall had a stock of dry goods there. John W. Cooke put up a two-story log house for a hotel at the northwest corner of the public square, and Maj. H. H. League opened a house of entertainment early in the fall of 1823. * * John Brown commenced building soon after the sale of the lots on the southwest corner of the square, and by fall had a stock of goods there. John Young also built on the west side of the square, and had a stock of dry goods on sale about the same time. So in the fall of 1823 there were five stores, as Col. Richard Porter had built on the east side of the square, and had his store opened early in the summer of 1823. Samuel McCorkle commenced building his brick hotel in the fall of 1823. It is on the south side of the public square.* Maj. Wm. Stewart and his brother Charles did the carpenter work." The stores that were opened in Paris in 1823 were mostly classified by Mr. Greer as dry goods stores, but it is to be presumed that they all kept groceries, hardware, etc. The establishing of five stores in the town within a few months after it was laid out in an uncleared forest speaks well for its rapid development. It grew and improved with the country, so that in 1860 it contained the following business houses, viz.: Howard & Powell, Dunlap & Bro., Wright & Son, J. V. Risen, McFarland & Aycock, Worthen & Cardwell, O. F. Brasswell, Rushing & McCullough, Blanton & James, B. Lowenstein & Bro., J. A. Brown, Crawford McNeal & Co., Moore & Wilson, Dunn & Crutchfield, A. L. Bradley, Jacob Alexander & Co., J. A. Nance, E. J. McFarland, Olive & Loving, Howard & Pearce, Williams, Clark & Co., and John M. Vondyke, together with the hotels, boarding houses, churches, schools, mills, etc. During the war all business was suspended in the town, and fortunes were swept away. But notwithstanding the disasters of that period, business has revived, and the town is in a flourishing condition, with the following business houses and business enterprises, to wit: Dry goods—Head & Carter, Joe H. Bullock & Co., McNeill Bros., Johnson & Vancleave, Wright Bros., J. P. Cooper, B. Lubin, G. T. Morris, W. C. Williams, T. F. Jones. Drugs—T. C. McNeill, E. W. Grove, G. H. Trevathan, J. T. W. Cole. Jewelry—George D. Van Horn, David Jones. Family groceries—W. T. Wrather, John M. Carter, F. E. Doty, Arthur & Stevens, J. B. Lemonds, Goldston & McGehee, J. W. Porter, W. F. Dawson, H. C. & F. W. McNeill, H. Mayne. Millinery—Mrs. F. A. Orr, Mrs. Fannie Robbins. Furniture—John V. Eaker, C. Frazier. Undertakers—W. E. Rogers, R. W. McCullough. Banks—Commercial, of Paris, Bank of Henry. Hotels—Carter House and Blanton House. Manufactures—Freeman, Lasater & Co., sash, doors and blinds; John T. Currier & Co.,

---
*Now known as the Carter House.

cotton factory; Williams & Hudson, tobacco factory; H. V. Freeman, cotton-gin and mill; J. N. Thomason, grist-mill. Churches—Methodist Episcopal South, Cumberland Presbyterian, Christian and Missionary Baptist. Colored churches—African Methodist, Methodist Episcopal South and Missionary Baptist. Schools—The Mrs. S. H. Welch High School, public male and female school of Paris, with 250 pupils, The Mrs. Bruce Infant School, Mrs. McAnulty's Primary School and the colored public school.

The town is exceedingly well supplied with churches and schools, and all are well sustained. Benevolent and secret societies: Masonic, Odd Fellows, Knights of Honor, Good Templars, Ancient Order of United Workingmen and Knights of the Golden Cross. Ministers: Rev. B. G. Mitchell, Cumberland Presbyterian; Rev. S. C. Hearn, Missionary Baptist; Rev. G. K. Brooks, Methodist Episcopal Church South; Rev. A. C. Smithers, Christian. Physicians: S. C. Edmunds, F. F. Porter, R. A. Grainger, Jr., J. B. Pillow, Jr., and J. M. Corum. Attorneys: See elsewhere. In addition to the foregoing there are five drinking saloons, two barber shops, three blacksmith and other mechanics' shops; also two good weekly newspapers.

Paris was incorporated September 30, 1823, under the name and style of "The Mayor and Aldermen of Paris." Under this charter the people elected the aldermen, and they chose the mayor. The charter was afterward amended, and finally repealed by an act passed March 30, 1883, and the town re-incorporated under the name and style of "The Mayor and Board of Aldermen of the City of Paris." Under the new charter the people elect the mayor, marshal, recorder and aldermen. The present city officers are W. A. Carter, mayor; J. T. W. Cole, recorder; E. H. Blanton, marshal, and T. C. Fryer, Geo. D. Van Horn, F. H. Upchurch, J. J. Head, John C. Sweeney and W. H. Lasater, aldermen. The population of Paris is about 2,000. Gen. Felix H. Zollicoffer, at the age of seventeen, in company with two other young men, commenced the publication of a paper in 1829 or 1830, in Paris. This was the first paper published in the county, and the enterprise soon proved a failure. Wm. Gates published a paper in Paris during the thirties, and S. B. Aden in the forties, and perhaps later. A Mr. Moise established the first Democratic paper in the county in 1852. This was followed in 1855 by the *Sentinel*, which was established by H. F. Cummins, and published a few years. The *Analysis* was published at some time prior to the war, by a Mr. Darwin, and the *Bee* by John W. Cook. The *Intelligencer* was established in 1866 by H. W. Wall and W. B. Porter. The *Gazette* was established in 1877 by Holsapple & Hutchins. It changed hands several times, and in 1879 the name was changed to the *Paris Post*. In 1883 the *Intelligencer* and *Post* were consolidated under the name of the *Paris Post-Intelligencer*. The latter is now edited and published by Squire J. R. Rison. It has a large circulation and is well sustained. The *Paris Tribune* was established in September, 1886, by James P. McGee and Headley Boyd, editors and publishers, and is meeting with merited success.

About the year 1821, Maj. John Randle, William Randle, George D. Randle and James Miller dug a well in a "lick" about four miles from the present station of Springville, on the Louisville & Nashville Railroad, prospecting for salt. At the depth of sixteen feet they struck a rock of brown marble. Subsequently they bored through the rock a depth of 374 feet, and there struck a large stream of sulphur, instead of salt water. This water issues from the well in quantities sufficient to turn a mill. The place is utilized to some extent as a summer resort. There are some mineral springs near it.

Cottage Grove, in the northwestern part of the county, and in the best agricultural district, was established about the year 1845, on lands belonging to Dr. Bowden. It contains six general stores. three or four tobacco houses, two or three cotton-gins and a grist-mill. The village does a large business, especially in the tobacco trade. Conyersville, in the northern part of the county, was established about the year 1846, on lands belonging to Pack. Conyer. It was once a flourishing village with about eight stores, but since the war it has declined to two dry goods stores and a family grocery. Henry Station, on the Louisville & Nashville Railroad, in the southwestern part of the county, was established in 1858, on lands of Peterson and Busby. It is a prosperous village, and has several cotton-gins and does a heavy trade in cotton. It has a steam grist-mill, four good stores and other business enterprises. Como, near the west line of the county, was established about the year 1859. It has several stores, cotton-gins and tobacco houses, and does a considerable amount of business.

Elkhorn, nine miles east of Paris, has two general stores. Buchanan, in the northeastern part of the county, was established during President Buchanan's administration. It contains two general stores which do a good business. Manlyville was established in an early day, on lands owned by William Manly. At one time it had five or six stores and did a considerable business, but has gone down and now only contains one store. At all the foregoing named villages, or in their immediate vicinity, are good schools and churches. Caledonia, in the southwestern part of the county, was, in an early day, a flourishing village, but since the completion of the railroads, and the establishment of other towns, it has entirely gone down, and the site has become a farm.

Among the pioneer school-teachers of Henry County were John Reavis, Henry Lightfoot, Samuel Hankins, Wm. Watson, Henry Harding and Samuel W. Fleming; and the pioneer schools, as is the case in all newly settled counties, were of a primary character. No free school system then existed, and the first schools were known as subscription schools," that is, a stated price per pupil for each month was paid directly to the teacher by the parent or guardian. As soon as villages were established and the population became sufficient to sustain them, academies were also established at the village sites, which were generally well patronized by those wishing to educate their children. The town of Paris nearly always had sectarian schools, some of which were very successful, but it is claimed that sectarianism was often exercised very much to their injury. No adequate means were provided for the education of the masses, and none whatever for the colored people, until the present free school system was inaugurated; and to show the working of this system, the following statistics are taken from the county school superintendent's report for the year 1885, it being the latest one to which the writer has access. Scholastic population: White—male, 2,935; female, 2,788; total, 5,723. Colored—male, 1,478; female, 1,447; total, 2,925. Number of pupils enrolled during the year: White—male, 2,283; female, 2,072; total, 4,355. Colored—male, 1,123; female, 1,037; total, 2,160. Number of teachers employed: White—male, 43; female, 56. Colored—male, 27; female, 7; grand total, 133. Number of schools: White, 92; colored, 33; total, 125. Number of days taught during the year, 95. By a study of the foregoing it will be seen that 76 per cent of the white scholastic population, and 73 per cent of the colored, attended the free schools. This is a tolerably good showing, the per cent of enrollment being larger than in many other counties, though not up to the highest. It is sufficient, however, to show that the free school system is agreeably accepted, and well sustained in Henry County. It is claimed by some that the daily sessions are entirely too short.

The Methodist Episcopal, Baptist and Cumberland Presbyterian were the pioneer churches of Henry County, and they have always been and are still the leading religious denominations, with their numerical strength in the order here named. The pioneer Methodist ministers were Benjamin Peeples, Rev. Couch, John Manly, Samuel Hankins, and others. Among the pioneer Baptist ministers were Rev. Trainer after whom Trainer Creek was named, Lewis Baldwin, Samuel McGowan, Jacob Browning, James Conyers, James Haynes and Lewis M. Edgar.

The latter, at present writing, is living about five miles northeast of Paris. William Henry, James Laws, Robert Baker, James Mackey and Richard Beard were among the pioneer ministers of the Cumberland Presbyterian Church. The latter was afterward president of the Cumberland University, at Lebanon. Rev. Benjamin Peeples was the first minister sent into West Tennessee by the Tennessee Conference of the Methodist Episcopal Church, and it is generally conceded that he was the real pioneer Christian worker in West Tennessee, being the first man who came west of the Tennessee River in the capacity of a minister. He was located, about 1819, at McLemoresville, in Carroll County, where the land office was first established, and was the first circuit rider in that and Henry County. He soon after located in this county, near Manlyville, where he became a farmer as well as a minister, and lived there until his death, which occurred recently. He was a great and good man, a devoted Christian, and most eloquent preacher, as all who knew him cheerfully testify. He was for many years a member of the county court, and at one time the judge thereof, as has already been stated. He reared and educated six sons, and sent five of them, viz.: William, Benjamin F., John R., Thomas and Samuel, out as ministers. He also reared and educated Richard, Thomas and John Randle, his three brothers-in-law, and Arthur Davis and John M. Steele, two orphan boys, and sent them all out as ministers. In all, ten ministers of the Gospel were reared, educated and sent out from his household, and all of them became prominent Christian workers. Can his record be surpassed? Rev. John Manly, then a local preacher, established the first church in Henry County about the year 1821. Rev. Couch was the second circuit rider. The three churches above named soon organized societies and erected church edifices throughout the county. Before such edifices were erected, each society held religious services at the dwelling houses of the members. Later came the Christian denomination and established a church in Paris, and recently the Adventists have established a church in the Twenty-fourth Civil District. These people regard the seventh day of the week as the true Sabbath, and persist in their right to labor on Sunday. Three of the members of this church were prosecuted in 1885 for laboring on Sunday, and were found guilty and fined $10 each and costs of suit. They appealed to the supreme court, where the judgment of the lower court was sustained, and they have just now, December, 1886, completed the task of working out their fines and costs, and been set at liberty. They are said to be honorable men, who willingly suffered this penalty to maintain their convictions of right. In 1831 the Tennessee Conference of the Methodist Episcopal Church held its annual session in Paris, with Bishop Joshua Soule presiding. In 1843 the Memphis Conference of the same church held its session at Paris, when Bishops Soule and Capers presided; and again in 1868, when Bishop McTyeire presided. The presiding elders of the Paris District have been as follows: Lewis Garrett, Jr., 1821–23; Robert Payne (afterward bishop), 1823–24; Joshua Boucher, 1824–27; Thomas Smith, 1827–31; George W. D. Harris, 1831–35; Thomas Joyner, 1835–39; Thomas Smith, 1839–41; Thomas Joyner, 1841–45; George W. D. Harris, 1845–49; James W. McFarland, 1849–52; George W. D. Harris, 1852–53; John Randle, 1853–56; Nathan Sullivan, 1856–60; John A. Vincent, 1860–61; Ephraim E. Hamilton, 1861–64; Richmond S. Harris, 1864–67; John H. Witt, 1867–71; John G. Acton, 1871–72; Joseph H. Evans, 1872–75; John H. Witt, 1875–79; Benjamin A. Hayes, 1879–82; Thomas G. Whitten, 1882-86; James H. Roberts, 1886. The first camp-meeting in Henry County was organized and held in 1822, at Manly's Chapel; and there the people have met annually and still continue to meet to worship God in nature's leafy bowers. Camp-meetings were also held for many years at Neill's Chapel, now Chapel Hill, and at the grounds known as Palestine, and Lebanon.

BENTON COUNTY.

BENTON COUNTY belongs to the western division of the State. It extends fifty miles along the west bank of the Tennessee River and is bounded on the north by Henry County, on the west by Henry and Carroll Counties and on the south by Decatur and the "Panhandle" of Carroll County. Including one half of the Tennessee River along its border, it has an area of about 400 square miles, lying partly in the Western Valley and partly in the plateau of West Tennessee. It has an average elevation of about 370 feet. The character of the surface is extremely varied. Near the center of the county, in the vicinity of Camden, it is gently undulating, while along the margin of the river valley are found many steep bluffs and spurs. The valley has an average width of about two miles and contains the most productive land in the county. Along the creeks which thread the county, are usually found flats or bottoms, averaging about one-half mile in width and fringed by low, but distinctly marked ridges. Along the ridges, especially in the southern part of the county, limestone is found at various depths and in the Third

Civil District on Birdsong Creek, there is found a variegated marble of handsome appearance, and capable of taking a fine finish. Some iron is also found along the Tennessee River but no effort has ever been made toward developing it. A marble quarry was opened and worked for some time, near Rockport, but was abandoned several years ago. The soil on the hills is mainly argillacious while that of the bottoms is sandy and black loam. The county is exceedingly well watered, possessing innumerable small streams fed by springs of pure water. The creeks emptying immediately into the Tennessee River are Eagle, Birdsong, Harmony, Sulphur, Crooked Lick and Cypress. The Big Sandy River forms the dividing line between Benton and Henry Counties. Its principal tributaries from the former are Rushing Creek, Ramble Creek and Sugar Creek. Cane Creek and Beaver Dam Creek are tributary to Cypress Creek. Sycamore Creek, Wolf Creek and Seventeen-mile Creek empty their waters into Birdsong Creek. The beds of the creeks flowing into the Tennessee River, with the exception of Cypress Creek, are covered with flinty rock. The timber supply of the county is good. The most abundant variety is oak, but distributed over nearly the whole are found some poplar, while in the southern district chestnut abounds. Hickory, gum, beech, cypress and other varieties are found in greater or less abundance. The principal agricultural products are corn, wheat, oats, hay, peanuts, tobacco, Irish potatoes, sweet potatoes, rye and cotton in small quantities.

The first settlement in Benton County, was made by Willis and Dennis Rushing, on Rushing Creek, six miles north of Camden, about 1819. A year later Nicholas and Lewis Brewer settled in Ramble Creek, twelve miles north of Camden, and at the same time M. Mimms located on Birdsong Creek. During the next four or five years the settlement went on quite rapidly, many coming from Hickman, Stewart and other counties lying on the east side of the Tennessee River. Among those who located along the Big Sandy River were David Watson, John and Wm. Pierce, Lewis Graham, Wm. Cottingham, George McDaniel and James Craig. The Arnolds (Wyatt, James and Wyly) settled on Beaver Dam Creek, while in the neighborhood of Cowell Chapel were Joseph Cowell, Charles Benjamin, and Matthew Williams, Zachary Barker, Thomas Jones, Wm. Thompson, Benjamin Holland and James Lee. The last two named were the first to locate. Ephraim Perkins, Dorsey P. Hudson and William Woods settled about two miles north of where Camden now is. On Eagle Creek were William Hubbs, John Lomaner, Michael Frey, John Barnett, "Cos" Matlock and David Lewis. Among the first settlers on Harman Creek were George W. Farmer, David and Samuel Benton, William Wheatley, Joseph Melton, Si Melton, John Phifer, Daniel Mason a "store keeper," and an old man from whom the creek took its name; Charles and Thomas Wheatley and Simon Nobles, located on Sulphur Creek; John Anderson, near Chalk Level; James Wyly, below Birdsong Creek; John Jackson, Charles Surratt and John B. Carnes, near the present site of Camden.

During the first few years, the settlers depended for a subsistence upon deer, turkey and other wild game, which was very plentiful, and upon bread made from meal ground either in hand-mills or horse-mills. The first water-mill in the county was built by Matthew Williams, on Cypress Creek in 1824. Another was erected at about the same time on the banks of the Big Sandy, by a man by the name of King. About 1832, a mill was built by James Hogg, on Birdsong Creek, not far from Chaseville. It was afterward owned and operated by Green Flowers. The mill on the same creek, now owned by John Allen, was built by Pleasant Mullinix, early in the thirties. The first cotton-gin in the county was built by Dorsey P. Hudson, on his farm northeast of Camden, in 1828. William Thompson also built one at very nearly the same time. The mills mentioned above were all grist mills at first, but later saw-mills were attached to them. Several other mills have been built on the various creeks of the county, but they have been most numerous along the Big Sandy. No other manufactories with the exception of a tobacco factory at Camden, have ever been established.

Previous to the year 1836, the greater portion of what is now Benton County, constituted a part of Humphreys County. The remainder, including about one civil district, was taken from Henry County. The county was established by an act of the General Assembly, passed November 24, 1835. A postoffice named Tranquility had been established on the great stage route from Memphis to Nashville, about one mile west of the present town of Camden, and there at the house of Samuel H. Burton, contracted from Samuel Haliburton, on February 7, 1836, the county was organized by the commissioners, Green Flowers, Ephraim Perkins, Lewis Brewer, John F. Johnson and George Camp. The magistrates constituting the first county court were George W. Farmer, chairman; John D. Rushing, Hezekiah Green, William Barnes, John Pope, John H. Williams, Charles W. Wheatley, John Anderson, William Hubbs, Lewis Brewer, Pleasant Mullinix, Jesse D. Hall, William Wright, Burrell Beard, David Benton, Edward W. Lynch, Robert H. Hawthorne, John Kilbreath, and Mansfield Barnett. The first term of the circuit court was held at the same place on April 11, 1836, J. W. Cook, judge of the Ninth Judicial Circuit presiding. Dorsey P. Hudson, qualified as clerk, giving the following persons as sureties: Dennis, Robert, Able and Willis Rushing, Lewis Brewer, G. W. L. Hudson, Ephraim Perkins, Robert Holmes, and Hosea D. Browning. James R. McMurray was the attorney-general. The grand jury empaneled was Robert Rushing, foreman, Matthew Presson, Robert Holmes, Samuel Presson, Willis, Dennis and Abel Rushing, John Presson, C. C. Poe, John Merritt, Hosea D. Browning, Wilson M. Surratt and John Jackson. The house in which court was held during the first year, was a one-story log structure with one door and with big cracks for windows. The next year a two story brick building thirty by thirty-six feet was erected on the public square. It was well arranged for the times, having a court-room above and offices below. This house was occupied until the latter part of 1853, when it was torn down, and a new building similar in size and arrangement was completed about January 1, 1855. Meanwhile court was held in the Baptist Church. This building in 1877 was found to be unsafe, and was torn down to make room for the present fine brick, which was erected at a cost of about $9,000.

The first jail was a log building erected in 1837 on the lot where the present jail stands. It was about twenty feet square with double walls eight inches apart, the space between being filled with upright poles. It was built by Irwin B. Carnes. About 1840 a brick jail was erected upon the same lot. It was used until about 1866, when it was burned by the prisoners confined within it, with the expectation of making their escape. In this they were disappointed, and it was with the greatest difficulty that they were rescued. Immediately afterward a second brick jail, similar to the one burned was erected. This was used until 1883, when the present excellent brick building was completed at a cost of about $8,000.

At the organization of the county it was divided into nine civil districts, and so continued until 1850, when the Tenth District was formed from a portion of the Fifth. to the remainder of which was added a part of the Fourth and Sixth Districts. In 1860 the Eleventh District was formed from fractions of the First and Third, and in 1872 portions of the Fourth and Sixth were constituted the Twelfth District. In 1883 two additional districts, the Thirteenth and Fourteenth, were formed. The former was composed of a fraction taken from Decatur County, added to a portion of the First District; the latter was constituted from part of the Second, Third and Fourth Districts.

The following is a complete list of the officers of the county from its organization to the present time:

County court clerks—Thomas H. Burton, 1836–38; G. R. Kelsey, 1838–43; Col. W. P. Morris, 1843–52; William M. McAuley, 1852–60; W. A. Jones, 1860–65; A. C. Presson, 1865–68; John Rushing, 1868–

70; D. A. Bruce, 1870-75; J. M. Holladay, 1875-78; A. C. McRae, 1878.*

Sheriffs—Thomas Jones, 1836-42; Allen C. Presson, 1842-44; David Brewer, 1844-48; William M. McAuley, 1848-52; Isaac Anderson, 1852-54; David Brewer, 1854-56; William W. Davidson, 1856-60; John H. Farmer, 1860-64; David Brewer, 1865-66; E. C. Smalley, 1866-68; Malcomb McKenzie, 1868-70; Burrell L. Utley, 1870-71; John P. Morris, 1871-72; Amos Corbett, 1872-73; John P. Morris, 1873-74; David A. Gossett, 1874-75; Robert J. Bomar, 1875-80; J. P. Lashlee, 1880-84; W. G. Kirk, 1884.*

Circuit court clerks—Dorsey P. Hudson, 1836-48; John W. Davidson, 1848-52; W. J. Greer, 1852-56; William A. Jones, 1856-60; W. W. Davidson, 1860-65; J. F. Presson, 1865-66; W. A. Jones, 1866-70; R. P. Haley, 1870-78; A. G. McDaniel, 1878-86; W. C. Benton, 1886.*

Trustees—John H. Williams, 1836-40; Amos Bruce, 1840-48; Merritt Melton, 1848-52; John H. Williams, 1852-56; David Quillin, 1856-58; John H. Williams, 1858-60; F. A. McElyea, 1860-65; J. C. McDaniel, 1865-68; W. L. McKenzie, 1868-70; J. M. Castile, 1870-72; James G. Hudson, 1872-74; Eli Hatley, 1874-76; James G. Hudson, 1876-82; William M. King, 1882-86; W. F. Baber, 1886.*

Clerks and masters—Dorsey P. Hudson, 1856-66; W. A. Steele, 1866-71; Green B. Greer, 1871.*

The county surveyors were Burrill Beard, 1836-40; W. A. Steele, 1840-44; Robert H. Hawthorne, 1844-48; A. C. Presson, 1848-52; Green Flowers, 1852-60; A. C. Presson, 1860-65; J. R. Childress, 1865-83; D. H. Van Huss, 1883*.

The superintendants of schools were George Hollowell, 1866-69; J. F. Presson, 1873-75; J. M. Castile, 1875-79; D. J. Allen, 1879-81; A. J. Farmer, 1881-83; D. J. Allen, 1883*.

The registers were G. W. L. Hudson, 1836-40; John W. Utley, 1840-44; W. C. Thompson, 1844-48; D. F. McElyea, 1848-52; B. H. Lightfoot, 1852-60; W. L. Gordon, 1860-65; B. H. Lightfoot, 1865-67; S. M. Atchison, 1867-68; T. J. Ward, 1868-69; T. A. Henry, February to April, 1869; Wayne Rye, 1869-78; A. H. Mitchell, 1878-82; Travis Davidson, 1882-86; A. H. Mitchell, 1886*.

The representatives to the Legislature resident in the county have been James Wyly, S. C. Pavatt, R. J. Lawrence, Ichabod Farmer, David Brewer, W. P. Morris and John P. Lashlee. Since 1881 the county has been entitled to a representation, and the last two above named served under the new apportionment. W. P. Morris represented the senatorial

*Present incumbent.

district, to which Benton County is attached, in 1861-62 and 1879-80. It was also represented by J. H. Farmer in 1885.

The commissioners appointed to organize the county and fix the county seat located it upon forty acres of land occupied by John Jackson who had no title to the land other than occupancy. He was allowed however a few choice lots for his own use as compensation for the land appropriated. The survey was made by John Doherty and Burrell Beard in December, 1836, and a public sale of the lots took place during the following month. The first dwelling in the town was erected by Irwin B. Carnes, a carpenter. At about the same time Thomas H. Burton built a small log store house on the northeast corner of the square which for a short time was occupied by Burrell Beard. Anderson Lashlee also erected a log store and dwelling-house combined on the southeast corner of the square. Edward and James Haywood opened a store on the south side of the square. In 1838 C. K. Wyly began selling goods in the house formerly occupied by Beard; just previous to that time Samuel H. Burton had built a brick hotel on the adjoining lot, the site now occupied by the Stigall House. The first physician to locate in the town was J. L. Williams, who was among the earliest residents. During the decade from 1840-50 the town continued to improve though somewhat slowly. Among the principal merchants of that period were C. K. and T. R. Wyly, Crawford and Alfred Rushing, Anderson Lashlee, John H. and Cave Farmer and John Phifer. In 1843 three or four young men of more than ordinary ability were added to the population of the town. Alvin Hawkins, afterward judge of the supreme court and governor of Tennessee, came as a young attorney just admitted to the bar. W. P. Morris came to take charge of the office of clerk of the county court, and M. L. Travis, for thirty years the leading physician of the county, came to engage in the practice of his profession. D. F. McElyea, afterward register of the county, also located during the same year.

The next decade, although a fairly prosperous period, witnessed no material increase in the population of the town. In 1850 the firm of Pickett & Morris engaged in the mercantile business, and since that time the latter has been one of the most successful men of the county. C. K. Wyly, as he has done since that time continued to be a leading merchant. Others engaged in the mercantile business during the fifties were T. K. Wyly, Hall & Sharp and Lewis Lashlee, who succeeded Anderson Lashlee. From 1855 to 1860 a tobacco factory producing chewing tobacco in considerable quantities was operated by William Pickett & J. C. McDaniel. Besides those already mentioned the principal physicians were R. B. Travis, James Moses and Thomas Douglass.

Since the war the business interests of the town have continued much the same as before. Several firms and individuals have been engaged in merchandising for short periods, but with the exception of C. K. Wyly and W. P. Morris, none has remained for many years. In 1872 the People's Company was incorporated with forty members, mostly farmers; two years later it had 175 members with a cash capital of $6,000 divided into shares of $25 each. At the present time it has about eighty members. It is reorganized every five years.

The present business interests of Camden are represented by the following individuals and firms: C. K. Wyly, W. P. Morris, Joseph G. Hudson, W. T. Hubbs, Bateman & Herrin, and a stock company, general merchandise; George Shelton, and James Jeffrey, family groceries; J. E. Totty, drugs and groceries; Revins & McAuley and R. M. Hawley, groceries and liquors: T. B. Totty, drugs; Aaron Arnold, saloon and hotel; Henry G. Stigall, hotel and livery stable; A. G. McDaniel & Bro., livery stable; F. G. & F. A. McElyea, blacksmiths; E. M. Cornell and John Arnold, shoe-makers; Mrs. L. E. Davis, millinery; Daniel Markham, jeweler; E. M. McAuley and J. W. Drain, dentists; W. T. Hubbs, R. B. Travis, F. C. Whitfield and W. R. Haman, physicians; C. N. Travis, *Camden Herald*.

Camden Lodge, No. 179, A. F. & A. M. was organized about 1845. Between 1850 and 1855, in company with the Baptist Church and the Sons of Temperance, a building was erected west of the public square. This hall was used by the lodge until 1876 when it was destroyed by fire. In 1878 a new hall was erected upon the same lot. The present membership of the lodge is about sixty. The I. O. O. F. organized a lodge in 1880, but on account of a lack of interest it was suspended after a few months.

Camden Lodge, No. 416, K. of H., was organized December 23, 1876, with the following charter members: I. C. Yarbrough, past dictator; R. P. Haley, dictator; William Stanford, assistant dictator; R. M. Hawley, vice-dictator; N. T. Strickland, guardian; Wayne Rye, reporter; L. H. Presson, financial reporter; F. C. Whitfield, treasurer, and E. M. Cornell chaplain; A. J. Morris, J. D. McAuley, and A. P. Lashlee. The lodge now has but twelve members.

In the spring of 1886 the Benton County Temperance Alliance was organized with a membership of about fifty.

The first newspaper in the county was the *Central Democrat*, established by William F. Doherty in 1852 and continued for two years. After its suspension the county was without a newspaper until June, 1875, when the *Benton Banner* was established. The first few numbers were printed at Huntingdon, and published from Camden by T. H. Baker. The venture proving successful an office was opened in Camden and its publication was continued by W. F. Moiden & Co. It changed hands frequently, being published successively by Travis & Crockett, Travis & McGee, R. B. Travis and H. K. Springer. It was a seven column folio, and was a credit to the county, but the patronage was not sufficient to retain it, and in the fall of 1879 it was suspended. The office was purchased by John C. Brown and J. L. S. Travis, and removed to Dresden. In 1881 the *Camden Herald*, a six column folio, was established by E. M. and C. N. Travis. It also changed proprietors several times until 1883, when C. N. Travis became the editor and sole proprietor. During 1884 it was changed to a five column quarto, and January 1, 1886, to a five column folio. Mr. Travis is an experienced printer, and is managing the paper successfully. He recently added a job press to the office, and is building up a good business in that line.

Since the completion of the railroad a little village known as South Camden has sprung up around the depot, about one half-mile south of the town. Its business men at present are I. C. Yarbrough, N. E. Finley, J. F. Presson and A. J. ——— general merchandise; Lindsey McElyea, groceries; P. W. McDade, produce; A. J. Hudson, saw and grist-mill.

Big Sandy is a thriving village on the Memphis division of the Louisville & Nashville Railroad, about fourteen miles north of Camden. It is located on land formerly owned by R. M. Graham. The first building erected was a saloon built by J. B. Lindsey in 1871. He also built the first store, about two years later, which was occupied by G. T. Morris and William Caraway. The first dwelling was built by A. C. McRae and J. B. Lindsey.

The business of the town at present is conducted by the following individuals and firms: William Caraway, G. T. Morris, J. F. Dowdey, Graham & Grainger, and Hudson & Son, general merchandise; Bullock & Cantrell, drugs; stave factory, Hudson & Son; saw-mill, William Caraway; blacksmiths, A. Bell, John DeBruce and J. E. Wilson & Son.

Big Sandy Lodge, No. 290, A. F. & A. M., was organized as Pleasant Ridge Lodge, No. 290, at Pleasant Ridge Church, in January, 1861, under a dispensation from the grand lodge, with the following officers: A. W. Russell, W. M.; L. Childress, S. W.; W. R. Pierce, J. W.; J. B. Lindsey, S. D.; W. Warmack, J. D., J. P. Byrn, Sec.; J. Askew, Treas.; T. J. Warmack, Tyler. Owing to the general suspension of lodges during the war no charter was obtained until December 6, 1866. From that time until 1879, meetings were held at Pleasant Ridge. At the latter date the lodge was removed to Big Sandy when, in partnership with the

Odd Fellows, a hall was erected about two years later, and in 1883 the name was changed to compare with that of the town.

Big Sandy Lodge, No. 185, I. O. O. F. was organized at Pleasant Ridge Church about 1876, and was removed to Big Sandy three years afterward. The first officers were E. N. Williams, N. G.; William Caraway, V. G.; G. T. Moses, Sec.; and P. M. Melton, Treas. The present membership of the lodge is about twenty.

West Danville is a station on the Memphis Division of the Louisville & Nashville Railroad on the west bank of the Tennessee River. It was established in 1860 on land owned by Calvin Bomar. Point Mason, Thompson Point, and Rockport are all steamboat landings on the Tennessee River. Coxbury and Chaseville, twelve miles southeast and fourteen miles south of Camden, respectively, are small hamlets, each having a postoffice and store. Mt. Carmel, situated in a fine agricultural section fifteen miles south from Camden, and Williamsburg in a broken but productive district six miles northwest, as well as Sawyer's Mill, six miles west, are small hamlets of more or less local importance.

The small amount of legal business in Benton County has precluded the possibility of its having a bar of great experience or large numbers. As has been stated, the first resident attorney was Alvin Hawkins, who located at Camden in 1843. As a young man, he displayed unusual ability and soon became desirous of a broader field in which to exercise his talents. Accordingly, after two years, he removed to Huntingdon. He was succeeded by Col. W. F. Doherty, who had been attorney-general of his judicial circuit. He continued a member of the Camden bar until his death in 1881. He possessed a fine vein of humor and was a good speaker. In 1870 he was chosen a member of the convention which framed the new State constitution. John W. Davidson, while clerk of the circuit court, took up the study of law, and afterward was engaged in its practice for some time.

About 1846 S. C. Pavatt removed from Huntingdon to Camden, where he remained until the Civil war. He was a man of great dignity of bearing and possessed unusual talents. He was at one time chancellor of his district. T. A. Henry located at Camden about 1866, and remained until 1882 when he removed to Texas. While not a superior advocate, he was an excellent office lawyer, and never failed to present his cases properly. He always preferred the chancery practice and obtained the greater part of the business in the county coming under that branch of his profession. The present bar is composed mainly of young men of good ability, who, in a great measure, have their legal reputation to make. W. F. Moiden and A. J. Farmer are the two eldest members, both having been licensed to practice about eight years ago. The former prepared himself for his profession in the office of T. A. Henry. He is a good lawyer before a jury, and has a fair practice.

Joseph E. Jones, the present attorney-general of the Twelfth Judicial Circuit, was admitted to the bar at Camden, in December, 1878. He immediately took high rank among the members of his profession in this section of the State, and in 1884 was elected to the responsible position he now holds. He is well grounded in the law, and is an advocate of no ordinary ability.

T. C. Rye began the study of law with Mr. Jones and since his admission to the bar has been located at Camden. He has secured a good practice for so young a man and is fast gaining an enviable reputation as an advocate.

Walter Ayres is a highly educated young man of good native ability. As yet, however, he has given but little attention to the practice of his profession, having been employed as private secretary to Congressman J. M. Taylor and clerk of the Congressional Committee on Naval affairs.

Travis Davidson, who has recently completed a term as register of Benton County, is a man of unquestioned integrity, and possesses good legal ability. He has recently engaged in the practice of his profession. J. F. Presson and —— Brandon, are also licensed attorneys.

During the first three or four years after the organization of the circuit court, it was presided over alternately by Judges J. C. Cook, William R. Harris, Benjamin C. Totten, Mortimer A. Martin and William C. Dunlap. Afterward, until 1845, Judge Totten occupied the bench. His residence was at Huntingdon. He was one of the ablest judges ever upon the bench in this judicial circuit, although in private life he was recognized as a genial gentleman, while in the discharge of his official duties he was exceedingly dignified and reserved, and maintained excellent order in the court room. He was succeeded by William Fitzgerald, who continued upon the bench until the suspension of the courts in May, 1862. He was an able jurist, and socially was very popular throughout the circuit. In 1865, L. L. Hawkins, of Huntingdon, was commissioned judge of the circuit court by Gov. Brownlow. He continued to preside until 1870, when he was succeeded by James D. Porter, of Paris, who four years later was elected governor of Tennessee. The remaining four years of the term were filled by Jo. R. Hawkins, of Huntingdon. At the election of 1878, Samuel B. Ayres, of Dresden, was elected judge of the judicial circuit, but died in less than a year after entering upon the office. Clinton Aden, of Paris, completed the unexpired term, and in 1886,

W. H. Swiggart, of Union City, was elected to the office for the succeeding eight years.

Benton County has never been deficient in patriotism nor military spirit. Promptly upon the breaking out of the Mexican war, a large company of volunteers was formed and organized, with Alvin Hawkins as captain; O. B. Caldwell, first lieutenant, and W. P. Morris, second lieutenant. They at once reported to the governor, but the quota of the county was filled and they were never called into service.

The first company organized in the county for the late Civil war was Company C, of the Fifth Tennessee Regiment, Volunteer Infantry. It was recruited in April and the early part of May, 1861. The following were the commissioned officers at its first organization: Captain, M. S. Corbett; first lieutenant, Calvin Rushing; second lieutenant, Alfred Rushing; third lieutenant, George Lashlee; orderly sergeant, Meredith Corbett. The company left on the 20th of May for Camp Dawson, Henry County, and thence went to Humboldt, where the regiment was organized. From that time until the close of the war, the movements of the company were identical with those of the regiment, an account of which is found in another chapter of this work. At the close of the first year, the term of enlistment having expired, the company re-enlisted, and was reorganized at Corinth. P. G. Swar, who had succeeded M. S. Corbett soon after the original organization, was re-elected captain, Meredith Corbett was chosen first lieutenant, Ed. Hudson, second lieutenant; Isaac Wyguf, third lieutenant, and J. H. Combs, orderly sergeant. At about the same time Company C was consolidated with Company A, and soon after, Capt. Swar having been placed on post duty, the consolidated companies were commanded by Capt. A. P. Wilson, of Company A. Near the close of the war the entire regiment, numbering scarcely more than a full company, was placed under the command of Benjamin Peeples. Company L, of the above regiment, was organized in May, 1861, with John T. Winfrey as captain.

B. L. Utley, first lieutenant; James Bellew, second lieutenant; John Matthews, third lieutenant, and "Bud" Fry, orderly sergeant. At the reorganization J. T. Winfrey was elected captain; James Bellew, first lieutenant; Henry Linderman, second lieutenant, and John Matthews, third lieutenant.

Late in the fall of 1861 Capt. R. W. Ayres organized a company of about 100 men, of whom J. W. Williams was first lieutenant, Samuel Gilbert, second lieutenant; Archibald Jordan, third lieutenant; and Austin Russell, orderly sergeant. Before being organized into a regiment, the company was ordered to the Tennessee River bridge, at West Danville, to superintend the reshipping of stores and munitions for Fort Donelson. After the fall of Fort Henry, the command was stationed as a guard along the railroad to Paris, until March 6, 1862, when it was ordered to Henderson Station. It remained there until June, when it marched to join Bragg, then entering upon his raid into Kentucky. It failed to reach Bragg's army, and dropped back to the Tennessee River, where about the 1st of October it captured the steamboat "Terry," together with her crew, two cannons, several stands of small arms and other supplies. Capt. Ayres then proceeded with his company to Tullahoma, the headquarters of Gen. Bragg, which place he reached about the last of November with sixty-eight men. The company was then reorganized and placed under the command of the provost-marshal general, in which position it remained until the close of the war. The new officers were J. W. Williams, captain; William Love, first lieutenant; J. T. Heggie, second lieutenant; and Thomas Scott, third lieutenant.

Company A, of the Fifty-fifth Tennessee Regiment, was organized in October, 1861, with William A. Jones as captain; W. Sharp, first lieutenant; Isaac N. Presson, second lieutenant; G. W. Ballard, third lieutenant, and W. R. Herrin, orderly sergeant. The company went to Trenton, Tenn., where it was attached to a battalion of infantry, and sent to Columbus, Ky., at which place the regiment was organized. With the remainder of the regiment it was captured at Island No. 10, and the privates and non-commissioned officers sent to Camp Douglas, where they remained, with the exception of six weeks spent at Madison, Wis., until exchanged in September, 1862. The commissioned officers during the same time were confined at Johnson's Island. Upon reorganization Solomon Jones, who had succeeded his brother in the command of the was re-elected captain; Green B. Greer was chosen first lieutenant; Isaac N. Presson, second lieutenant; and Orrin E. Hawley, third lieutenant. It was soon after consolidated with Company B. Company B was organized at about the same time as Company A. P. M. Milton was chosen captain; J. K. Wheatley, first lieutenant; B. F. Hall, second lieutenant; Charles J. Wheatley, third lieutenant; and G. A. Kemp, orderly sergeant. Upon reorganization the same officers were re-elected with the exception of Charles J. Wheatley, whose place was filled by E. A. Pierce. After consolidation some of the officers were placed upon post duty, while others were retained as supernumeraries.

Company I, of the Forty-ninth Regiment Tennessee Volunteer Infantry, was organized at Camden in the fall of 1861, with Alonzo Napier as captain; "Mira" Nunnery, first lieutenant; Henry Roberson, second lieutenant; H. K. Camp, third lieutenant, and A. H. Mitchell, orderly sergeant.

The company then went to Fort Donelson, where the regiment was organized, and where, in February, it was captured. After about seven months' imprisonment, the commissioned officers at Johnson's Island and the privates and non-commissioned officers at Camp Douglas, they were exchanged, and the company was reorganized at Clinton, Miss. The officers chosen were captain, Isaac Anderson; first lieutenant, Henry Robertson; second lieutenant, H. K. Camp, and orderly sergeant, A. H. Mitchell. At Port Hudson the company was consolidated with Capt. McClellan's company, and he assumed command of the combined forces, Capt. Anderson having been placed upon detached duty. The company thus continued until the close of the war.

Company A, of the Twenty-seventh Tennessee Regiment, was organized in July, 1861. Aaron Lawler was elected captain; A. J. Hicks, first lieutenant; D. A. Bruce, second lieutenant; Jasper Hooten, third lieutenant; A. C. Hall, orderly sergeant. During the first year Bruce and Hooten were both discharged on account of disabilities. The latter's place was filled by John Bibbs, and at the reorganization which took place at Tupelo, Miss., A. C. Hall was chosen first lieutenant.

The first school taught in Benton County was on Rushing Creek, in 1822 or 1823. Prominent among the early teachers were Allen C. Presson, who taught the first school in what is now the Sixth Civil District in 1830; his brother, William Presson, and George R. Kelsey. The last named taught for several years, and was the first teacher in Camden. In 1839 W. A. Steele took charge of the Camden school and continued for several months. He had between fifty and sixty scholars, whom he taught in a house on a lot near where the jail now is. January 25, 1838, the General Assembly of Tennessee passed an act incorporating the Benton Male and Female Academy, with the following board of trustees: W. Rushing, D. P. Hudson, James S. Scales, Elijah Woods, A. B. Wilson, Berry Vester, Willis Arnold and Green Flowers, and soon after a school was opened and Jordan G. Sims and wife were installed as teachers. They were excellent instructors and maintained one of the best schools ever in the county. Sims was succeeded by W. A. Steele, who, in 1859, built a house of his own near the depot, where he taught for some time. The academy is still continued. A portion of the year it is supported by the public school fund and the remainder of the time by private subscription.

Under the public school system established in 1866 George Hollowell was elected county superintendent. Only a few schools were opened, however, as the portion of the school fund allotted to Benton County for that year amounted to only $1,514.20. The next year it was increased to $3,581.10, and in 1869 the superintendent reported that 23 white and

1 colored schools had been established, with an aggregate enrollment of 666 white and 50 colored pupils. The General Assembly of 1869 repealed the law establishing a school system, and no more public schools were held until 1873. In October of that year the county superintendent reported: "We have had no public schools and few private schools for several years; I think in the course of the next month we will have all our schools under way; there will be about forty in the county." A year later he reported the scholastic population of the county as white, 2,578; colored, 135; the aggregate number of pupils enrolled, 2,112; average attendance, 1,437; number of schools, white, 35; colored, 2; amount of school money received, $3,189.58. During the year an election to determine upon levying a special school tax was ordered, and was held in a portion of the district. It resulted in a vote of nearly four to one against the tax. The schools, however, continued to improve slowly and to grow in popular favor. In 1885 the superintendent reported 49 white and 5 colored schools, with an aggregate enrollment of 2,756 and 206 pupils, respectively. The average length of term was fifty days. In January, 1886, the county court levied a special school tax of 50 cents on each poll and 5 cents on each $100 worth of property. The additional fund thus raised increased the length of the term to nearly four months.

In the early history of the county the leading religious denomination was the Primitive Baptist. The first congregation was organized on Cyprus Creek in 1823, by George Turner and Levi Kirkland, the latter of whom became its pastor. Another congregation was organized soon after on Rushing Creek, by the same preachers. As the settlement increased, congregations multiplied, to meet the wants of the growing communities. Services were usually held at private residences until it became possible to erect a house of worship.

The Methodists were scarcely behind the Baptists in the organization of congregations and the building of churches. About 1824 Benjamin F. Peeples, the pioneer circuit rider and presiding elder of West Tennessee, organized the church since known as Cowell Chapel, about two miles southwest of Camden. At nearly the same time a congregation was organized on Eagle Creek, near the residence of William Hubbs. Mt. Carmel and Rushing Chapel were also established at an early date. In 1836 a camp ground, which was used for more than —— years, was constructed on Beaver Dam Creek. A congregation was organized at Camden soon after the town was established and services were conducted in the courthouse until about 1849, when a church was erected upon a lot donated to the trustees by Mrs. J. G. Sims. At the same time the trustees of the Presbyterian Church at Camden, Daniel McElyea, Anderson Lashlee, Henry C. Camp and Samuel Madden, purchased a lot of Irwin B. Carnes, and erected a house upon it. At about the same time a Presbyterian Church was organized at Pleasant Ridge, in the north part of the county.

About 1835 the schism in the Baptist Church began to manifest itself in Benton County, and it is believed that the first division occurred at Rumble Creek Church, the larger part of the congregation adopting the Missionary faith. Rushing Creek Church was converted at about the same time, and other churches rapidly followed. Among the earlier ministers of this denomination were Jacob Browning and his son Benjamin, Lemuel Herrin, Merritt Melton, Josiah Arnold, M. S. Corbett, Obediah Hardin, Josiah Arnold, George Hollowell and Scott Brewer, the last three of whom are still actively engaged in the ministry.

Most prominent among the Presbyterian ministers have been Samuel T. Thomas, Abner Thomas, Abner Cooper, H. Babbitt, H. R. Reid, Allen Justice, William Guthrie, R. M. Gillum and J. H. McKnight.

Among the early presiding elders and circuit riders, who administered to the Methodist congregations of Benton County, were Thomas Smith, G. W. D. Harris, E. J. Williams, Robert Collins, Levi B. Lee, and E. E. Hamilton. At the present time the Methodist Episcopal Church South is the leading denomination of the county, the aggregate membership reaching about 1,200. There are two circuits embraced within the county. The following constitute the Camden Circuit: Cowell Chapel, Shiloh, Palestine, Salem, Mt. Zion, Nanley Chapel, Morris Chapel, Camden, Mt. Carmel, Post Oak Grove, Liberty and Bethlehem. Those in the Big Sandy Circuit are Prospect, Rushing Chapel, Flatwoods, Harmon Creek, Sulphur Creek, Crooked Creek, Lick Creek, Sugar Creek, Big Sandy and New Hope.

The following congregations belong to the Northern Methodist Church: Chestnut Hill, Mt. Zion, Mt. Vincent, Pleasant Hill, McRae Chapel, Wesley Chapel, and possibly two or three others. The aggregate membership of the Cumberland Presbyterian Churches is about 300. They are Camden, Pleasant Ridge, Pleasant Valley, Mt. Zion Chapel, Hudson Grove, Caney Fork and Matlock Chapel.

The Missionary Baptists of the county number about 700, distributed among the following congregations: Cross Roads, Chalk Level, Union Birdsong, Mt. Zion, Unity, Shiloh, Rushing Creek, Chalk Hill and Ramble Creek.

The Primitive Baptists now have only two congregations in the county, Cypruss and Ebenezer. The Congregational Methodists have a church on Lick Creek, the only one of that denomination in the county. The Christians also have one church at Mt. Carmel.

CARROLL COUNTY.

G. J. Adams was born in Halifax County of the Old Dominion, in December, 1826, one of four children born to Meads and Jane (Irby) Adams, who were born in Virginia, in 1799 and 1807, respectively. They were married and reared their family in their native county. The father was a stone mason by trade, and died in 1832. The mother departed this life in 1858. Our subject was reared by his relatives and was educated in the common schools. At the age of fourteen he began working in the foundry of Geo. Avery. October 23, 1850, he married Armon E., daughter of Joseph and Mary Fuqua. Mrs. Adams was born in Halifax County, Va., June 12, 1833, and became the mother of six children: James A., Joseph M., George W., William E., T. H. and C. D. After his marriage, Mr. Adams and J. P. Fuqua, his wife's brother, built the first foundry ever erected in Carroll County. They continued to do business together until after the war, then our subject disposed of his interest to Mr. Fuqua, and began farming. He owns about 700 acres of very fine land, 500 acres being under cultivation. Mr. Adams is a good business man, and is well respected by all who know him. He is a Democrat but was formerly a member of the Whig party. He is also a Mason.

W. W. Algea, farmer, was born in Carroll County, Tenn., in 1847, and is one of a family of three children. He was reared under the parental roof and received his education mostly at McLemoresville. September, 1873, he married Caroline Williamson, a native of Carroll County, born in 1852 and the daughter of Samuel and Mary Williamson. To our subject and wife were born four children: James A., Mary E., Grace E. and Peter. In 1880 Mr. Algea located where he now lives, two miles northeast of McLemoresville, and has a fine farm of over 400 acres all well improved. He is a Democrat in politics and he and wife are worthy church members. His parents, James and Sarah (Wilson) Algea, were natives of Kentucky and North Carolina, respectively. The father was born April 6, 1815, and came to Tennessee when quite young being one of the early settlers of the county. He was a farmer by occupation and died in Dyer County, October 30, 1854. The mother was born September 23, 1821 and is now residing with her son, W. W. Algea.

John G. Belew, farmer and machinist, was born in Carroll County, Tenn., 1830, and is one of seven children, four of whom are living. The father, Jacob Belew, was born in South Carolina in 1796 and had very meager advantages for an education. He was a saddler by occupation in his younger days and when about twenty-two years of age, married Sarah Wilburn. In about 1819 they emigrated to Carroll County, and purchased land in the Thirteenth District on which he passed the remainder of his days. He was one of the very early pioneers of Carroll County having settled there when the county was a vast wilderness. He died in 1855. The mother was born in South Carolina about 1794, and died about 1869. Our subject was reared under the parental roof and received his education in the old log schoolhouses of that period. He learned the carpenter's trade, which he followed exclusively till about 1860. In October, 1858, he married Adaline Parker, of Henderson County, and then located in Clarksburg, where he has since resided. By this union they had one child deceased. In June, 1859, Mrs. Belew died and in October, 1860, he married Miss Mitchell, a native of Kentucky, born about 1840 and the daughter of Scott Mitchell. This union resulted in the birth of eight children—seven now living: William E., Ludie, James S., Robert L., Mettie, Ada and Thomas. Mrs. Belew died in 1880. She was a devoted wife and mother, and a consistent member of the Methodist Episcopal Church. During the late Civil war, Mr. Belew, in August, 1862, enlisted in Company G, Seventh Tennessee Cavalry, Confederate Army, and was captured in December of the same year, taken to Camp Chase where he was held on parole till September, 1863. He then returned to Salisbury, Miss., and rejoined the service. At the end of fifteen months of hardship and suffering he returned home. Previous to the war, in 1860, he engaged in the milling business, manufacturing both lumber and flour, which pursuit he has since continued with evident success. His mill is situated two and a half miles northwest of Clarksburg. He also owns about 700 acres of land, the most of which is producing and in a high state of cultivation. The home farm consists of 158 acres at Clarksburg. In politics Mr. Belew was formerly a Whig and cast his first presidential vote for Gen. Scott, Since the war he has affiliated with the Republican party. He is a Mason of long standing, and an advocate of universal education and is a liberal supporter of charitable, religion and all public enterprises.

John G. Blount, farmer and cotton dealer of the Fourteenth District, and son of Isaac and Lovey Blount, was born in Carroll County, Tenn., in 1821, and is one of a family of ten children, six of whom are living. The father was born in North Carolina about 1781, and was of English lineage. At the age of eighteen he commenced the life of a sailor, and followed this for about twenty-five years. When thirty-five years of age he married, and in about 1815 immigrated to Carroll

County, being one of its very early settlers. He established a grist-mill in what is now Benton County, and afterward built one on Blount's Creek, named in his honor. He assisted in building the first courthouse in Carroll County, and was one of the very first magistrates of that county. At the time of his death, which occurred about 1871, he was ninety years of age and the owner of a good farm. The mother was also born in North Carolina, about the same time as her husband, and died soon after his death. Our subject received a fair education, and at the age of twenty-five years married Miss E. Brewer, by whom he had three children: Wiley W., Larcena (Mrs. M. A. Sanders) and Aquilie (Mrs. C. J. Bruce). Mr. Blount then settled in the Fourteenth District on a farm of about 200 acres, where he has since resided, and which he has increased to 1,400 acres. He is now one of the most extensive landholders in the Fourteenth District. Mrs. Blount died about 1856, and in the following year Mr. Blount married Miss Keziah A. Brewer, sister of the first wife. By this union they had four children—three now living: Josephine (Mrs. Paley Rosser), Frances Elizabeth (Mrs. James Rosser) and Lovey L. (Mrs. Barney Bruce), deceased. Mrs. Blount died about 1868, and in 1870 our subject married Mrs. Winnie R. King, daughter of Noah Hampton, by whom he had two children: Isaac C. and Rosena. Soon after the war Mr. Blount was elected to the office of constable, but soon after resigned. He was formerly a Whig in politics, and cast his first presidential vote for Henry Clay in 1844. He is a Mason, and Mrs. Blount is a member of the Missionary Baptist Church.

J. H. Bramley, a merchant of McLemoresville, Tenn., was born in Carroll County of that State, in 1858, and is one of a family of seven children born to J. P. and S. D. (Smith) Bramley, both natives of Tennessee, and both born in 1831. The father was educated in Bethel College, and came to this county about 1852. He is now a resident of this county, living in the Twentieth District. The mother was also educated at Bethel College. Our subject was reared at home, and received his education mostly at Trezevant. In 1880 he married S. A. McKinney, a native of Tennessee, born in 1856, and the daughter of Ralph and Mary McKinney. This union resulted in the birth of one son, Dossie P. Until 1882 Mr. Bramley was engaged in tilling the soil; he then went to McLemoresville and engaged in merchandising, which occupation he still follows. He keeps a general stock of groceries, hardware and drugs, and has a good and increasing trade. He is a Democrat in politics, and a member of the Methodist Episcopal Church.

Alfred Briant, farmer and old resident of Huntingdon, was born in Spartanburg District, South Carolina, 1809, and is the son of Reuben and

Nancy (Tolerson) Briant. The father was of Irish descent; he was born in Virginia, and followed farming. In his youth he went to South Carolina, where he married and remained until his career ended. He died at the advanced age of one hundred and three years, about 1870. His wife, Nancy Tolerson, was born in South Carolina; she died in 1813, at the age of about thirty-five. By this union they had ten children. Mr. Briant was married three times, and was the father of fourteen children. Alfred is the youngest child by his first wife; he was reared at home, receiving a common school education, and made his home with his father until he was nineteen years of age. January 18, 1831, he married Miss Polly Stone, daughter of Aaron and Susanah Stone. Mrs. Briant was born in 1810, in the same district and State as her husband. By this union they had these children: Gardner M., who lives in California; Thomas J. (who in died May 15, 1886, at the age of forty-one; he was town marshal of Huntingdon for twelve years and occupied that position at the time of his death); Sarah A., widow of R. J. Johnson; Aaron R., Reuben A., Albert D., David B.; William H., who was killed by a falling tree near Huntingdon, at the age of sixteen years, and an infant (deceased). In 1838 Mr. Briant left his native State and immigrated to Carroll County, W. Tenn. He bought 400 acres in the Second District, and lived there until 1858 when he came to Huntingdon, bought 152 acres on the outskirts of the city, where he located and now resides. Mr. Briant is one of the substantial and influential citizens of Carroll County. Previous to his coming to Tennessee he was constable for several years. In 1841 he was elected magistrate and served for six years; was deputy sheriff several years previous to the year 1852. In 1852 he was elected tax collector of Carroll County, and served two years; in 1858 was elected sheriff of Carroll County, and 1860 was re-elected and served until the breaking out of the war, when he became one of the "boys in gray." He organized Company H, Fifty-fifth Regiment, Tennessee Infantry and Mr. Briant was elected captain of the company. He led his men at Island No. 10, and numerous severe skirmishes. At Island No. 10 he was captured and made prisoner of war. He was taken to Camp Chase, Ohio, thence to Johnson's Island where he was retained until September 1862, when he was taken to Vicksburg, exchanged, and being honorably discharged returned home. In 1870 he was again elected as sheriff and held the position two years. Capt. Briant is highly esteemed for his sterling qualities and honesty of purpose. During the many years he has been a resident of the county he has always proved to be a man above reproach, and his character without blemish. He is well to do financially, owning 360 acres in the county, and several houses and lots in Huntingdon. In politics he is a Democrat, casting his first vote for H. Clay in 1832. He is a Royal Arch Mason, and he and wife are members of the U. O. of G. C. and Methodist Episcopal Church South.

A. D. Bryant, proprietor of the Quin House, and city marshal of McKenzie, Tenn., was born September 15, 1842, in Carroll County, and is one of six sons and one daughter, surviving members of a family of ten children born to Alfred and Polly (Stone) Bryant, both of whom were of Spartanburg District, South Carolina, where they were raised together in the same vicinity; were schoolmates, and were married in the same district, and he engaged in farming until 1830, then moved to Carroll County, Tenn., locating at Huntingdon in 1859, where they now reside. Alfred Bryant, the father, was at one time tax collector of Carroll County, also sheriff one term before the war, and two terms since the war, and is at present county coroner; he was born in 1809, and his wife in 1810. Our subject remained with his parents until the commencement of the war, then enlisted in the Twenty-second Tennessee Confederate Infantry, remaining three months; he was then transferred to the Fifty-fifth Infantry, with which he remained until it was consolidated with the Forty-second Regiment, and was then color bearer of the consolidated regiment until December, 1864, when he returned home, and in October, 1866, married Aletha M. Quin; from this marriage were born four daughters and one son; three daughters are still living. He resided in the vicinity of Trezevant, Tenn., for two years after the war and then moved to Huntingdon, and from there to McKenzie in 1884. March, 1884, he was elected to his present office, but soon resigned and moved to Oxford, Miss., but after a few months returned to McKenzie, and was re-elected. He has recently taken charge of the Quin House, and by the hospitality of himself and wife have gained for the place considerable popularity. Mrs. Bryant's parents, S. R. and Emily (Harvey) Quin, are both natives of South Carolina, but were married in this State in 1842, and followed farming in Carroll County until 1884, when they moved to Lafayette County, Miss., and engaged in the hotel business; then they returned and are still living in McKenzie. They had four sons and eight daughters; one son and seven daughters are still living. Mr. and Mrs. Quin are members of the Cumberland Presbyterian Church.

John J. Burrow, farmer and one of the pioneer settlers of Carroll County, was born in North Carolina, November 22, 1806, and is one of a family of eight children. The father, Banks M. Burrow, was born in North Carolina, January 4, 1781, was reared and married in his native State, and then moved to Georgia, where he remained until 1812; at that time he came to Tennessee, located in Bedford County, and in 1821 emigrated from there to Carroll County. He came to this county at a very early date, even before the county was organized, and engaged in farming. He was a local preacher of the Methodist Episcopal Church, was magistrate and a trustee of the county for a number of years; he died in 1851. The mother, Mary (Blanchard) Burrow, was born in Gates County, N. C., in 1786 and died in 1856. Our subject was reared at home and received most of his education in Bedford County, at the district schools, but afterward completed his education at the University of Nashville. In 1832 he married Eliza Snell, a native of Rutherford County, born in November, 1808, and the daughter of Roger Snell. By this union were born two children; George H., who died February 4, 1880, and Harriett E. (Mrs. J. W. McKelvy). After marriage Mr. Burrow located near McLemoresville, and remained there until 1845, when he moved to the place where he is now residing. He is a Democrat in politics, and cast his first presidential vote for Andrew Jackson. He has been a member of the Masonic fraternity for many years, and he and Mrs. Burrows are members of the Methodist Episcopal Church.

E. M. Canon, citizen and farmer of the Twenty-first District, was born in Rutherford County, Tenn., June 1, 1826, and is one of eight children, five of whom are living, born to John and Elizabeth (Dickson) Canon. The father was born in 1791, in North Carolina, and came to Tennessee when eleven years of age, located in Rutherford County, was married, and in 1832 went to Henry County, and five years later came to Carroll County; he followed agricultural pursuits, and died January 5, 1865. The mother was born in North Carolina in 1794, and died September 1, 1874. Our subject received a good practical education in the country schools, and in the year 1849 wedded Elizabeth Hamilton, a native of Carroll County, born in 1823, and the daughter of Thomas and Elizabeth Hamilton. The father of Mrs. Canon was born near Nashville, Tenn., about the year 1787, in the blockhouse, which was a protection against the Indians at that early day. He came to Carroll County about 1822, and died at the advanced age of ninety years, three months and eighteen days. The mother was born in North Carolina about two years after the birth of her husband; she died when about sixty years of age. To our subject and wife were born five children: R. F., a merchant at Atwood; T. W., a Cumberland Presbyterian minister, and a resident of McKenzie; Emma E. (deceased), J. M. (deceased), and A. H., a farmer, residing with his father. In 1856 Mr. Canon located where he is now residing, on an excellent farm of 184 acres. He has been a life-long Republican in politics, and he and wife and entire family are members of the Cumberland Presbyterian Church, of which he has been an elder for nearly thirty years.

M. DeWitt Carnal, farmer, was born in Henderson County, Tenn., in 1837, and is the third in a family of six children born to Joshua and Sarah W. (Dunn) Carnal. The father was a native of North Carolina; born in 1808; he received a fair education, and followed the occupation of a farmer. In 1832 he removed to Henderson County, Tenn., and about 1844 came to Carroll County, where he purchased land in the Thirteenth District; he remained here until his death, which occurred in 1850. The mother was born the same year, and in the same State as her husband; she died in December, 1885. Our subject grew to manhood on the farm and received a good practical education; he taught several terms of school and in December, 1863, enlisted in Company G, Second Tennessee Mounted Infantry, Confederate Army. He was at Paducah and in several sharp skirmishes, but was principally engaged in guarding the Nashville & Chattanooga Railroad, between Huntingdon and Nashville. At the end of thirteen months' hard fighting and suffering, he returned home. In 1865 he began clerking in a mercantile house, where he remained two years; he then, in company with W. P. Smith, established the firm of Smith & Carnal, and engaged in the mercantile business. This firm continued until 1875, when they disposed of their stock, and in 1878 he and P. E. Parker, Jr., formed a partnership and continued the business in the building where Mr. Parker now is. In 1879 Mr. Carnal purchased the stock and engaged in the business on his own responsibility; in December, 1883, he sold his stock and since that time has been farming. He has several farms in Carroll County, considerable town property, and some land in Kansas. In December, 1875, he married Martha A. Johnson, daughter of A. J. Johnson, and to this union were born five children: William, Martha D., Fannie L., Lizzie P. and James E. Mrs. Carnal was born in Carroll County, about 1853. Mr. Carnal has been a Republican since the war, and is a member of the Masonic fraternity.

William M. Carson was born April 5, 1834, in Carroll County, Tenn., and is one of six children—three sons and three daughters—born to Wm. H. and Sarah H. (Dinwiddie) Carson; himself and a sister Mrs. Dr. Curtis, of McKenzie, Tenn., are the surviving members. The father was born in Butler County, Ky., January 30, 1806, and lived there until 1826, having served an apprenticeship in the tanning trade; then moved to Carroll County, and married, in 1827, our subject's mother, she being also a native of Kentucky. His father continued the tanning business alone until 1850, then combined cotton spinning with it, until 1856, then also embarked in the mercantile trade in the county, which he continued until 1860; then farmed a few years, but re-engaged in the cotton and leather manufacturing until about 1864, when he gradually retired from business, still residing in the county until his death, January 12, 1882. His wife died October 26, 1843, and after her death, in 1845, he married Elizabeth M. Reed, *nee* Dinwiddie, who also died before he did. Our subject stayed with his parents, working at the cotton factory until 1856; he then assisted his father in his mercantile business four years; then he returned to the old homestead and farmed, in connection with the tanning business, until 1865, and in three years closed out the business, after which he accepted a clerkship in McKenzie; then superintended the Shiloh Cotton Mills, of the county until 1872, when he moved to his present residence, a farm of 165 acres two miles southeast of McKenzie. January 15, 1862, he married Sarah A. Ridley, who is still living. The farm is known as the old Pigeon Roost, so called from wild pigeons congregating there formerly in sufficient numbers to break down timber. Mr. Carson and family are Cumberland Presbyterians and he is a member of the F. & A. M.

Rev. A. E. Cooper was born in Halifax County, N. C., October 12, 1803, and was one of seven children, two now living, of Isles and Nancy (Edwards) Cooper. The former was of Scotch origin, born in 1767, and reared his family in Halifax County, N. C. He died about 1812. The mother was born in North Carolina, and was a few years younger than her husband. Our subject was taken to South Carolina when a small boy and was educated in the common schools of the Palmetto State. In December, 1839, he married Mary H., daughter of Hon. Robert Clendening of York District, South Carolina. Mrs. Cooper was born near Yorksville, S. C., December 11, 1811, and has the following living children: S. C., a farmer living in Henry County, Tenn.; William F., a professor of music and a resident of McLemoresville; Mary A. (Mrs. J. J. Wingo); Martha L. (Mrs. William Fuqua); Robert A., a farmer residing near McLemoresville; Eliza A. (wife of George Ferrell, who is a lawyer by profession and is now editor of the Humboldt *Weekly Messenger*). In 1830 Mr. Cooper located at McLemoresville, where he has since resided. Mr. Cooper began his ministerial labors in 1846 and has since been actively engaged in preaching the doctrines of the Cumberland Presbyterian Church. He assisted in establishing Bethel College and was president of the board of trustees when the school was organized, and with the exception of a short time has since held the position. About 1870 the college was moved to McKinzie, and about one and a half years Mr. Cooper devoted his time and interest to the endowment fund of the college, the same being raised to nearly $50,000. He has always been an energetic worker, and although eighty-three years of age, preaches at three regular appointments.

James B. Cox, M. D. was born in Carroll County, Tenn., near Hollow Rock, December 20, 1856, son of Green D. and Mary P. (Williams) Cox who are natives of West Tennessee. Our subject is the fifth in a family of ten children and his early years were spent on the farm and in attending the country schools, and West Tennessee Seminary at Hollow Rock. He began the study of medicine in 1876 at Hollow Rock under the direction of W. A. McCall, who died in 1879. He also attended medical lectures at the University of Tennessee, and graduated in 1878. The same year he located at Hollow Rock and there practiced his profession until 1885 when he came to Huntingdon and formed a partnership with Dr. J. W. McCall. In 1882 and 1883 he attended lectures at Bellevue Hospital Medical College at New York City. He is an uncompromising Republican in politics and cast his first presidential vote for James A. Garfield. He is a member of the I. O. O. F. and the Methodist Episcopal Church, and is one of the prominent and successful young physicians of West Tennessee.

Dr. W. E. Curtis, was born March 27, 1833, in Henry County, Tenn., and is one of seven children born to John and Sarah (Sessams) Curtis, two daughters and our subject being the present surviving members of the family. The father was born in North Carolina, moved to Humphreys County, Tenn., when young, married there, then moved to Marengo County, Ala., about 1815, remained there engaged in farming two years, then moved to Stewart County, Tenn., and in 1826 to Henry County, being one of the early settlers in both counties. He resided in Henry County, farming, till his death in 1872. His wife died in 1854. Our subject remained with his parents until he attained his majority, then accepted a clerkship in a store at Paris, Henry Co., Tenn., remaining there until 1856, when he embarked in the drug business at the same place, which he continued a few years, when he commenced the study of medicine, attending the medical university at Nashville, during the sessions of 1859-61, and graduated. He began the practice of medicine in Carroll County, locating at McKenzie in 1878. During the war he was surgeon in 1861. Dr. Curtis married Harriet Looney, daughter of Dr. J. D. Looney, now deceased. From this union were born two daughters: Harriet Ella, and Alice, both living. Their mother died in 1865, and in 1866 Dr. Curtis married Ann E. Carson; from this marriage resulted these children: two sons and a daughter—John William, Lillian Howard and Thos. C., deceased. On Dr. Curtis' father's old place in Henry County is a very large Indian mound forming a perfect square and containing one and a half acres; the elevation is about seven feet and is used as a building site. The Doctor has two farms in Carroll

County of 100 acres each; on one is located a grist-mill; also has a residence in McKenzie. He and his family are members of the Cumberland Presbyterian Church. He is also a member of the F. & A. M.

B. A. Denney, farmer, was born in Smith County, Tenn., July 8, 1824, and is one of a family of four children, all living, born to George and Mary (Winfrey) Denney. The father was born in North Carolina, October, 1800, and came to Tennessee with his parents when but six years of age. They located in Smith County, where he lived until about thirty-five years of age, and then moved to Alabama. He acted as overseer here and died in 1865. The mother was born in Virginia about the same year as her husband. She died in 1833. Our subject received a rather limited education in the Alabama schools, and in October, 1866, married Martha J. Utley, a native of Carroll County, Tenn., born January 16, 1835, and the daughter of Green and Elizabeth Utley. Four children were the result of our subject's marriage: James T., Robert C., Maggie M. and John D. April, 1856, Mr. Denney located where he now lives, and owns, in all, about 1,600 acres of land. He has nearly 500 acres in the home place, all well improved, and about seven miles nearly east of Milan. In 1882 he was elected magistrate, a position he continues to hold. He is a life long Democrat in politics, and he and wife are members of the Cumberland Presbyterian Church.

J. L. Dickens, A. M., B. D., was born March 3, 1853, in Gibson County, Tenn., and is of a family of seven children born to Robert G. and Mary M. (Dickey) Dickens, of which our subject and two sisters are surviving members. The father was born in North Carolina and moved to Gibson County, Tenn., when thirteen years of age; that is also the native county of his wife, and they were married there in 1846, farming until 1862, when they moved to Marion County, Ill., continuing farming until the father's death, December 27, 1864. The mother then returned to Gibson County with the children, and afterward married G. W. Dickey, and they are at present residing on a farm in Dyer County. Our subject remained with his parents until he was nineteen years of age, then attended Newbern Seminary two years, acquiring the necessary means by the assistance of friends, added to his own industry and economy. He was then licensed to preach in the Cumberland Presbyterian Church, and in 1876 was ordained to the ministry. He did mission labor until November, 1874, then entered Bethel College, which he attended until he graduated in the classical course, in 1879, then he continued in the ministry in Tennessee until November 1880, accepting at that date a call to become pastor of the Cumberland Presbyterian Church at Fayetteville, Ark., which he filled until the spring of 1882, then he responded to a call from a church at Biggsville, Ill., which terminated abruptly, owing to throat disease that caused him much trouble. In September, 1882, he entered Lane Theological Seminary at Cincinnati, Ohio, and remained two years, then entered the theological department of Cumberland University, graduating June, 1884, with the degree of B. D., and accepted the position of professor of *belles lettres* and moral and mental science in Bethel College, McKenzie, Tenn., of which he was elected president June 1, 1886. August 21, 1879, he married Miss Mattie J. Tiner, of Gibson County. Her parents, J. A. and Mary J. Tiner, are still residing in Gibson County. Mr. and Mrs. Dickens are Cumberland Presbyterians, and he is a member of the F. and A. M.

W. H. Eason, proprietor of the Eason House at Huntingdon, Tenn., is a son of Stephen and Rittie Moore (Trice) Eason. The father was born in Green County, N. C., in December, 1800, and in 1832 came to Carroll County, Tenn., and purchased 160 acres of land. He died in 1870, and was the father of nine children, five of whom are living. At the time of his death his possessions amounted to 600 acres of good and well improved land. His wife was born in North Carolina in 1807 and died in 1879. Our subject, W. H. Eason, was educated in the common schools and at Bethel College and McLemoresville, Tenn. In June, 1861, he enlisted in Company G, Twenty-second Regiment Tennessee Infantry, and was elected sergeant and first corporal of his company. He was at Belmont, Shiloh, Richmond, Ky., Perryville and Murfreesboro. He was wounded in the head by a ball at Belmont, and in the left arm at Murfreesboro, the wound being so severe that amputation of his arm between the elbow and shoulder was found necessary. He was in the hospital at Chattanooga from January until May, 1863. He then rejoined the army, and until July was forage master. After his return home he erected a still-house and made apple and peach brandy during the summer of 1864. In 1866 he began teaching and taught ten months. The following fifteen months he attended school at McLemoresville, and was assistant teacher in the college the following seven months. In 1868 he began working with a firm of marble dealers at Evansville, Ind., but in 1870 was elected clerk of the Carroll County Court by a majority of 197 votes, being re-elected in 1874. In 1871 he bought the livery and feed stable of J. E. Southerland & J. R. Johnson, and continued in the business until 1885, with the exception of from 1874 to 1878 when he had it rented. In 1885 the barn burned. Since 1881 he has kept hotel. He owns 1,068 acres of land and five houses and lots in Huntingdon, and an interest in two others. Since 1883 he has been engaged in the retail liquor business. In December, 1877, he married Beverly A., daughter of Beverly S. and Lizzie Allen. Mrs. Eason was born November 28, 1857, in Carroll County. They have two children: Stephen Allen and William Howard. Mrs. Eason died January 1, 1885. Mr. Eason is a Democrat, and belongs to the I. O. O. F. and K. of H. fraternities.

E. Falkner, ex-county court clerk, was born November 22, 1846, in the Thirteenth District of Carroll County, and is the son of G. J. and Jane (Tosh) Falkner. The father was of Scotch descent. He was born in 1806, in Anson County, N. C., and was a farmer by occupation. In 1826 he left his native State and immigrated to Carroll County, Tenn. In 1830 he married Miss Nancy Sellars. She died the following year. In 1833 he married Miss Jane Tosh, who was of Irish extraction. She was a native of Christian County, Ky., born in 1804. Mr. Falkner bought 250 acres in the Thirteenth District, where he settled and lived until 1860, when he moved to the Twelfth District and remained until 1875, when he broke up housekeeping and he and his wife went to live with their son, E. He died December 1, 1884, and his wife five days subsequently. He was the father of six children, four by his first wife and two by his second, only two of whom are living, one by his first wife (Nancy, wife of E. P. Philips,) and Mr. Falkner, our subject. He was reared at home, receiving his education in the native county, making his home with his parents until he was nineteen years of age. After becoming his own master he hired to P. E. Parker as clerk in his dry goods store, and worked for him two years, and the following year, or 1870, he was appointed as census taker of Carroll. In 1871 he clerked for Jo. McCracken & Co. In 1872 he was appointed as assistant assessor in the United States revenue department for a part of the Eighth District, or three counties, Benton, Henry and Weakley. He served two years. In 1874 he commenced merchandising on his own responsibility in Huntingdon and continued three years. In 1878 he was elected as county court clerk on the Republican ticket. In 1882 he was re-elected, and in 1885 he resigned. February 13, 1873, he married Miss Bettie Scott, who was a native of Carroll County, and was born in September, 1846. They have five children: Lula, Joe, Birdie, Elijah J., Wayne. Mr. Falkner resides one mile southeast of Huntingdon, and is the owner of 360 acres. He is a member of the Masonic fraternity, Lodge No. 106, and himself and wife are members of the Christian Church.

Hon. J. M. Gilbert, Sr., was born in Hancock County, Ga., June 17, 1800, and is the only surviving member of a family of four sons and five daughters born to Benjamin and Amelia (McKenzie) Gilbert, both of whom were of Virginia, where they were married, and directly after moved to Georgia and raised their family there, and followed farming until 1811, then moved to Livingston County, Ky., continuing farming until 1826, then moved to Weakley County, Tenn., where they died. Our subject remained with his parents until he was twenty years old, and was appointed constable at the early age of nineteen, and at twenty was appointed deputy sheriff of same county. October 9, 1821, he married Frances W. Busey, of Kentucky; they followed farming there until 1823, when they moved to Carroll County, locating near the present site of McKenzie. The whole county at that time was barrens, covered with wild grass, there being then but very few families in the county. He began farming, and was one of the pioneer farmers of the county. About 1834 he, with several others, made the old Paris and Huntingdon road. He built the first house on the present site of McKenzie, but the town did not commence building until many years afterward. Mr. Gilbert knows of but three men living who were in Weakley, Carroll and Henry Counties at the time he came. They are William Hamilton, Reuben Edmonson, and Tilman Johnson, all of Weakley County. He was engaged in the commission business at Memphis in 1867–69, and during the same time was engaged in the mercantile business in Weakley County. | The town of McKenzie began to build in 1857, at the building of the Louisville Railroad. Mr. Gilbert was coroner of Henry County about 1876. Although temporarily out of the county a few months at a time, he has made his permanent home in Carroll County since first settling there. From his marriage with Miss Busey he had four sons and five daughters, five of the latter and two of the former are now living; their mother died July 4, 1867, and in 1870 Mr. Gilbert married Mrs. Louisa Dumas who is still living. In 1885 Mr. Gilbert was elected mayor of McKenzie, and still fills the office. During the first of the war he was employed by the Confederate Government to furnish labor and provender until the evacuation of Columbus. He then went to Texas, where he remained until the close of the war. He is a member of the Cumberland Presbyterian Church, also of the F. & A. M., of which he is Knight Templar, and has filled all of the prominent state offices of the fraternity.

Granville Goodloe, M. A., was born at Tulip, Ark., January 23, 1857. He was the eldest of twelve children of the Rev. Dr. A. Theodore Goodloe and Sallie Louise, daughter of Granville La Force Cockrill and Louise M. Turner. Dr. Goodloe was a native of Maury County, Tenn.; was educated at the University of Virginia, took the degree of M. D. at Hampden Sidney College, Virginia, and practiced two years in Bellevue Hospital. Just before the war he settled with his brother in St. Francis County, Ark., and engaged in farming. He entered the Confederate service in April, 1862, as third lieutenant in the Thirty-fifth Alabama Regiment; the same year he was promoted to first lieutenant, for gallantry; he served through the war, and in 1868 entered the ministry of the Methodist Episcopal Church South, as an itinerant preacher, in which he is still engaged. His wife is a native of Tuscumbia, Ala., and a relative of the Cockrills and Hardings, of Nashville; her great-grandfather, John Cockrill, was the first white man married in Middle Tennessee. His wife was a sister of Gen. James Robertson. The subject of this sketch, Mr. Granville Goodloe, was a pupil of the Culleoka Institute (Webb School) for three and one-half years. In 1873-75 he was a student of Emory and Henry College, Virginia, and from 1875 to 1879 of the Vanderbilt University, where he was the first to take the degree of M. A., May 30, 1879. In 1879-80 he was principal of the Black River High School in Smithville, Ark. In the summer of 1880 he became associated with his classmate, the Rev. E. R. Chappell, as joint principal of McKenzie College, as McTyeire Institute was then called. He still presides over this institution. He is a member of the Methodist Church.

Dr. R. D. Guin was born in October, 1829, in Carroll County, Tenn., and is one of two sons and one daughter, surviving members of a family of five children, born to Edward and Margaret (Bowden) Guin. The father was born in Sumner County, Tenn., in February, 1799. The mother was from North Carolina. Both moved to Carroll County when young. The mother taught school in the county before they were married, in the old primitive school building with dirt floor. They were married in 1824, and kept a hotel at the present site of Huntingdon, from 1824 to 1827, it being the first hotel of Carroll County. He was also first county court clerk of the county, holding the office a number of terms. In 1832 he located on a farm in Carroll County, and remained there until their death, the mother dying in 1873, and the father in 1874. Dr. R. D. Guin graduated at Princeton, Ky., and then graduated in medicine at Jefferson College, Philadelphia, and practiced his profession at his father's residence, from 1856 until the commencement of the war. He then enlisted in the Twenty-second Tennessee Infantry, and at the organization was appointed assistant surgeon, remaining in this position until the disorganization at the battle of Shiloh, when he was detailed to hospital service for six months; he was then assigned the duties of surgeon in the Thirteenth Tennessee Infantry, and was afterward surgeon of Johnson's brigade, with which he remained until the close of the war, when he returned to his home, and in 1866 embarked in the drug trade, and resumed the practice of medicine at McKenzie, Tenn., which he still continues. He has a good stock farm of 600 acres, five miles south of

McKenzie, well supplied by several good springs of freestone water; there are also Indian mounds on the place. In September, 1877, Dr. Guin married Sarah E. Bomac, by which marriage he had three sons and one daughter, all now living.

Dr. Andrew E. Hastings, trustee of Carroll County and native of Marshall County, Ky., was born September 9, 1855, son of John and Diana (Francisco) Hastings, who were Tennesseans, born January 13, 1831, and April 22, 1833, respectively. The family came originally from North Carolina and settled in Henry County. Dr. Hastings' boyhood days were spent on his father's farm. He attended the common schools, and for some time was a student of the West Tennessee Seminary, at Hollow Rock. He came to Carroll County in 1876, and the following year began teaching school, which he continued until 1880. In 1881 he began the practice of dentistry in Hollow Rock, but in 1884 came to Huntingdon, where he resided until August 5, 1886, when he was elected to the office of county trustee on the Republican ticket. He is an ardent Republican, and cast his first presidential vote for Hayes. He was elected circuit court clerk of Carroll County in 1884, and in October, 1881, was married to Miss Zoe Martin, who was born in Carroll County October 8, 1862. They are members of the Methodist Episcopal Church, and have two children: Rufus B. and Guy M. January 1, 1887, Mr. Hastings assumed the editorship of the *Tennessee Republican*, and continued in that capacity for one year.

Hon. Alvin Hawkins, ex-governor of Tennessee, like his two immediate predecessors, is a native of Kentucky. Mr. Hawkins was born in Bath County, of that State, December 2, 1821. His father, John M. Hawkins, was the descendant of an ancient English family, and quite a number of his early ancestors were prominent in English history. The mother of our subject was Polly G. Ralston, whose mother was a Neely, a family prominent in Indiana and other Western States. Alvin Hawkins is the eldest of thirteen sons, eleven of whom reached man's estate, and eight of whom are now living. All of them have held important public positions. When Mr. Hawkins was about five years of age he with his parents removed to Maury County, Tenn., and there remained two years. The family then came to Carroll County. The father of our subject died in Carroll County in 1852, greatly respected. The boyhood of Mr. Hawkins was spent assisting his father in the gun shop and attending the country schools, although his mother was his principal teacher at home. Later in life he engaged in farm labor, and at the age of eighteen became a student at McLemoresville Academy. When twenty years of age Mr. Hawkins entered the law office of Hon. Benjamin C. Totten, and studied under his direction. One year later he was admitted to the bar and became a co-partner in the law practice with Isaac R. Hawkins, and soon gained prominence in the legal profession. He had for his colleagues such men as Parvatt, Allen and James, of Huntingdon; Isaac B. Williams and the Harrises, of Paris; R. P. Raines, of Trenton; McCorry and the Browns, of Jackson, and others. In politics he was formerly a Whig, and is now a Republican. In 1845 he made the race for the Legislature for Benton and Humphreys Counties, but was defeated, owing to the counties being largely Democratic. In 1847 he was married to Miss Justinia M. Ott, of Murfreesboro, Tenn., by whom he had seven children, but two of whom are now living. In 1853 he was elected to the Legislature, but declined a re-election, and continued his law practice until 1860, when he was nominated presidential elector on the Bell and Everett ticket for his district. In 1864 he was appointed by one of the justices of the supreme court of the United States to the office of district attorney for West Tennessee, and was re-appointed in 1865 by President Johnson to the same office. In September of the same year he resigned, and was appointed to a position on the supreme bench of Tennessee, but resigned in 1868 and returned to private life. President Johnson appointed him consul-general of the United States at Havana, but he soon resigned, and in 1869 was elected judge of the supreme court of Tennessee. He joined the Methodist Episcopal Church in 1875, and has held some important positions in that church. In 1880 he was elected governor of Tennessee on the Republican ticket, and was a candidate for re-election in 1882, but was defeated by Gen. William B. Bate. Mr. Hawkins is now engaged in the practice of law at Huntingdon, Carroll Co., Tenn. He made a good governor and judge, and as a lawyer is one of the most prominent in West Tennessee. He is one of the leading citizens of the State, a man of the highest character, and a prominent leader of his political party.

Hon. Albert G. Hawkins, judge of the Ninth Chancery District, was born near Huntingdon, Carroll Co., Tenn., April 24, 1841. (For early history of the family see sketch of Alvin Hawkins, a former governor of Tennessee.) He was reared to man's estate on a farm and was educated in the early country schools and at Huntingdon Male Academy. In January, 1861, he went to Shreveport, La., and for five months was engaged in teaching school. After his return to his native county he enlisted in Capt. Briant's company, Fifty-fifth Tennessee, Confederate States Army Infantry, and served until 1862, when he came home on account of illness. Recovering, he joined Forrest's cavalry and in that capacity served until the close of the war. He was wounded at Brice's Cross-roads in 1864 and surrendered at Gainesville, Ala., May 11, 1865. He began studying law in 1861 and resumed it in 1865. He was admitted to the bar in 1866 and since then has been engaged in the practice of his profession, and is one of the able lawyers of West Tennessee. In politics he is a Democrat. In 1876 he was elected to represent the counties of Carroll and Gibson in the Tennessee Senate. In 1880 he was the Democratic elector for the Eighth Congressional District, and in August, 1886, was elected chancellor of the Ninth Chancery Division. He is one of the popular men of West Tennessee and is a Mason and K. of H. In 1869 he married Ellen Prince, of Carroll County, born in 1849. They have three children: Prince A., Clarence M. and Leslie O. Mr. and Mrs. Hawkins are members of the Methodist Episcopal Church South.

Capt. Samuel W. Hawkins, attorney at law, was born in the town of Huntingdon, Carroll Co., Tenn., January 6, 1844. His father was Hon. Isaac R. Hawkins, born in Maury County, Tenn., in 1818, and was a son of Samuel Hawkins, a native of Bath County, Ky., born about 1793. His wife was Nancy Roberts, daughter of Gen. Roberts, extensively known in Tennessee history, The father of our subject came to Carroll County in 1828. He was by profession a lawyer, and in politics was formerly a Whig. He was a Union man during the war, and since that conflict, to the time of his death in 1880, has been a leading Republican. He was a Mexican soldier. In the Rebellion he was colonel of the Seventh Tennessee Cavalry. He was a member of the Peace Congress, which sat at the city of Washington in 1860. The same year he was elected circuit judge of the Twelfth Judicial Circuit, but on account of the war did not accept the office. In 1860 he was elected to represent the Eighth Congressional District in Congress, and was re-elected to the same office in 1865 and in 1867. He was the man, perhaps, above all others, that saved the State of Tennessee from reconstruction. He was a profound lawyer, an eminent statesman, a true and brave soldier, and one of the early settlers and benefactors of Carroll County. An omission of his name would leave the history of Carroll County incomplete. The mother of Capt. Hawkins was Ellen A. Hawkins, whose maiden name was Ott, a native of Rutherford County, Tenn., born in 1822, and died in Carroll County in 1884. Our subject is the oldest of three children, two surviving. He attended school at Huntingdon Male Academy. In 1862 he enlisted in Company F, Seventh Tennessee Cavalry, United States Army. The same year he was commissioned second lieutenant. He afterward raised Company I, of the same regiment, and was mustered in as first lieutenant and later commissioned captain. He was taken prisoner in 1865, and held as a prisoner of war for some time. During a portion of 1863 he was with the Eighty-eighth Ohio, and later had charge of the Third Infantry. He was a true and brave soldier, and was discharged at Nashville in 1865, and the same year began the study of law under the direction of his father in Huntingdon. Since then he has been engaged in the practice of his profession, practicing in the courts of Carroll and surrounding counties. He is without question one of the best informed men of this section. Politically, he is a Republican, and for many years has been prominently identified with the interests of that party. He was married in 1867 to Miss Hester B. Gardner, a native of Humphreys County, born in 1847. They have three children, viz.: Hugh R., William W. and Isaac G. Mr. and Mrs Hawkins are members of the Methodist Episcopal Church South. He is a leading citizen and an active man.

Albert Hilliard, farmer of the Twelfth District, and son of William and Elizabeth (Shelley) Hilliard, was born in Carroll County in 1829, and is one of a family of eight children, six of whom are now living. The father was born in North Carolina about 1816, and immigrated to Carroll County with his parents when a young man. At the age of about twenty he married and settled in the Twelfth District, where he remained till his career ended, about 1839. The mother, Elizabeth (Shelley) Hilliard, was born in Virginia about 1814, and died January 10, 1884. Our subject was reared on the farm and had little or no advantages for an education, as he was obliged to stay at home and assist in the maintenance of the family, his father having died when Albert was quite a child. When about twenty-two years of age he married Irene Milam, of Henderson County, by whom he had one child (deceased). After spending a short time in Henderson County, he removed to the old home farm and about eight years after came to the farm on which he now resides, which consists of 400 acres of valuable land and is situated four miles south of Huntingdon. Mrs. Hilliard died about 1853, and January 8, 1857, Mr. Hilliard married Emily Holladay, daughter of George and C. Holladay. This union resulted in our subject's becoming the father of the following children: John B., William S., Minnie Lee, Albert E., Richard H., Walter G., Linnie E. and Arthur. Mr. Hilliard in politics was formerly a Whig but is now a Democrat and cast his first presidential vote for Gen. Scott. He is a long standing and prominent member of the Missionary Baptist Church.

W. H. Hilliard, farmer of Huntingdon, was born in 1834, in Carroll County, Tenn. He is the son of Rightmon and Delany (Jones) Hilliard. The father was born in 1800 near Raleigh, N. C., and was a farmer by occupation. When a young man he went to Alabama, near Huntsville, where he married a Miss Jones, by whom he had one child. Mrs. Hilliard died, and he afterward married Delany Jones. She was born in 1803. About 1820 Mr. Hilliard came to Carroll County and located in the Twelfth District. He was one of the pioneer settlers of the county. He bought 300 acres, settled, and where he always remained. He died in 1856 and his wife in 1867. They had ten children who lived to be grown, six of whom are now living—Eliza, widow of J. P. Johnson; W. J., Emma, wife of Joel A. Watson; Delia, wife of John D. Crider; Fannie, wife of A. C. White, and W. H. He was reared at home receiving his education in the schools of his native county, making his home with his parents until he was twenty-one. November 30, 1856, he married Miss Cordila Johnson, daughter of James M. Johnson. Mrs. Hilliard was born in 1829, in Carroll County. They had one child, Sebron J., who resides in the Twenty-fourth District and is a farmer. Mr. Hilliard lost his wife in September, 1874, and December of the same year he married Miss Louisa E. Johnson, sister of his first wife. Mrs. Hilliard was born in 1842, in Carroll County. They have two children—Eddie May and Louisa Essie. After marrying, Mr. Hilliard bought 118 acres in the Twelfth District, and began his career as a farmer on his own responsibility. In 1883 he moved to Huntingdon, where he has since resided. Mr. Hilliard now owns 850 acres, and is a well-to-do farmer. He commenced in life as a poor boy, but by his energy, industry and close application to business he has succeeded nicely, and is now in easy circumstances. In politics he is a Democrat, casting his first vote for Fillmore in 1856. He and his wife are members of the Methodist Episcopal Church, and his oldest son of the Christian Church.

G. W. Humble, judge of Carroll County, Tenn., was born in Henry County, September 20, 1827, son of Jacob and Jane (Nesbitt) Humble, and is of Dutch-Irish lineage. His father was born in Georgia in 1798 and his mother in Middle Tennessee in 1806. His paternal grandfather, George Humble, was a North Carolinian born about 1772. He died in Middle Tennessee in 1827. He was a soldier in the war of 1812 and participated in the battle of New Orleans. Jacob Humble came to West Tennessee in 1822 and was the second man who was married in Carroll County, the event occurring in July, 1822. He resided in Henry County from 1823 until 1831 and at the latter date came to Carroll County. He died in Huntingdon in 1884, his wife dying in 1864. G. W. Humble is the younger of two children and was reared on a farm. He received a common school education and at an early day engaged in farming, continuing until 1874, when he moved to Huntingdon and here has since resided. Politically he was formerly an old line Whig. He was a Union man during the war and since that time has been identified with the Republican party. In 1860 he was elected justice of the peace and has since been an incumbent of that office. In 1872 he was elected judge of Carroll County and served by re-election up to the present time. December 23, 1853, he married Caroline Pinson, who was born August 21, 1837. They have one child—Benjamin. Mr. Humble is a Mason and a prominent old citizen of West Tennessee.

William Johnson was born in 1830, about two and a half miles from where he now lives; son of James and Margaret (Mebane) Johnson. The father was born in Johnson County, N. C., in 1806, and was a farmer by occupation. He came to Carroll County, Tenn., about 1825, and became one of the well-to-do farmers of the county. He died in 1876. His wife was born in Orange County, N. C., in 1803. She is yet living and resides with her son William. The latter was educated in the common schools of Carroll County and made his home with his parents until he was twenty-seven years of age. November 27, 1857, he married Sophia Britt, daughter of John Britt. Mrs. Johnson was born in Carroll County in 1840 and became the mother of the following children: James Clarence, Annetta D. and Dora, who is deceased. Mr. Johnson owns 800 acres of land in the county and a saw and grist-mill, which he purchased in 1880 for $1,600. He has the respect and esteem of all who know him, and in his political views is a Democrat and cast his first presidential vote for Franklin Pierce. His wife is a member of the Cumberland Presbyterian Church.

B. F. Jones, citizen and farmer of the Twenty-first District was born in South Carolina in 1825, and is one of eleven children, eight of whom are living, born to the union of John and Austocia (Floyd) Jones. The father was a native of South Carolina, born in 1774, was a cabinet workman and also a gunsmith. He was married in his native State and remained there till 1835, when he went to Gibson County and lived there till his death in 1852. The mother was born in Virginia in 1784 and died in 1860. Our subject was reared at home and received a good practical education in the Gibson County schools. In 1847 he married Sarah Moore, who was born in Virginia in 1829 and who is the daughter of Yancy and Mary Moore. Eleven children were the result of our subject's marriage, nine of whom are living: Mary C. (deceased), J. H., C. C., R. L., Laura (Mrs. T. B. Ruff), C. F., W. B. (deceased), Annie, S. L., B. B., and R. R. Soon after marriage Mr. Jones located in the First District of Gibson County and began farming, which occupation he has continued to follow up to the present time. In 1857 he came to Carroll County and located where he now lives, four miles due south of Trezevant. He owns 181 acres of very desirable land and is one of the county's best farmers. He is a stanch Democrat, casting his first presidential vote for James K. Polk. He and wife are worthy members of the Methodist Episcopal Church and all the children except two who are members of the Baptist Church.

J. H. Keaton, farmer, of the Twenty-first District, and a native of Carroll County, Tenn., was born May 30, 1831, and is one of a family of nine children born to C. W. and Mary (Hays) Keaton, natives respectively of Virginia and South Carolina. The father was born in Patrick County, in 1797, and when about ten years old came to Tennessee, located in DeKalb County, where he was married, and remained there till 1819. He was a farmer by occupation and was magistrate of his district for twenty-five years. He died in 1871. The mother was born in 1799 and died in 1873. Our subject grew to manhood on the farm and received his education in the schools near home. December 29, 1851, he married Martha M. Leach, a native of Carroll County, born in October, 1832, and the daughter of Abner and Sallie Leach. Seven children were born to our subject and wife by this union: Laura A., Mary, Elizabeth, Emma, Ella, Beatrice and John D. Mr. Keaton owns 500 acres of well improved land situated one mile east of Atwood, and also about the same number of acres in Arkansas. In 1871 he began the milling business, by sawing lumber; this he continued until March, 1885, when he built a saw and grist-mill combined, at Atwood, and is now engaged in doing a good business. He is interested in a saw and grist-mill in Gibson County, at Cade's Switch, on the Illinois Central Railroad. He is a Republican in politics, a Mason, an Odd Fellow, and he and wife are members of the Cumberland Presbyterian Church.

Adam Kilmer, M. D., homœpathic physician at Clarksburg, was born in Essex County, N. Y., 1847. The father, Daniel Kilmer, was of Dutch ancestry, and was born about 1825. He married Cornelia Ray, and afterward settled in Essex County, N. Y., where at the early age of twenty-seven he was killed, by the accidental breaking of a large wheel belonging to some machinery. Mrs. Kilmer, a native of Essex County, N. Y., was married the second time about 1877, and is now living in Saratoga N. Y. Our subject found parental care and protection with his aunt, who was living in Bouquet, N. Y., with whom he remained until he was twelve years of age, when his aunt died and he was again left without a home. He was soon apprenticed to learn the wagon and carriage trade, which he followed for several years. His educational interests had been very much neglected, and he soon saw the benefits an education would bring him, and began to occupy his spare time in the improvement of his mind.

He attended school in winter and worked during vacation until he acquired sufficient knowledge to enter the ministerial profession, under the Methodist Episcopal doctrine. About 1860 he began the study of medicine in connection with his duties as minister. In 1866 he took a practical course in his medical studies at Philadelphia, and the rest of his study was at St. Louis, Mo. In April, 1877, he married Miss Gertrude, daughter of Minor Felt, of New York, and by this union became the father of several children, only one of whom is living, Mabel. In 1878 he removed to Savannah, Tenn., where he spent a portion of his time practicing. Our subject is now living in Clarksburg, where he has made his profession a complete success, having secured an extensive and lucrative practice. Mr. Kilmer and wife are both prominent members of the Methodist Episcopal Church.

Robert G. Kyle was born December 7, 1813, in Williamson County, Tenn., and is a farmer by occupation. He is of a family of eight children—four sons and two daughters still living—born to Barney C. and Elizabeth (Gilbert) Kyle, both from Georgia, his father of Irish descent, and his mother of Scotch-English; they were married in Georgia, and about 1812 moved to Williamson County, Tenn., remaining a few years, and then moved to Madison County, Ala., for a short time, and then located in Giles County, Tenn., remaining there six years, and moved to Weakley County, Tenn., in 1827, and followed farming until 1839, when they moved to Panola County, Miss., where his father died in 1861, his mother in 1873. Mr. Robert Kyle remained with his parents until of age, then attended and taught school one year in Weakley County, after which he spent one year in Georgia, then returned to Weakley County, and was elected constable in 1839, serving eight years; then he engaged in stock trading two years, and in 1849 embarked in general merchandising at Caledonia, which occupied his time for four years, when he returned to stock trading a few years, and in 1855 began farming on a tract of land he had previously purchased in Weakley County. He filled the office of county trustee in 1856–57, and in 1858 married Flora Elizabeth Crittendon, and continued farming until 1872, when they moved to McKenzie, Tenn., where they have since resided. By his marriage he has four sons and two daughters: Jno. S., William M., Emma D., Robert B., James D. and Mora. His farm in Weakley County contains 570 acres. He is a member of the F. & A. M., and himself and family belong to the Cumberland Presbyterian Church.

H. C. Lawhon, the editor of the *Tri-County News*, was born March 21, 1850, and is one of a family of six children born to F. E. and Miranda (Martin) Lawhon, our subject and a sister being the only surviving members. His father was a Virginian, and his mother a North Carolinian; both moved to Sumner County, Tenn., when young, were married there, and soon after moved to Weakley County in about 1838, his mother dying there in 1850, his father then moving to Arkansas, where he followed farming, and where he died in 1856. Our subject after his father's death lived with his brother in Dyer County, Tenn., and had the benefit of limited educational advantages. In 1863 he enlisted in the Twelfth Kentucky Confederate Cavalry, with which he remained until the close of the war; he then engaged in mining in Colorado until 1880, when he returned to Arkansas, and embarked in journalism, continuing in the business there until 1884, when he moved to McKenzie, Tenn., and succeeded J. B. Gilbert in the publication of the *Tri-County News*, which he has since edited and controlled. In 1884 he married Miss Ella Allen, daughter of Rev. W. J. F. Allen, and has had three daughters, two of whom are living. Mr. Lawhon is an Episcopalian and Mrs. Lawhon a Baptist.

Dudley S. Laws, M. D., of Clarksburg, was born in Carroll County, Tenn., in 1829, and is the second of six children, three of whom are living. The father, Hiram Laws, was of English ancestry, born in Orange County, N. C., November 17, 1803. His father, George Laws, is supposed to be a son of one of three brothers, John, George and James, who emigrated from England about 1620, and settled in Maryland, where they figured quite prominently among the business men of that State. Hiram was reared by a mother's tender care, his father dying while he was quite small. He acquired sufficient education to enable him to enter the teacher's profession, which he followed for a number of years. About 1825 he married Jincey Ann Sims, and immediately started for Maury County, Tenn., where he remained one year. He then came to Carroll County and settled in the Twelfth District, and in 1834 removed to Alabama, but in 1836 returned to Carroll County, where he passed the remainder of his days. He died in 1879. Mrs. Laws was also a native of North Carolina, born May 2, 1807, and died in 1878. Our subject was reared under the parental roof, and received his education in the country schools and in Huntingdon, but acquired the most of his knowledge and ability through his own application. He possesses an intellect of extraordinary brilliancy, and soon became master of all the mathematical branches, and had a good knowledge of the languages. He afterward spent twelve years teaching, and was one of the most successful and popular educators of this portion of the State. In 1861 he commenced the study of physic, and two years later entered Rush Medical College, and at the close of the Rebellion entered as a partner with his former preceptor, and began the practice of his chosen profession. In 1871 he entered the medical department of the University of Nashville and Vanderbilt University, and graduated in 1873. He then returned to Clarksburg and continued his practice with well-deserved success. He was for eight years school commissioner of his district, which position he declined to hold longer. He is at present one of the trustees of Clarksburg Male and Female Academy. He is a Republican in politics, a Mason and the owner of 700 acres of land.

T. B. Manning, farmer, of the First District, was born in Carroll County, Tenn., in 1840, and is one of a family of three children, he being the only surviving one. His parents, Alfred and B. Manning, were both natives of North Carolina, the former born in 1805, and the latter in 1807. The father came to Tennessee at an early day, and settled in the middle part of the State, where he remained a short time. He then came to Carroll County, and remained there until his death in 1856. The mother died in the fall of 1877. Our subject grew to manhood on the farm, and received his education in the schools in his neighborhood. In 1869 he married Martha, daughter of Abraham and Pernelia McLemore, and a native of Franklin County, Tenn., born in 1847. This union resulted in the birth of seven children: Pernelia, Alfred, Lucy, Mike, Beulah, William and Thomas Edward. After marriage Mr. Manning located on the old home place, and began tilling the soil, an occupation he has since followed. In 1882 he located where he now lives, two miles west of Lavinia, and has been quite successful in business. He is one of the county's best men and a Republican in politics.

Joseph W. McCall, M. D., is a native of Henderson County, Tenn., born January 20, 1832, son of Andrew McCall, who was born in South Carolina, September 2, 1790, and is a descendant of some of the immigrants who came to the United States in the Mayflower. He was one of the early schoolmasters of Tennessee, a member of the Old School Presbyterian Church, and was an old line Whig in politics. He was a soldier in the war of 1812, and in about 1830 or 1831 came to Tennessee, and located in Henderson County, where he died October 11, 1841. His wife was Jane Todd. She was born in Ireland, March 4, 1795, and was brought to America in 1798. She died in Henderson County, Tenn., in 1875. Our subject is the ninth of ten children, six of whom are living. He was raised on a farm and attended the early schools of the county. He began the study of medicine at Clarksburg, Tenn., in the office of his brother, Dr. Henry McCall. He graduated from the medical department of the University of Nashville in 1857. In 1862 he became assistant surgeon in the United States Army for the Seventh Tennessee Cavalry.

Since 1865 he has been a resident of Huntingdon, and is the oldest physician in the town; in 1869 graduated from the College of Physicians and Surgeons in the city of New York. June 16, 1858, he married Victoria A. Wilson, who was born in Henderson County, Tenn., October 15, 1841. They have four children: Lenora J., Emma J., Fannie J. and James H. Mrs. McCall died August 24, 1884. Dr. McCall is a Republican, and for the last eighteen years has been local examining surgeon of pensions. His most important case, perhaps, was the first authenticated case in Tennessee of trichinosis. He successfully treated the family of James Espey, seven in number, in 1885.

George T. McCall, a leading member of the Huntingdon bar, was born at Clarksburg, Carroll Co., Tenn., October 21, 1854, son of Dr. Henry and Frances (Bowlin) McCall, and is of Scotch-Irish descent. His father was born in South Carolina in 1817, and his mother, who was a Virginian, was born in 1827. Dr. McCall came to Carroll County about 1845, and for thirty-seven years was a successful physician of the county. He died May 2, 1880. George T. McCall is the third of their eight children, and was educated at Bethel College and McNairy Institute. He began his legal studies in 1876 in the office of Judge L. L. Hawkins, and July 4, 1877, was admitted to the Carroll County bar. Since then he has been engaged in the practice of his profession. He is an ardent Republican, and in 1880 was elected mayor of Huntingdon, and was re-elected in 1886, and also in 1887. As a lawyer he has been prominent and successful, and as a citizen is well known and esteemed.

J. C. McCollum, prominent citizen and successful farmer of the Twenty-first District, was born in South Carolina in 1828, received his education in the schools near home, and in 1852 married Mary E. Chements, a native of South Carolina, born in 1839, and the daughter of Calvin and Cynthia Chements. Mrs. McCollum died August, 1871, leaving a family of seven children: A. C. H., D. A., R. G., Lucus B. (Mrs. J. M. Roberts), M. I. (Mrs. Dr. G. W. McKinney), C. C. (Mrs. W. R. Crossett) and M. L. D. Mr. McCollum lives at the old home place where his father settled in 1839. He owns 300 acres of very desirable land quite well improved, and one and a half miles south of Atwood. In 1873 Mr. McCollum married M. C. Giles, a native of Carroll County, Tenn., born January 10, 1842, and died April 6, 1885, leaving five children: Hugh L. W., C. C., S. F., E. C. and Jo. Our subject has given his children the advantages of a good English education, and has always been one to aid and support all laudable public enterprises. He is a Democrat in politics—was formerly a member of the Whig party—a Mason and a member of the Cumberland Presbyterian Church. His parents, Aaron and Sarah

(White) McCollum, were both natives of South Carolina, born in 1778 and 1788, respectively. The father was married and reared his family in his native State. In 1839 he came to Carroll County, and engaged in farming. He died here in 1853. The mother died in 1865.

Joseph McCracken, merchant of Huntingdon, Tenn., began business in 1868, with Frank Travis as partner. The firm, for sixteen months, was known as McCracken & Co., and the following four years Isaac R. Hawkins was Mr. McCracken's partner. Since 1876 Mr. McCracken has been in business by himself. He was born in Huntingdon in 1845, and is a son of Robert and Cynthia (Lashlie) McCracken. The father was of Scotch-Irish descent and was born in North Carolina in 1783, and was a hatter by trade. He came to Tennessee in his youth, and married Jane Priest, who afterward died. His second wife, Cynthia Lashlie, was born in North Carolina in 1801 and was of Welsh extraction. She died in 1877 and Mr. McCracken in 1865. He was the father of nine children—six by his first wife and three by his last. The following are living: William, Licurgus and Joseph (who was educated in Huntingdon). At the age of thirteen he began clerking in a general store for A. C. McNeill, with whom he remained until the breaking out of the war. November 27, 1862, he joined Company F, Seventh Regiment, Tennessee Cavalry, United States Army. He was captured and taken to Andersonville Prison, where he was kept thirteen months and seven days. He weighed 150 pounds when captured, and only seventy-five pounds when released. He served until the close of the war; then returned home and resumed work for Mr. McNeill, with whom he remained until 1868; then engaged in business for himself. May 28 of that year he married Bettie McEwen, who was born in Henderson County, Tenn., May 30, 1852. They have one child, Linnie. In March, 1885, Mr. McCracken established a livery and feed stable, and is now keeping one of the best establishments of the kind in the city. He is a Republican and cast his first vote for A. Lincoln. In 1868 he was elected county register, and served two years. He is a Mason (Huntingdon Lodge, No. 106,) and is an elder in the Cumberland Presbyterian Church. He is a man of good business capacity, and is a successful dry goods merchant of the town. His wife died June 4, 1886.

Harris B. Mebane is a farmer and was born in Carroll County, Tenn., June 19, 1833. He is the sixth of ten children born to William and Elizabeth Mebane. His father was also a farmer, and held the office of magistrate in his district a number of years, and he was born in Alamance County, N. C. He was reared and married in his native State; he settled in Carroll County, and remained there until his death, which occurred at his home in 1883. The mother of our subject was born in North Carolina and died at the homestead about 1875. Harris B. Mebane was raised on the farm and received a limited education, and has made farming his chief occupation. He was married in Carroll County January 11, 1854, to Miss Martha J. Fields, daughter of Alexander Fields. Of this union there were thirteen children, nine of whom are now living: Newton H., Vandela (Rogers), Lon F., Maranza D., Mattie S., Sarah E., Mary B., Pitt and Yancy. William A. died March 17, 1873, and the other three died in infancy. Mr. Mebane enlisted in the Confederate Army and belonged to the Twenty-second Infantry, under Col. Freeman. He was at the battles of Belmont and Shiloh, and served until the fall of 1862, when he was discharged on account of physical disability. Mr. Mebane is a Democrat and a Mason, also a member of the Wheel. His wife and all of the family are church members, Mrs. Mebane belonging to the Cumberland Presbyterian Church and the children to the Methodist Episcopal Church South. He is a man of broad views, strict integrity, and of a generous disposition, readily responding to all calls made upon him for charitable purposes, so far as his means will justify. He has 287 acres of land, on which he raises stock, cotton, tobacco, and the cereals in about equal proportions. The farm is situated about eight miles east of Huntingdon, Tenn., near the Nashville, Chattanooga & St. Louis Railroad, and the residence is well located and surrounded with numerous comforts and conveniences.

H. D. McGill, M. D., was born in Henderson County, Tenn., in 1858 and is one of a family of eight children born to E. T. and Sarah (Meals) McGill. The father was born in Giles County, October, 1825 and was of Scotch-Irish extraction. He was reared on a farm by a Mr. William Legg, of Alabama, and had no advantages for an education. In 1849 he was married and December of the same year removed to Henderson County. He was engaged in the mercantile business for many years at Metropolis, Huntingdon and other places and also dealt somewhat largely in cotton. In 1870 he went to Nashville and engaged in the cotton business there for McCray & Co. He is now acting as traveling salesman for a firm in Cincinnati, Ohio. Our subject received a good academic education and finished at Nashville. In 1875 he began the study of medicine under Dr. J. B. Stephens, of Nashville, and in 1877 entered Nashville Medical College and graduated from this institution in 1878. He soon located at McLemoresville and practiced there two years, after which he came to Clarksburg and has continued there ever since. In 1884 and 1885 he attended a course of lectures at the University of Tennessee where he graduated in 1885. Since his residence at Clarksburg he has established an extensive and lucrative practice and is fast becoming one of the most popular and successful physicians of the county. January 12, 1881, he married Gracie McDowell, daughter of Rev. J. L. and M. S. McDowell. Mrs. McGill died September 29, 1885, leaving three small children: Arthur, Maggie May and Gracie M. Mrs. McGill was a consistent member of the Cumberland Presbyterian Church, a fond parent and a true companion. Our subject is a Republican in politics and cast his first presidential vote for Gen. Garfield.

A. C. McNeill, merchant of Huntingdon, Tenn., began business in 1851. He was born in 1821 in Fayetteville, N. C., and is a son of William L. and Rachel B. (Clark) McNeill, who were natives of North Carolina. The father was born in 1787 and in 1826 came to West Tennessee and after residing one year in Weakley County, came to Carroll County and purchased land and erected a grist-mill and cotton-gin and in connection followed merchandising. He died in 1837 and his wife in 1862. Of their eleven children, eight are now living. A. C., the fourth child, was reared at home and at the age of fourteen began clerking for his brother James at Paris, Henry County. He remained with him four years and the following two years clerked for Mr. Crawford at the same place. In 1841 he came to Huntingdon and clerked for his grandfather, Col. John Clark. The Colonel died in 1850 and A. C. succeed him in the business. March 8, 1854, he married Sarah W. Murray, daughter of Robert and Mary (Gwin) Murray. Mrs. McNeil, was born in Carroll County in 1835 and died in 1859 leaving one son, William L. In 1862 Mr. McNeil, married Mary E. Baker, daughter of Rev. Robert Baker. She was born in Carroll County in 1841 and is the mother of five children: George H., Robert B., Kate, Addison W. and Maggie E. Mr. McNeil, keeps a fine stock of general merchandise and is noted for his honesty. He is a Democrat and a member of the G. C. and he and wife are members of the Cumberland Presbyterian Church.

David McMackin, a farmer by vocation, was born in North Carolina February 14, 1821. He is the second of five children—three sons and two daughters—born to James and Elizabeth (Frick) McMackin, and of Scotch-Irish descent. His father was born in North Carolina in 1791, and was raised and educated in his native State. On attaining his majority he married and soon after immigrated to Tennessee. He lived one summer in Humphreys County, not far from Waverly. At the end of this time they moved to Carroll County and settled on the homestead now occupied by our subject. The father of our subject was an early settler of this county, and one of the prominent and respected citizens of the locality in which he lived. He aided in cutting out the first road in this part of the county, now known as the Huntingdon and Camden road, extending from Sandy River to Huntingdon, the county seat of Carroll County. He died at his home September, 1864. The mother of our subject was born in North Carolina and died at the homestead in 1858. David McMackin was raised on the farm, receiving the usual education afforded by the common school in the country, and has given his time to agricultural pursuits. He was married in Carroll County in 1844 to Miss Mintie Rogers. Six children resulted from this union, of whom four were raised to maturity: James William, Nancy E., Eli A. and Mary A. James W. died August 23, 1876, and Eli A. died December 29, 1878. The mother of this family was also born in Carroll County, and died July, 1857. Our subject was married the last time September 11, 1860, to Miss Sarah E. Driver, daughter of William Driver, a farmer. This lady was born in North Carolina June 20, 1834. Mr. McMackin is a zealous Republican, and Mrs. McMackin is a member of the Primitive Baptist Church. He has nearly 700 acres of land, about 400 of it being in the home place. He raises stock to some extent, but devotes his chief attention to cotton and grain. The farm is situated two miles east of Hollow Rock, on the line of the Nashville, Chattanooga & St. Louis Railroad, and is pleasantly located with the best water in this part of the county. The residence is well located, and is in every respect a most desirable home. Mr. McMackin is highly esteemed by all who know him as a man of fine character and sterling worth.

J. D. Moore, an enterprising farmer, was born in North Carolina in 1840, son of A. W. and Nancy Moore. The father was born in North Carolina in 1813, and followed the occupation of an overseer. In the spring of 1844 he came to Tennessee and located in Carroll County. He died in 1852. The mother was also a native of North Carolina and a few years younger than her husband. She died in 1844. Our subject was reared by his grandmother Moore, received his education in the schools near home and at the Caledonia Institute, Henry County. April, 1866, he married Mary Townes, who was born in 1843, and who died in 1873, leaving four children: Stephen H., James A., Robert S. and Mary A. In 1874 Mr. Moore married Mrs. Mattie A. Henderson, who was born in 1841. By this union they had three children: Eliza B., A. R. and Dennis V. In 1872 Mr. Moore located at the place where he is now residing. He owns 100 acres of excellent land, situated two miles southwest of Lavinia. He is a Democrat in politics, a Mason, and he and wife are worthy members of the Methodist Episcopal Church.

Gen. W. W. Murray, a prominent lawyer of West Tennessee, was born at Blairsville, Ga., on the 27th of June, 1838, and was educated in the common schools. When a small lad he was taken by his parents to Arkansas, and at an early day became a citizen of Carroll County, Tenn., where he has since made his home. Having a predilection for the medical profession, he began studying and became a graduate of two of the leading medical colleges of the country, Rush Medical College at Chicago, Ill., being one of them. During the late war he espoused the Union cause and in September, 1862, joined the Federal Army as a private and was soon raised to the rank of second lieutenant, and was afterward captured with his regiment, the Seventh Tennessee Cavalry, at Union City, by Gen. Forrest's command, and was taken south as a prisoner of war. He made his escape at Macon, Ga., by digging a tunnel under the prison walls, and after suffering many hardships, finally reached the Federal lines at Pensacola. He was then promoted to the rank of first lieutenant and soon after to adjutant, holding the position until the close of the war. He commenced the practice of law in 1868, and the same year was elected to represent Carroll County in the State Legislature. In 1872 he was the Republican candidate for Congress in the Eighth Congressional District, and on June 27, 1873, was appointed United States District Attorney of West Tennessee, by President Grant. He was re-appointed by President Hayes in 1877. During his official career he became an eminent lawyer and his speeches were noted for their power and logic. In 1884 he was elected railroad commissioner of Tennessee, and in 1885 he was one of the Republican nominees for supreme judge. In 1887 he received the unanimous vote of his party in the Legislature for the office of United States senator. January 1, 1869, he married Mary H. Strange, born in 1853, and daughter of Henry and Lucinda Strange. Mr. and Mrs. Murray have three children: Joseph, born in 1871; Eddie, born in 1873, and Charles H., born in 1878. In 1860 Mr. Murray was married to Mary Cox, of Mississippi, who died in 1861, leaving one son—Dr. Robert M. Murray. Our subject's early ancestors were from Perth, Scotland. He is a son of Rev. James W. and Amelia Murray, whose maiden name was Reid. Her parents were Jesse and Elizabeth Reid. James W. Murray was born in Georgia, in 1813, and died in 1860. His wife was born in North Carolina, and died in 1863.

W. R. Newsom, M. D., physician of McLemoresville, Tenn., was born in Springfield, Robertson Co., Tenn., February 14, 1831, and is a son of Green B. and Malinda (Dickerson) Newsom, natives respectively of Virginia and Tennessee. The father was born in 1796, and came to Tennessee when a young man. He was in the war of 1812 and filled the position of regimental quartermaster. He was a teacher by profession, having taught in Columbia, Franklin and Lebanon, and died in 1859, after a long and well spent life. The mother was born in 1798, and died in 1845. Our subject received the rudiments of his education in the schools near home, but subsequently attended Andrew College, Trenton, Tenn., where he graduated in 1856. He then entered the University of Nashville, and graduated from that institution in 1859. July 7, 1859, he married Mrs. M. A. Roach, a native of Jackson, Tenn., born in 1825, and the daughter of Jones Newsom; this marriage resulted in the birth of two children: W. R. and Dr. N. D. After graduating, the Doctor located at McLemoresville and began practicing medicine, which he has followed with evident success ever since. In 1858 he was elected trustee of Bethel College and held the position until 1872, when the school was removed to McKenzie. He was also school director for many years of the public schools at McLemoresville. Dr. Newsom is a life member of the Tennessee Historical Society, from which he holds a diploma; he is also director of the Tennessee Central Railroad. The Doctor is a Democrat in politics and cast his first presidential vote for Franklin Pierce. He is a Mason. Mrs. Newsom has one daughter, Eliza J., by her former husband, Rev. J. N. Roach, who was the founder of Bethel College, its first president, and filled that position until his death, which occurred in 1852.

W. Albert Palmer, farmer, and prominent citizen of the Thirteenth District, was born in Carroll County in 1845, and is one of a family of six children, three of whom are living. The father, William Palmer, was born in Anson County, N. C., in 1808, and his father, Marcus Palmer, was also a native of the same county, and was of English descent. He was magistrate in his native county thirty-six years, and died in 1828. William was married in 1829 to Nancy Harris, and in 1830 he, in company with his mother and one brother, came to Carroll County and settled in the Twelfth District, where the mother died about 1842. In 1837 he settled on the farm where our subject now resides, and here ended his days. He died in 1876. The mother of our subject was a native of the same State and county as her husband, and was born in the same year. She is still living with her son, W. A. Our subject grew to manhood on the farm and received a good practical education. In October, 1868, he married Martha Belew, who died four months after her marriage. In March, 1875, he married Susan Hart of Henderson County, and the daughter of James and U. Hart, also of Henderson County. Our subject has always lived on the farm where he was born and reared, and has been so far successful in the management of it as to increase the number of acres to 274. Mr. Palmer is a man of considerable information and good judgment, fully understanding the true method of farming. In politics he is a Democrat, but cast his first presidential vote for Gen. Grant, in 1868. He is a member of the Masonic fraternity. Mrs. Palmer was born in Henderson County, in 1855, and is an active and devoted member of the Christian Church.

Charles F. Phillips was born in McMinn County, Tenn., November 27, 1830. He is the third of ten children born to William and Mahala (Davis) Phillips, who were of Irish and Welsh descent. William Phillips, his father, was a farmer, and was born in East Tennessee, where he was raised and married; when his son Charles was ten years old he moved to West Tennessee, and settled in Henderson County, remaining there eight years, and then removing to Carroll County, where he lived three years, dying in August, 1849. The mother was born in East Tennessee also, and died in Henderson County in 1846. The subject of this sketch was raised on a farm and received a common school education. In 1855 he went into the family grocery business at Marlboro', Tenn., and continued the business until the war. March 4, 1853, he was married to Miss Cynthia A. Roberts, daughter of R. W. Roberts, a promising farmer and mechanic. Mr. Phillips had twelve children, eight of whom are living, and are named Rosalinda A. (Watkins), Mahala P. (Horn), John W., James M., Robert P., Edgar, Marina T. and Claude. The mother of the first five children above mentioned was born in Rutherford County, N. C., and immigrated to Tennessee with her parents at an early age, and died at the homestead November 24, 1874. Mr. Phillips was married the second time in Carroll County, February 27, 1876, to Mrs. Mary Martin, and from this marriage was one son, Edgar. Mrs. Martin was born in Carroll County, and died February 13, 1879. He was again married February 28, 1882, to his present wife, who was Miss Alice A. Cook, daughter of John Cook, of Nashville, Tenn. She was born June 27, 1849, and they were married in Nashville, February 28, 1882. Of this union were two children: Marina T. and Claude. Mr. Phillips is a stanch Republican, and takes pleasure in the success of his party. He is a member of the Masonic fraternity, and his wife and himself are members of the Missionary Baptist Church; he is liberal in disposition, conservative in politics[]and upright in business and aids in all laudable enterprises, such as will benefit schools, churches and public and private charities. He has been in the mercantile business since 1868, always carrying a good stock of general merchandise. He has 750 acres of good land, eighty acres of which is in the home place at Hollow Rock, on the Nashville, Chattanooga & St. Louis Railroad, ten miles east of Huntingdon, Tenn. He devotes his farm to raising stock, and, to some extent, cotton, but gives chief attention to the cereals. The home place is nicely located, within a quarter of a mile of the station. The residence is commodious and comfortable, the location elevated and healthy, and with the convenient surroundings is one of the pleasant homes of the county.

Benjamin S. Pritchard, farmer and stock dealer of the Thirteenth District, was born in Carroll County in 1835, and is one of a family of ten children, only three of whom are living: Martha J. (Mrs. Henry Cox), B. S. and Susan (Mrs. Thomas L. Key). The father of our subject, Charles Pritchard, was born in Anson County, N. C., in 1797, and his father, Jesse Pritchard, immigrated from North Carolina to Carroll County in 1834, where he passed the remainder of his days. In about 1817 Charles was married to Martha Williams, and in 1833 came to Carroll County, where he settled and engaged in farming. He died March 4, 1872, and at that time was the owner of 3,000 acres of land. The mother of Benjamin was also a native of North Carolina, born about 1800 and died in October, 1883. Our subject grew to manhood under the parental roof and received a common-school education. In February, 1860, he married Amanda Philips, and by this marriage had five children, two living: J. Homes and Sherad. After marriage Mr. Pritchard located in Henderson County, where he remained till 1882 and then removed to the farm on which he now resides. This consists of 323 acres of excellent land about three miles south of Clarksburg. He also owns 800 acres of land in other tracts, 325 of which is in Henderson County. He is one of the most extensive and enterprising farmers in the county. Mrs. Pritchard died January 7, 1874, and in November of the same year he married Lou Parker, who was born in Carroll County in 1833, and who is the daughter of J. C. and Elizabeth Parker. Previous to this, in April, 1864, Mr. Pritchard offered his services in defense of his country by enlisting under Capt. James Gooch and served under Gen. Forrest's command. He was at Harrisburg and Brice's Cross-roads, and returned home in August of the same year. He is a Democrat in politics; was formerly a Whig and cast his first vote for John Bell. He is a member of the I. O. O. F. and a liberal supporter of religion and charitable institutions.

A. G. Propst, is the proprietor of Beechwood farm, six miles east of Milan, breeder of blooded stock, such as shorthorn Durham cattle, Southdown and Cotswold sheep and fine mules; any of the above stock is on hand and for sale at all times. Mr. Propst was born in Catawba County, N. C., in 1838, and was one of a family of five children born to the union of John H. and Susan (Peacock) Propst. The father was born in Catawba County, N. C., in 1810. He was a farmer and resided in his native county. The mother was born in North Carolina and was ten years younger than her husband. She died about 1876. Our subject was reared at home and received his education in the common schools of North Carolina. When nineteen years of age our subject learned the carpenter's trade in South Carolina, and was engaged in this capacity at the breaking out of the Civil war. He enlisted in Company F, Twenty-third North Carolina Infantry, and was made sergeant; participated in the battles of Seven Pines, Chancellorsville, where he was severely wounded in the head. He was at Fredericksburg and around Spottsylvania Court House where he was twice badly wounded. He was captured at Winchester, September, 1864, and taken to Point Lookout, where he was confined six months. He was then taken to Camp Lee, paroled and allowed to return home. He was a brave soldier and rendered valuable service to the Confederate Army. November, 1866, he came to Tennessee, located and remained in Gibson County until January, 1876, when he came to Carroll County, where he located and now resides. He has about 800 acres of fine land especially adapted to stock farming. November 3, 1876, he married Sarah A. Cunningham, a native of South Carolina, born October 6, 1836, and the daughter of John and Amanda Cunningham. Three children were born to our subject by this union: Nena, Joseph and Mary. Mr. Propst is a man well known and much esteemed throughout the county, both as a citizen and neighbor. He is a Democrat in politics, and he and his wife are members of the Cumberland Presbyterian Church.

E. G. Ridgley, editor and proprietor of the *Tennessee Republican*, was born near Olney, Ill., September 7, 1848, son of Daniel and Sarah (Ingman) Ridgley, and is of German-English lineage. His father was born in Maryland, and his mother in Ohio; the former died in Illinois in 1882 and the latter in 1861. At the age of eleven our subject began learning the printing business in the Olney *Times* office. In 1864 he enlisted in Company F, Forty-eighth Illinois Infantry and served twenty-one months; was discharged in Springfield, Ill., in 1865. He was wounded at the battle of New Hope Church in 1864, and after the war resumed the printing business in Olney, Ill. April, 1868, he came to Huntingdon, and in March, 1870, he established the *Tennessee Republican.* November 28, 1869, he married Mollie Denman, a native of Hamilton County Ohio, born July 7, 1848, and by this union had one child—John D. Mr. Ridgley is a Republican in politics, a member of the I. O. O. F. and he and wife are members of the Methodist Church. In 1878 he was elected register of Carroll County, and held the office one term. March, 1885, he engaged in the grocery, book and stationery business. He is one of the leaders of the Republican party in this part of Tennessee, and was one of the famous "306" at the Chicago convention. He was a member of the National Republican Convention in 1876 and in 1880.

Furmon C. Sanders, sheriff of Carroll County, Tenn., was born in Anson County, N. C., August 6, 1837, son of James and Martha W. Sanders. His parents were born in North Carolina, the former in 1812 and the latter about 1814. The family came to Carroll County about 1841, and here the father died in 1854 and the mother in 1883. Our subject is the second of seven children and was raised on a farm. He received a limited education and in 1862 enlisted in Company D, Seventh Cavalry, United States Army, for twelve months. He was taken prisoner at Trenton, Tenn., December 20, 1862, and was paroled and came home. Since the war he has farmed; he is a Republican in politics but was formerly a Whig. In 1876 he was elected justice of the peace of the Fourteenth Civil District, and was re-elected in 1882. In 1884 he was elected sheriff of Carroll County, and was re-elected in 1886. In 1859 he married Elizabeth McCauley and five children have blessed their union: James B., Ollie P., Elias C., Lavisa V. and Furmon A. Mrs. Sanders died in 1879, and in 1881 Mr. Sanders married Mrs. Susan Weake, formerly a Miss Garrett, born in Benton County in 1856. They have three children: Nancy O., Lutie L. and an infant yet unnamed. Mr. Sanders is a Mason and a member of the I. O. O. F. and K. of H. He is a member of the Missionary Baptist Church and his wife of the Primitive Baptist Church.

James F. Sloan was born in South Carolina December 2, 1825, and was one of five children (two of whom are living) born to William and Mary Robertson) Sloan. The father was born in Ireland in 1786. He was married on the "old sod" and there remained until 1819, when he came to America, locating in South Carolina. In 1827 he came to Carroll County, Tenn., and followed farming until his death in June, 1870. His wife was also born in Ireland in 1789 and departed this life January, 1862. Our subject was educated in the schools near his home, and in January, 1870 married Rebecca, daughter of Joseph and Sarah Swinney. Mrs. Sloan was born near Trezevant in 1846 and died August 20, 1874, leaving two children: Oliver Cromwell and Minnie. Previous to his marriage Mr. Sloan remained at home and took care of his aged father until his death. Mr. Sloan is a good financier and has been quite successful in his business enterprises. He owns 400 acres of valuable land and is conservative in politics although formerly a Whig. He is a member of the Masonic fraternity.

Robert M. Stofle, was born in Weakley County, Tenn., April 16, 1850, and is one of two sons and eight daughters, surviving members of a family of twelve children born to Thomas and Frances (Hoggard) Stofle.

His father was of Henry County and his mother of Weakley County, Tenn. They were married in 1849, and engaged in farming in Henry County until his death in 1885. His mother still lives in Weakley County. Our subject remained with his parents until he was twenty-three years old, and October 9, 1873, married Johanna Johnson. Three children have been the issue of this union: John Thomas, deceased; William and Robert. In 1874 Mr. Stofle was elected constable of his district, in Weakley County, serving four years; he then removed to McKenzie, Tenn., and engaged in the mercantile business, under the firm name of Gilbert, Stofle & Co., which copartnership was continued three years, when he embarked in the livery and live stock trade, which he still continues, supplying McKenzie with first-class livery stock, carriages, buggies, etc.

E. B. Teachout, ticket agent, express agent and telegraph operator of Huntingdon, was born July, 1845, in Ohio, and is the son of S. M. and C. A. (Bolton) Teachout. The father and mother were natives of the Buckeye State and he was a farmer by occupation; for the past few years have been living in the city of New York. They have three children living; Frank, who resides in Memphis, railroading; Clara, wife of Joseph Payne, who lives in New York, and E. B., our subject. He was educated in the schools of his native State, remaining with his parents there until he was fifteen years old. The first year after leaving home he worked on a farm. In 1863 he enlisted in Company I, Ninth Regiment Ohio Cavalry, United States Army. He took an active part in the battles at Decatur, Florence, Nashville and numerous minor engagements. After the battle at Nashville, and while on his way to Athens, he injured his right heel, as the result of which a surgical operation was performed. He has never fully recovered from the wound, receiving $4 per month as pension. He was honorably discharged six months previous to the surrender, on account of disability. During his illness he commenced the study of telegraphy, at Brownsboro, Ala. In 1866 he assumed charge of an office at Tantallon, Tenn. While there he was attacked by a catamount while seated in his office. A long and bloody hand to hand fight ensued. As Mr. Teachout was about to get the better of the animal an assistant entered, and the animal was soon dispatched. In 1867 he went to Dresden, Weakley County, and was railroad operator at said place six or seven years. He then went to New York City and was proprietor of a hotel for eighteen months. In 1877 he came to Huntingdon and entered upon his duties at this place—the railroad office, which position he has since held with good satisfaction. In July, 1868, he married Miss Addie Ross, daughter of W. R. and Adeline Ross. Mrs. Teachout was born in 1846, in Weakley County. They have four children: Charles, Olla,

Stanley and Alva. Mr. Teachout is a man of good business capacity, courteous, obliging and very popular as a railroad official. He has a nice home and a beautiful residence. In politics he is a Democrat, voting for S. J. Tilden in 1876; and is an ancient member of A. O. U. W. He and wife are members of the Cumberland Presbyterian Church.

Haywood B. Thomas, a farmer by occupation, was born in Carroll County, September 10, 1832, and is of a family of five sons and eight daughters, born to Luke and Elizabeth (Burradelle) Thomas, himself and four sisters being the surviving members of the family. Both parents were born in Burke County, N. C., and moved to Trigg County, Ky., when young, and were married there; moved to Carroll County, Tenn., in 1825, and remained there farming until his father's death in 1862. His father was an elder in the Cumberland Presbyterian Church for many years. His mother remained in the county until her death in 1870. Our subject, Haywood B. Thomas, attended Bethel College a few terms after his majority, then taught school one year in Carroll County, after which he was engaged in the marble trade until 1858, in the interest of a firm in Hickman, Ky. He was then employed in the construction of the Northwestern Railroad until 1862, when he enlisted in the Fifth Tennessee Confederate Infantry, remaining a year, and was then transferred to the Twelfth Kentucky Cavalry as first lieutenant, and held this position until Capt. Falkner's death at Dresden, when he returned home, and remained until he married, November 7, 1867, Miss Ann Roach, the issue of this union being four sons and five daughters, all living but one son. After the war, he purchased a farm in Carroll County, which he still owns, but in June, 1885, he moved to McKenzie. On his farm, which contains 250 acres, are Indian mounds, and a number of fine springs of freestone water. Mr. Thomas is an extensive cotton grower, paying but little attention to the cultivation of the cereals. He and family are members of the Cumberland Presbyterian Church, of which he is an elder. He is also a member of the board of aldermen of McKenzie and board of trustees of Bethel College, and vice-president of the State Agricultural Wheel, and president of the Carroll County Agricultural Wheel.

Hon. Henry C, Townes, attorney at law, and native of Carroll County, Tenn., was born June 10, 1840, son of Col. James and Julia B. (Clark) Townes, and is of Welsh-English lineage. His father was born in Virginia in 1788 and his mother in North Carolina, 1795. The Townes family came to Tennessee about 1828 and here James Townes died in 1858, and his wife in 1870. The Clark family located in the county about the same time. They were among the early settlers. Our subject is the youngest of seven children and was educated at Huntingdon Male Academy and at Hamden Sidney College in Virginia, where he was attending school at the breaking out of the war. He enlisted in the Hamden City Company Twentieth Virginia, Confederate States Army, and was captured at the battle of Rich Mountain. He was subsequently exchanged and then joined the Third Virginia Cavalry and with this continued until the close of the war. He was in many important battles and in 1865 came home and began the study of law. He was admitted to the bar in 1867, and from that time until the present has been engaged in practicing his profession, with Albert G. Hawkins as his partner since 1874. He is a Democrat and was married in December, 1868, to Alice Crockett of Carroll County. She was born in 1847. They have five children: Eva, Charlie M., Cora, Lida and Herbert C. Mr. Townes is a K. of H., and he and wife are members of the Cumberland Presbyterian Church. Mr. Townes was a delegate to the National Democratic Convention at Chicago in 1884, and is now a member of the Senate of Tennessee, having been elected in November last to that position.

Alexander C. Tucker, farmer of the Twenty-fourth District and son of Joseph and Nnaommaah (Johnson) Tucker, was born in Carroll County, Tenn., in 1837 and is one of a family of ten children, eight of whom are living. The father was born in Raleigh, N. C. about 1817 and is of Irish extraction. He emigrated to Carroll County, with his parents when a child and was married at the age of twenty. He settled in the Twelfth District, where he still resides. In 1862 he married his second wife, Caroline Black. He is a Christian and a much respected citizen. Our subject was reared under the parental roof and received his education in the country schools. Soon after reaching his majority the main support of the family devolved upon him, as he was the eldest boy, and as a result his education was rather neglected. In December, 1864, he married Martha Bell, a native of Carroll County, Tenn., born in 1849 and the daughter of William and Nancy Palmer. By this union our subject became the father of eight children, six now living: Nancy E., Percy Alex., S. Y. (deceased), Minnie Belle, Emma L., L. M. (deceased), Marietta and William Albert. Soon after marriage Mr. Tucker settled on the farm where he now resides, which then belonged to the family. He is now the owner of about 368 acres of productive and valuable land. He has always been a hard working, industrious man and has accumulated his fine property by his own efforts and good business management. He was formerly a Whig in politics but since the war has affiliated with the Democratic party. He is a Mason of long standing and he and Mrs. Tucker are prominent members of the Christian Church. The mother of our subject was born in 1819 and was a devoted member of the Christian Church. She was a kind parent, a true companion and a woman who was worthy the title of wife and mother. The children are all members of the same church.

E. W. Williams was born in Carroll County, five miles east of Huntingdon, April 17, 1832. He is the sixth of seven children—six sons and one daughter—born to Rowland and Mary (Mills) Williams. His father was born in North Carolina, where he was raised and married, and soon after this he moved to Tennessee and settled in Carroll County, where his family was reared. He died at his home in 1836. The mother of our subject was born in North Carolina, and died at the homestead in 1841. Mr. Williams was raised on the farm, having the benefit of the schools in the county, and has made farming his business. He served as constable of his district in 1865, and also served as deputy sheriff of the county from 1866 to 1870. He was in this year, after the expiration of his deputyship, elected as magistrate for six years, but resigned to accept the office of sheriff, tendered him by the voters of the county. He served as sheriff three terms, which is the constitutional limit. In 1881 he was elected notary public by the county court, and has served in that capacity ever since; he is also magistrate of his district, and has served three years in this office. Mr. Williams was married in Carroll County July 30, 1850, to Miss W. J. Edwards, daughter of Nathaniel Edwards, a farmer. From this union were nine children, of whom eight are living: Sarah A. (Rogers), William A., John E., James N., Elizabeth J., Washington H., Loruza M. and Ella Alpine. Rowland N. died July 30, 1880. The mother of this family was born in Carroll County in 1829. Mr. Williams is a firm Republican, a member of the Masonic fraternity, and is exceedingly popular in his county, possessing the respect and confidence of his fellow citizens, being a man of liberal ideas and correct principles. He has 360 acres of land on which he raises cotton and tobacco and large quantities of the cereals. The farm is two miles east of Hollow Rock, and with its comfortable dwelling house is a desirable home. He belongs to the Methodist Episcopal Church, as does his wife and all of the children, except one.

Sanford N. Williams, general merchant, is a native of Madison County, Tenn., and was born June 8, 1842, son of B. T. and Margaret (Longmire) Williams, and is of Scotch-Irish lineage. His father was born in North Carolina in 1811, and his mother in Alabama in 1805. The family came to West Tennessee about 1837, and settled in Madison County. The father died in Carroll County in 1870, but his widow is residing in Huntingdon. Mr. Williams is the second of six children, and is self educated. He continued to reside on the farm until 1862, when he enlisted in Company G, Seventh Tennessee Cavalry, United States Army, and served fourteen months. In 1867 he began clerking in the store of E. T. McGill in Huntingdon, and from 1868 until 1870 was deputy revenue collector for what was then the Seventh District. In 1875 he engaged in general merchandising, and is now one of the leading business men of Huntingdon. Fredonia Adams became his wife in 1868. She was born in Henderson County, Tenn., in 1847, and is the mother of two children: Benjamin J. and Thomas N. Mr. Williams is a Republican, and cast his first presidential vote for A. Lincoln. He joined the Masons in 1865, and became a Royal Arch Mason in 1867. His wife belongs to the Christian Church. Mr. Williams is not a member of any church, and is rather liberal in his religious views.

Lorenzo F. Williams, farmer and citizen of the Twenty-fourth District, was born in Carroll County in 1843, and is the ninth in a family of ten children, six of whom are now living. The father, Thomas Williams, was born in North Carolina about 1795, and was of English ancestry. He received a good common-school and business education, and in 1817 married Harriet Blair. In about 1832 he immigrated to Carroll County and settled in the Thirteenth District, where his career ended. He was an active, industrious man, and at the time of his death, which occurred about 1848, was the owner of about 450 acres of land. The mother was also a native of North Carolina, born in 1809 and died about 1857. The father having died when Lorenzo was but a child, he was reared under the tender care of a mother's watchful eye. He received his education in the neighboring schools, and partly at Parker's Cross Roads in Henderson County. November, 1866, he married Caledonia McCall, a native of Carroll County, born in 1849, and the daughter of Dr. Henry and Frances McCall, of Clarksburg. Eight children were the result of our subject's marriage: Thomas H., Sidney H., Lorenzo P., Lizzie Frances, George W., Marietta, Bertha Mabel and John H. After marriage our subject settled in the Thirteenth District for one year and then removed to the farm on which he now resides, having owned it three different times. He was in the mercantile business for some time and also lived in Kentucky a year. He is now the owner of 160 acres of valuable land all well improved, three and a half miles northeast of Clarksburg. He is a liberal supporter of all charitable and religious institutions and a Democrat in politics, casting his first presidential vote for Horatio Seymour. He was formerly a member of the Masonic fraternity but is now demitted. Mr. and Mrs. Williams are both prominent members of the Christian Church and are much esteemed citizens.

W. M. Wright, M. D., was born in DeKalb County, Tenn., November 6, 1838, son of Dr. Ebenezer Wright, who was born in Massachusetts in 1800. He came to Tennessee when a young man, and in 1841 removed to Huntingdon where he was engaged in the practice of medicine for twenty years. He was a man of extended learning and a prominent physician of his day. He died in Huntingdon in 1860, lamented by all who knew him. The mother of our subject was Olivia A. Wright whose maiden name was Moore. She was born in 1812, and died in 1841. She was a daughter of Col. William Moore, who was editor of one of the first newspapers of Tennessee. He was a man of distinction, and died in Carthage, Middle Tenn. The subject of this biography is the youngest of three children and is of Scotch-Irish extraction. He has one sister, Mrs. E. M., wife of Judge L. L. Hawkins, of Huntingdon. The only brother of our subject was Col. Moses H. Wright, who was born in Dekalb County, Tenn., in 1836. When only a few years of age, he was brought by his parents to Huntingdon and here he passed his early life and received an academic education. In 1854 he was appointed by Hon. Emerson Etheridge (then a member of Congress) to a cadetship at West Point where he graduated with high honors in 1859 in the class with such men as Gen. Horace Porter, of the Federal Army and Gen. Wheeler, of the Confederate Army. During the war he served in the Confederate Army with the rank of colonel in the ordnance department, and gained a high degree of prominence, ranking second only to the chief of his department. In 1863, near Atlanta, Ga., he married Miss Sallie Lehon, of Nashville, daughter of Rev. E. W. Lehon, who was a prominent divine of the Methodist Episcopal Church South. At the time of Col. Wright's death, January 8, 1886, he resided in Louisville, Ky., and was a member of the firm of J. Balmforth & Co., of that city. He and J. Balmforth, one of his partners, were killed on the day above stated, by the falling in of their business house. He was an earnest Christian and one of the most prominent business men of Louisville. Dr. W. M. Wright received an academic education at Huntingdon and began the study of medicine in 1859 under the direction of his illustrious father. During the war he was assistant surgeon in the Confederate Army and was commissioned such in 1862. He was graduated from the Mission Medical College at St. Louis. Since 1865 he has been located at Huntingdon, and is one of the leading physicians of West Tennessee. He is a Democrat politically, and for quite a number of years has taken an active part in politics. He was a member of the constitutional convention, which met at Nashville in 1870. In 1871 he was appointed superintendent of prisons four years and was a delegate to the National Democratic Convention at St. Louis in 1876. Dr. Wright was married in 1870 to Erin Hanna, of Paris, Tenn., born in 1850. They have four children: Jamie McNeill, Charles Hanna, William Eben and Thomas McNeill. Dr. and Mrs. Wright are members of the Methodist Episcopal Church South and are among the prominent people of the county.

HENRY COUNTY.

Judge Clinton Aden, was born in Paris, Tenn., October 12, 1835, and is a son of Harvey E. and Louisa M. (Brown) Aden. The father was born in Charleston, S. C., in 1808 and when young moved to Simpson County, Ky., and from there to Williamson County, Tenn., where he married in 1829. He was a carpenter by occupation and died October 27, 1884. The mother was a native of Lunenburg County, Va., born in 1811, and came to Williamson County, Tenn., when a girl; she is still living in Paris. Judge Aden was reared and educated in Paris and also attended Bethany College, Virginia, under Alexander Campbell for two years. He worked at the carpenter trade until about twenty-three years of age when he began reading law under Judge McCampbell. At the end of eighteen months he attended one term of law school at Cumberland University and was licensed by Judge Fitzgerald and Judge Williams in 1859. He practiced until 1861 when he enlisted in the Confederate Army in Capt. Conway's company of the Fifth Regiment and was promoted to captaincy in a cavalry company of the Tenth Tennessee. He remained in the service till the close of the war and then resumed his profession, which he continued until 1874 when he was elected to the State Senate for one term. He then resumed his practice until April 30, 1879, when he was appointed judge of the Twelfth Circuit. He was elected to the office in 1880 to fill the unexpired term closing in 1886. As a practitioner Judge Aden has been very successful. In 1865 he married Mary Fuqua of Carroll County, and the fruits of this union were seven children, viz.: John B., Harvey F., William H., Clinton, Sheila, Thomas B. and Mary L. The mother of these children died December 13, 1884, having been a member of the Christian Church. Judge Aden has always been a Democrat in politics and an active member of his party. As a judge his decisions have always been characterized by deliberation and impartiality.

Capt. X. F. Alexander, liveryman of Paris, senior member of the firm of Alexander & Barton, established in 1865 the business which he has continued up to the present time. In 1883 Mr. C. C. Barton became a partner and has so remained from that time up to this date. Mr. Alexander was born in Henry County in 1838 and is one of two children born to Dr. Marion and Delilah (Crutchfield) Alexander. The father was a native of South Carolina, and a physician and surgeon by profession. He also followed mercantile pursuits for some time. About 1842 he went to sea and has never been heard from since. His wife was a native of North Carolina, and died about 1878 at the age of nearly forty-nine. Our subject was reared at home and received his education in the schools of Paris. He remained with his mother till twenty years of age, when he went to Salisbury, Tenn., and began clerking in a dry goods store. At the breaking out of the late war he enlisted in the Confederate Army May 20, 1861, in Company F, Fifth Regiment Tennessee Infantry, and was elected sergeant. After the reorganization of the army in 1862 he came home and organized the escort company for Gen. Lyons, Mr. Alexander being made captain of the same. He fought at Belmont, Hopkins (Ky.), Shiloh, Ft. Donelson and numerous minor skirmishes. In one of the battles he was wounded in the right thigh, which resulted in keeping him from active duty nearly a year. He is yet lame from the wound. In May, 1865, after an absence of four years, he returned home and in the same year established his livery and feed stable. December, 1865, he married Nellie Wright, a native of Paris, Tenn., and the daughter of Thornton Wright. They have two children: Eva and Mattie. Mr. Alexander has been one of the leading business men of Paris for the past twenty-four years, and is the oldest liveryman in the city. He has been in the business so long that he knows thoroughly the wants of the traveling public. He keeps on an average, eighteen horses, nine single buggies, four hacks, three wagons, and all else that is necessary for a first-class stable. Mr. Alexander is a stanch Democrat in politics and he and wife are members of the Methodist Episcopal Church South.

John Anderson, carriage and wagon-maker, of Paris, was born in Pennsylvania in 1825; son of Robert and Elizabeth Anderson. The father was a native of Pennsylvania, born about 1797, and was a stone-cutter and mason in early life, but later a farmer. He was a man of marked honesty, morality, integrity and great firmness of character. Mrs. Anderson was born in Pennsylvania, and was of Scotch ancestry; she died in 1882. Our subject was reared principally by his mother, as his father had died when our subject was but fourteen years of age. When about nineteen years of age he was apprenticed to A. B. and R. Patterson, of Pittsburgh, Penn., to learn the carriage and wagon trade, with whom he remained for several years. In 1849 he came to Henry County and located at Manlyville, established his business at that place, and continued there till 1854. He then came to Paris and has followed the carriage and wagon making trade till 1877, with the exception of a few years during the war when his industry was greatly damaged. In 1855 he married Isabella W. Brown, a native of Pennsylvania, born in 1829, and a devout member of the Cumberland Presbyterian Church. By this union they had six children, five of whom are living: Robert A., Nellie (Mrs. Mitchum), Charles B., Anna and Elizabeth L. (Mrs. James Thomason). Soon after the war Mr. Anderson was appointed circuit court clerk and in 1866 was elected to the same office, which he continued to hold for one term. He has served several terms as mayor of the city of Paris and in 1882 was appointed postmaster of the same place, holding this office for a term of four years to the entire satisfaction of the people. He started in life a poor boy but has managed his business affairs in a highly successful manner. He is the present owner of considerable real estate in town, also of a farm a short distance from town. In politics Mr. Anderson was formerly a Whig, and cast his first vote for Gen. Taylor in 1848. Since the war he has been a Republican. He is a prominent member of the K. of H. and the K. and L. of H. *Died 1890*

Hon. J. D. C. Atkins was born near Paris, Henry Co., Tenn., June 4, 1825, son of John and Sarah (Manly) Atkins, natives of Anson County, N. C. After moving to Montgomery County and soon afterward to Stewart County, Tenn., they finally, in 1823, removed to Henry County, and here passed the remainder of their days. The mother's death occurred in 1827 and the father's in 1847. The father was a farmer and a dealer in real estate, etc., and was a man of fine financial means. He took great interest in his county's affairs and was one of its most respected citizens. Both parents were members of the Methodist Episcopal Church. Our subject grew to manhood on the farm, and graduated from the East Tennessee University in 1846. He then read law, but on account of bad health left his profession and soon became enlisted in political pursuits. In 1849 he was elected to the Legislature, and re-elected in 1851. In 1855 he was elected to the State Senate and in 1856 was an elector on the Buchanan ticket, being, of course, one of the electoral college for Buchanan and Breckenridge. He was nominated to represent the Ninth District in Congress in 1857, and carried his election against a standing Whig majority by a very spirited contest. He was defeated in 1859 by a majority of eight votes, and although pressed by his friends to contest the election declined to do so. In 1860 he was a delegate to the Charleston convention and advocated the compromise or Tennessee platform. He was also a delegate to the Baltimore convention, and was an elector in the Ninth Congressional District of Tennessee on the Breckenridge ticket.

In 1861 he advocated the Crittenden compromise, and took an active interest in public discussions; was elected lieutenant-colonel of the Fifth Tennessee, Confederate States Army, May 20, 1861, and was elected to the provisional Confederate Congress, without solicitation on his part. In Nov., 1861, he was elected to the permanent Congress, and re-elected in 1863 by the soldiers, receiving the largest number of votes of any member of the Congress. He served on the committee of postoffices, post roads and military affairs, and at the conclusion of his services was on the committee of foreign affairs. He introduced the resolution which effected the Hampton Roads conference. At the close of the war he resumed farming, and has continued that occupation ever since. In 1867 he, with two other gentlemen, founded the *Paris Intelligencer*, and continued several years as editor. In 1872 he was nominated over Dorsey Thomas and elected over Col. Travis and W. W. Murray, to Congress; renominated without opposition, and re-elected in the years 1874, 1876, 1878, 1880 and 1882. He retired in March, 1883, not allowing his name to be again presented before the convention. He was a member of the committee on appropriations eight years, four of which he was chairman of the committee. He remained at home until March, 1885, when he was nominated by the President, and unanimously confirmed by the Senate without reference to a committee, as commissioner of Indian affairs. He was chairman of the State convention to appoint delegates to the National convention in 1884, was elector of the State at large on the Cleveland and Hendricks ticket, but, owing to ill health, made a limited canvass. Mr. Atkins is a man of home enterprise; always patronizes schools, churches and other institutions of that character. In 1847 he married Miss Elizabeth Porter, a daughter of Col. William Porter, a very prominent and dearly beloved citizen of Henry County. To our subject and wife were born five children: Sarah (Mrs. Hugh P. Dunlap), Bettie (Mrs. Prof. F. H. Hunter), John D., Mattie and Clintie (wife of Dudley Porter, second son of Gov. J. D. Porter). Mr. Atkins and wife and Mrs. Hunter are members of the Cumberland Presbyterian Church. Mrs. Dunlap is a member of the Christian Church. Mr. Atkins is politically a firm State-rights Democrat.

J. S. Barger, merchant, was born April 1, 1861, in Henderson County, Tenn., and is the son of W. O. and Catherine (Gray) Barger, natives, respectively, of Tennessee and Mississippi; the father born February, 1829, and the mother May, 1831. J. S. Barger's paternal grandparents were natives of North Carolina and of Dutch extraction. Our subject was reared on a farm, and worked on the same till he was about twenty-one years of age. He then engaged in business for himself as clerk in a dry goods store at Huntingdon, Carroll Co., Tenn., where he continued three years. He then engaged in agricultural pursuits which he followed for twelve months and for about eight months acted as salesman for J. P. Parker & Co., Decatur County. In the fall of 1884 he began business on his own responsibility at Bargerton, Henderson Co., Tenn. In 1886 he began the general merchandise business at Henry, Tenn., and is doing well in his business. July 19, 1882, he married Dollie Vickers of Carroll County, Tenn., born February 20, 1863, and the daughter of William R. and Martha Vickers. To our subject and wife was born one child, Sammie Eva. Our subject is a self made man and has accumulated considerable property by his own unaided efforts. He received good educational advantages and is highly spoken of by all. In politics he is Democrat, and prohibitionist.

J. Wade Barton, farmer and tobacco dealer of the Eleventh District, and son of Benjamin J. and Rebecca (Killebrew) Barton, was born in the Eleventh District, Henry County, in 1824, and is one of five children, only two of whom are living. The father was supposed to be a native of Kentucky, born in 1798, and in that State grew to manhood and was married. He came to Henry County at a very early day and settled in the Fifth District when the country was a dense wilderness abounding in wild and ferocious beasts. He afterward settled in the Eleventh District where he remained till his death in 1830. Mrs. Barton was also born in Kentucky, in 1800, and died in 1875. Our subject having been bereft of his father when but six years of age, was reared by the tender care of a mother. He had a very poor chance for schooling as the main support of the family devolved upon his shoulders. At the age of nineteen he began the battle of life for himself as a laborer, and attended school a portion of the time till he acquired sufficient education to enable him to engage in teaching, which occupation he followed for several years in this and Weakley Counties. September 17, 1846, he married Mary Ann Hardy of Kentucky, and soon after came to his native county. This marriage resulted in the birth of nine children, six now living: Adolphus H., Orion C., Eldorado, Scott W., Hamilton H. and Mary A. (Mrs. John Swanson). Our subject settled in the Eleventh District, where he taught and also carried on agricultural pursuits. He is now engaged in farming and has been quite successful, having accumulated his property by his own diligent labor. He is one of the most enterprising farmers of the Eleventh District and owns about 200 acres of good productive land. During his early life he served four years in the Eleventh District as constable and also several terms as magistrate, both prior to and since the war. In 1861 he enlisted in the Forty-sixth Tennessee Infantry,

Confederate Army, and was soon appointed assistant quartermaster, which position he held during his service. At the bombardment of Island No. 10, he returned home and soon after entered the cavalry and spent some time in that service. He returned home in the fall of 1862, and in February of the next year his wife died, after which he did not again re-enter the ranks. March 22, 1864, he married Louisa E. Bowden, a native of Henry County, Tenn., born in 1837, and a member of the Primitive Baptist Church. Mr. Barton was formerly a Whig in politics, casting his first presidential vote for Taylor in 1848, but since 1856 has been a Democrat. He is a man of strictly temperate habits, never having indulged in liquors of any kind, and having no use for tobacco or coffee. He is a long standing and prominent member of the Masonic fraternity, having taken the highest degree that that body confers upon its members. He is also an active member of the Missionary Baptist Church, having served as clerk in that organization for thirty years. Mr. Barton had a son, A. O., killed during the late war, at the battle of Harrisburg in 1864.

John J. Blake, farmer and leading citizen of the Third District, and son of James and Martha (Page) Blake, was born on the farm on which he now resides in 1826. The father was born in North Carolina, about 1776, grew up and married in his native State, came to Maury County, Tenn., in 1821, and in 1822 came to Henry County, settling in the Third District, where he passed the remainder of his days tilling the soil. He ran a grain-mill on the Obion River for several years, and led an active and industrious life. He died about 1846. Mrs. Blake was also a native of North Carolina, born about 1792, and died in 1873. John J. was reared at home and like the average farmer boy received his education in the common schools. He spent five years of his early life as an overseer and then purchased his father's farm, where he has remained ever since engaged in tilling the soil. In September, 1862, he enlisted in Company G, Seventh Tennessee Cavalry as second lieutenant and afterward as first lieutenant. He took part in many important battles, and received a wound at Athens which rendered him unfit for duty. He returned home the latter part of 1864, and did not again rejoin the service. December 31, 1864, he married Harriet Lee Diggs, and they had one child, Charley Waterfield. Mrs. Blake died in 1866, and in May, 1867, he married Mrs. Paralee, daughter of Milton and Lucy Wakeland, and the result of this union was four children: Francis Eugene, Bettie Lee, Sallie and Luna. Mrs. Blake was born in Henry County in 1841, and is a member of the Missionary Baptist Church. In politics Mr. Blake is a Democrat and his first presidential vote was for Lewis Cass in 1848. He is a long standing and active member of the Masonic fraternity, and one of the county's best farmers, owning at the present 200 acres of well tilled land.

George H. Browne, one of the proprietors of the Paris roller-mills, entered the business in 1880, and has continued the same up to the present time with the exception of about one year, when he was engaged in the furniture and saw-mill business at Big Sandy, Henry County. The firm is now known as Browne & Co., the other member being M. F. Trevathan. The mill has a capacity of about 150 barrels of flour per day, and is the most complete enterprise of the kind in the county. Our subject is a son of William Browne, who was a native of Virginia, born in 1809, and who emigrated to Missouri with his parents when quite young. He received a good business education, and when about twenty years of age went to Kentucky where he was soon married to a Miss Robinson. They had one child, who died. Mrs. Browne died in a few years and he took for his second wife a Miss Trevathan; by this union they had seven children, six of whom are now living. After the death of his second wife, Mr. Browne married Eliza Tinin, by whom he had ten children, eight of whom are now living. The parents are both now living at Wadesboro, Ky., where Mr. Browne is engaged in tanning. Our subject was born in Paducah, Ky., in 1857, and received a good business education. When about fourteen years of age he began dealing in tobacco and spent several years in the South. In 1879 he came to Paris, and in October, 1882, he married Jessie Trevathan, a native of Mississippi, born in 1866, and the daughter of A. G. and Martha F. Trevathan, of Paris. One child, Albert Gentry, was born to this union. Mr. Browne is a Democrat in politics and his first presidential vote was for Gen. Hancock. April, 1886, he was elected city treasurer and recorder of Paris, which position he still holds to the entire satisfaction of the people.

J. W. Buchanan, a prominent citizen and farmer residing in the Twenty-second District, was born in Henry County, June 23, 1830, son of Thomas and E. Buchanan, both natives of North Carolina, the father born in Gilford County, 1808, and died in 1847; the mother born in Edgecomb County, in 1812, and is now living with her daughter, Mrs. Allen Freeland. J. W. received but a limited education in the district schools of Arkansas and in 1858 was married to B. H. Walker, who was born in Smith County in 1833 and who died in 1860. They had two children, both deceased. In 1861 he married Mary A. Edmonds, a native of Kentucky, born in 1842, and by this union had one daughter, Sallie E. Our subject located where he now lives, in 1861, and has always been an energetic enterprising man. In 1850 he began traveling in the sale of manufactured tobacco and this continued for about seven years. He is a member of the county court having been elected magistrate each succeeding election since 1870. He joined the Masons in 1852 and has had many honors conferred upon him by that order. He is a Democrat in politics, and he and wife are members of the Christian Church.

Col. Robert D. Caldwell, farmer, tobacco raiser and general trader, is a prominent citizen of the Twenty-first District. He is a native of Sumner County, born in 1811, and is one of seven children—two now living—born to James and Mary (Davis) Caldwell. The father of our subject was of Irish ancestry, born in Virginia. He was a wheelwright by trade and came with his father, who was a native of Ireland, to Sumner County where he married and afterward moved to Montgomery County. In 1826 he came to Henry County where he lived until his death in November, 1848, Mrs. Caldwell was a native of Sumner County, and died in 1824. Robert D. lived at home and received his education in the common schools of Montgomery and Sumner Counties. In February, 1832, he married Miss Sarah Dupree and to them were born nine children, four of whom are living; Dr. Samuel H. Caldwell of Paris; Mary, wife of Alex Wilson; Alice, now Mrs. James Ray, of North Carolina, and Minerva, now Mrs. Samuel Miller. February 25, 1856, the mother died and November, 1857, Col. Caldwell married Mrs. Emily Mitchum, daughter of Reddick and Mary A. Hillsman, of Carroll County. They have one child, Yancy Quitman. Col. Caldwell first settled on the farm on which he now resides, fourteen miles from Paris, owning at that time 1,000 acres, but through his untiring energy and unceasing devotion to business and being possessed of extraordinary financial and business capacity, has become one of the most extensive land owners of Henry County, owning nearly 3,000 acres of land in that county. He owns 200 acres within the corporation of Dallas, Tex., which is very valuable, and several thousand acres in Mississippi. He is a man of considerable information and ability and in early days was for several years constable, and in the days of general muster served as captain, major and colonel. In politics he is a lifelong Democrat; cast his first presidential vote for Martin Van Buren in 1836, and has been an active member of the Methodist Episcopal Church for over forty years. Mrs. Caldwell was born in Wilson County, Tenn., in 1824, and is a member of the Missionary Baptist Church. Her parents were natives of Franklin County, N. C. The father died in 1857. The mother still lives at the age of eighty-seven years and resides in Carroll County. Mrs. Caldwell bore her first husband two children—Mary R., wife of W. D. Morris, and Albert B.

Dr. S. H. Caldwell, one of the leading citizens of the county, was born December 10, 1836, near Paris in Henry County, Tenn., and is a son of R. D. Caldwell, now an extensive farmer and tobacco manufacturer at what is locally known as Pine Hill. Our subject grew to manhood on a farm and in 1855 graduated from the Cumberland University of Lebanon. He entered upon the study of medicine, and in 1858 graduated from the Jefferson Medical College of Philadelphia. He then located in Paris and began practicing, where he continued very successfully until 1874, when he retired from practice and engaged in stemming and handling leaf tobacco, which he now continues prizing about 500 hogsheads per year. He also carries on his farming interest. In 1861 he married Mary R. Thompson, a daughter of William H. Thompson, who was a merchant of Paris. Four children were born to this union—two sons and two daughters: Alice, Juliett, William H. and Robert D. Mrs. Caldwell is a member of the Cumberland Presbyterian Church. Mr. Caldwell is a Democrat in politics and has been chairman of the Democratic County Committee. He has also served as delegate to the State Convention, etc., and is a very active member of his party.

William L. Carter, Jr., attorney at law at Paris, was born in Henry County, Tenn., in 1848, and is one of a family of four children born to William L. and Mary (Biles) Carter. The father was born in Davidson County, Tenn., in 1804, and received his education in the rustic schoolhouse of the forest. He came to this county in 1824, being one of its first settlers, and is one of the few men who settled in the county at that early day who is living. Mrs. Carter died in 1829, and in 1831 he married Arabella Sessum, of Humphreys County, who died in May, 1886. Mr. Carter is now living on the farm, where he settled in 1831 two miles south of Henry Station. Our subject grew to manhood on the farm, and received his education in Henry Station Academy. He began life by clerking in his father's store, and in 1868 commenced the study of law without any preceptor. He was admitted to the bar in 1874, and since that time has been actively engaged in his profession in Paris, where he has an extensive and lucrative practice. In 1880 he formed a partnership with W. M. Janes, the firm being familiarly known as Carter & Janes. In 1874 our subject was elected magistrate of the Paris District, which position he held six years. In about 1876 he was appointed county revenue commissioner, which position he continues to hold. March 7, 1871, he married Sarah Alice Gallion, a native of Carroll County, Tenn., born in 1854, and the daughter of Frank B. and L. Gallion. To our subject and wife were born three children: Alice Ray, May F. and William L. In politics Mr. Carter is a Democrat, and cast his first presidential vote for Horace Greeley. He is a member of the Masonic fraternity, I. O. G. T. and O. O. of H., also of the Cumberland

Presbyterian Church. In 1884 he, in company with F. B. and R. E. Gallion (his brother-in-law), established a pottery manufactory in Paris, in which enterprise he is still connected. Mrs. Carter is a member of the Christian Church.

L. Cherry, of the firm of Cherry & Purath, established his livery barn, etc., in 1871, and has continued it successfully ever since, taking in E. Purath as a partner in January, 1886. Mr. Cherry was born March 15, 1841, and is a son of Albert G. Cherry, a farmer of this county, and a native of Davidson County, who died in 1856. He was also a merchant for some time when a young man. The mother of our subject, Eliza Bradley, was born and reared near Lebanon, Tenn. Our subject was reared on a farm, and when a young man, in 1861, he enlisted in the Fifth Tennessee Regiment of Infantry and served four years. He was wounded with a bayonet by bushwhackers, and by a gunshot in the shoulder. After returning from the war he engaged in the retail grocery business in Paris, where he continued till he engaged in his present business. He is also transfer agent for the Louisville & Nashville Railroad out as far as Murray, Ky. In 1865 he married J. L. Martin, of Ballard County, Ky, and they have three children: Mattie, who died at eleven years of age; Albert G. and Lafayette. Mrs. Cherry and oldest son are members of the Christian Church. In politics Mr. Cherry is a firm and active Democrat, and is an enterprising business man. He has one of the best livery stables in the city, with a stock of about $7,000.

William M. Coffman, merchant and prominent citizen of Cottage Grove, was born in Henry County, Tenn., in 1833, and is one of seven children born to John M. and Elizabeth (White) Coffman. The father was born in Davidson County, Tenn., about 1799, and was of German extraction. His father, Isaac Coffman, was a native of North Carolina, and settled in Davidson County, Tenn., at a very early day, where he died. John M.'s educational advantages were very meager, and at the age of twenty-one he married and settled in Benton County, and afterward in Henry County, where he owned at one time 600 acres of land. He was a soldier in the war of 1812, and was an active, energetic man. He died about 1848. His wife, Elizabeth (White) Coffman, was born near Louisville, Ky., about 1797, and was of English descent. She was a cousin of Detective W. L. White, and died in 1871. Our subject was reared by the tender care of a mother and educated in the common schools of Henry County. He commenced life as a tobacco manufacturer, and thus continued for six years. At the breaking out of the Rebellion he enlisted in Company G, Seventh Tennessee Cavalry, Confederate Army, and continued in the service during the entire time of hostilities, taking an active part in all but two of the battles in which his command was engaged. After the surrender he returned home and soon after engaged in the mercantile business at Trezevant, Carroll County, where he remained thirteen years. He then came to Henry County and tilled the soil for three years, after which he again engaged in the mercantile business at Cottage Grove, where he remained till 1885, when he retired from business. Mr. Coffman is the owner of about 250 acres of good, productive land in the Eleventh District, also other property. In politics he is a stanch Democrat, and cast his first presidential vote for James Buchanan, in 1856. He is a member of the Missionary Baptist Church.

Simeon W. Cooley, general trader and prominent citizen of Paris, is a son of William M. and Eliza (Booth) Cooley. The father was born in Stewart County, Tenn., in 1822, and received a good practical education. When about twenty-one years of age he was married and became the father of nine children, six of whom are living. In 1878 he removed to Houston County, where he has since resided, engaged in farming, and is considered one of the leading farmers of that vicinity. The mother was also a native of Stewart County. The subject of this sketch was born in Stewart County in 1845, at the same place where his mother was born. He received his education in the common schools, and by his own efforts has since acquired sufficient education to enable him to transact all ordinary business. He is now one of the most practical business men of the city. In 1863 he entered the Confederate service by enlisting in Company B, Eleventh Kentucky Cavalry, and served as first lieutenant during the remainder of the war. June, 1865, he married Addie Sexton, of Stewart County, and by her had three children, one of whom is now living, Mamie. Mrs. Cooley died in 1871, and April, 1873, he married Mattie Brandon, daughter of Col. N. and Minerva Brandon, of Stewart County. By this union our subject became the father of eight children, six of whom are now living: Maurice, William, Minerva, Daisy, Henry and Harry. Mr. Cooley commenced life as a tiller of the soil, but at the end of one year he engaged in the grocery business at Dover. He was proprietor of the Commercial House for one year, and while a resident of Stewart County was made deputy sheriff, which office he held for four years. In 1875 he removed to Houston County, where he remained till 1882, engaged in the mercantile business, etc. He then came to Big Sandy Mills, Henry County, and at the end of two years moved to Paris, purchasing a one-third interest in the Paris Roller Mills. He now owns a two-thirds interest of the same, which is one of the best mills in this part of the State. Mr. Cooley is also the owner of 247 acres in Fayette

County, 200 acres in Stewart County, 537 acres in Henry County, and also an eleven-acre tract in the south part of Paris, on which he has a fine residence. Mr. Cooley is a Democrat in politics, and cast his first presidential vote for Horatio Seymour in 1868. Mrs. Cooley was born in Stewart County in 1854, and is an influential member of the Christian Church.

John T. Currier, cotton manufacturer of Paris, was born in Henry County, Tenn., in 1856, and is one of a family of eight children, only two of whom are living: Bettie Ann (Mrs. W. E. Weldon) and our subject. The father, Nathaniel Currier, was born in Salisbury, Mass., in 1807, and was of Scotch ancestry. He received a good literary and business education, and in 1833 he and his brother, James C., immigrated to Henry County. In 1842 Nathaniel married Martha Manly, by whom he had two children, one living, Mrs. Ann Mathewson, of Florida. Mrs. Currier died about 1847, and in 1849 he married Maria L. Blanton, of Frankfort, Ky., born in 1824, and who is still living on the old farm. When he first came to Henry County, he and his brother, James C., purchased 309 acres of land, one and a half miles northeast of Paris, on which they established their manufacturing business, and where they continued till 1869, when Nathaniel purchased J. C.'s interest. They established the business in a wooden building 30x40 feet, and in 1879 superseded it by a more commodious brick structure, 40x100 feet, erected by J. T. Currier and mother. In 1882 Mrs. Weldon entered as a third party, and the firm is now known as John T. Currier & Co. Mr. Nathaniel Currier continued his business without intermission during the Rebellion, it being the only establishment of the kind not disturbed at that time. He died in 1877. Our subject was educated in Lexington, Ky., at the Transylvania University, and in 1878 married Belle Shepard, a native of Illinois, born in 1859, and the daughter of C. R. and L. Shepard, of Arkansas. By this union our subject became the father of three children, only one now living, John Nathaniel. In politics Mr. Currier is strictly conservative, casting his first presidential vote for Gen. Hancock. Mr. and Mrs. Currier and mother are members of the Missionary Baptist Church.

Dr. H. Diggs, physician and farmer, residing in the Twenty-fifth District, was born within four miles of where he now lives, January 29, 1825, son of John H. and Sarah (Webb) Diggs, natives of North Carolina, born, respectively, in 1790 and 1799. They were married in their native State, and came to Henry County in 1823, being among the early settlers of that county. He was a farmer by occupation, and died in 1848; the mother died in 1869. Our subject received a good literary education and soon entered on his medical studies at Paris, where he read medicine for about one year and a half, afterward taking a course of lectures at the Transylvania Medical College, at Lexington, Ky. At the end of four years he entered the Louisville Medical College and graduated from that institution in 1852, after which he located in Holmes County, Miss., and practiced successfully for six years; at the end of this time, on account of ill health, he was obliged to leave that place, and while recruiting attended the Nashville Medical College, where he graduated in the spring of 1859. In the fall of 1860 he married Martha E., daughter of Dr. J. D. Looney, and by this union they have three children: R. K., J. D. and Lula B. In 1861 the Doctor located near where he is now residing, and has been actively engaged in the practice of his profession ever since. He is a Democrat in politics and cast his first presidential vote for Lewis Cass. He has been a Mason for many years, and is a member of the Henry County Medical Association.

J. R. B. Dinwiddie, son of James and Mary (Carson) Dinwiddie, was born in Henry County, Tenn., on the farm where he now resides, February 2, 1828. The father was a native of Virginia, immigrated to Tennessee about 1823, and located in Henry County, where he died in September, 1860. The mother was also a native of Virginia. Our subject was one of six children born to his father's second marriage; he worked on the farm until twenty-one years of age, after which he began life depending on his own resources. After the death of his father he hired a portion of the home farm and bought the remainder, on which he worked for some time. He is a member of the firm of Dinwiddie & Co., who are engaged in the manufacture of cotton goods, The machinery is situated in the Tenth Civil District—Spring Creek Cotton Mills. Mr. Dinwiddie is also engaged in merchandising at the same place in this county. February 22, 1860, he married Sallie Lee Gordon, and they have nine children: Mary M. (Mrs. Dr. J. H. Broach), Priscilla Gordon, Nancy Lee and Eliza Ellen (twins, the latter being Mrs. J. A. Dinwiddie), James M. B., Thomas B., John N., Callie C., and William Floyd. Our subject is a member of the Cumberland Presbyterian Church, and in politics is a Democrat.

R. E. Douglass a prominent citizen and farmer, was born in Sumner County, Tenn., May 23, 1825, and is a son of W. J. and Eliza (Watkins) Douglass. The father was a native of Sumner County, born 1792, and always lived in that county; was a farmer and died March, 1866. The mother was born in 1795 and was the daughter of Maj. Charles Watkins, a Virginian by birth and a prominent citizen of Sumner County. She died in 1837. Our subject received his education in the schools of

Sumner County, and in 1849 united his fortunes with those of Miss Sarah Walton, a native of Sumner County, Tenn., born 1827 and the daughter of Josiah Walton. By this union our subject became the father of eight children, viz.: J. W., Mary J., Sallie, Emma, Loula, R. C., R. E., Jr., and I. G. After marriage Mr. Douglass located in his native county and began tilling the soil, a business he has since continued to follow. In 1883 he came to Henry County and located on the Paris and McKenzie road seven miles from his former place. Mr. Douglass has reared quite a family of children, has given them the best advantages for a good education and a part of them follow the teacher's profession. In politics he is a Democrat and he and wife and all the family except the youngest child are members of the Methodist Episcopal Church.

Hon. W. A. Dunlap, a leading attorney of Paris, is the son of John and Marietta (Beauchamp) Dunlap. The father was born November 14, 1801, in Knoxville, Tenn., and was reared in Roane County, where he received a good education. He read law when a young man and entered upon his profession in 1823 at Reynoldsburg, Tenn. In the spring of 1824 he came to Paris, and here spent the remainder of his days in practicing his profession, attending strictly to this and accumulating quite a fortune. He was a member of the Christian Church and was a patron of all benevolent institutions, schools in particular. He reared six children, five of whom are now living, viz.: Mrs. Susan E. Porter (wife of ex-Gov. J. D. Porter), Bethenia A. (wife of Dr. T. C. Harcourt), John H. (who died in 1869), Hugh P., Richard W. and William A. The father of these children died December 24, 1874, and the mother is still living at the age of seventy-two, a consistent member of the Christian Church. William A., our subject, was born December 17, 1834, in Paris and received a good literary and law education, being a graduate from the literary department of the Cumberland University in 1854, and from the law department in 1857. He then began practicing law and has continued it ever since very successfully. He served one term in the lower house of the Legislature in 1861–62 as floater. In 1870 he married Sandal Stewart, of Memphis, and this union resulted in the birth of two children: John H. and Marietta. Politically Mr. Dunlap has always been a Democrat and is one of the respected citizens of Paris. Hugh P. Dunlap is a farmer living near Paris, in this county. He was born September, 1843, and in 1869 wedded Sallie Atkins, daughter of Gen. J. D. C. Atkins, of Paris. Richard W. Dunlap was born November 30, 1851, and in 1875 married Charlie B. Lamb. He is a minister in the Christian Church. The grandparents of our subject were early settlers of East Tennessee. The grandfather, Hugh Dunlap, was of Irish birth, born in 1769, and was one of the founders of Knoxville. The grandmother, Susanna Gilliam, was born in Virginia, and was a daughter of Devereaux Gilliam. The grandparents had quite a numerous family, eleven of whom lived to be grown. They came to this county in 1825 bringing with them several members of the family who lived to be prominent men in the county—James T., a lawyer, and Ripley E., who was a prominent citizen and lived here for several years. James T. was born in 1812 and practiced law in this place till 1857. In 1847 he was elected representative and in 1851-53 he was elected State senator. In 1857 he was elected comptroller of the State. He died in 1879, and Ripley E., who was born in 1817, died in 1881.

Robert Eastwood, proprietor of the Henry County Woolen Mills, was born in England in 1823, and is one of a family of eight children, four of whom are now living. The parents, John and Alice (Woodcock) Eastwood, were born in 1776 and 1778, respectively. The father was a native of England, and followed merchandising there till 1843, when he came to America, locating at Massachusetts. After remaining there a short time he went West to Ohio, and spent the latter part of his life in tilling the soil. He died in 1853. The mother died in 1855 in Massachusetts, having moved back to that place after the death of her husband. Our subject came to America one year previous to his parents, and after stopping in Massachusetts went to Ohio, and from there came to Tennessee in 1851. He located in the middle part of the State and married Angeline Longford, a native of Tennessee, born in 1833; by this union he became the father of seven children: Richard, Robert, Abel, Alice, Hannah, Mary and Joseph. In 1856 our subject came to Henry County, and built the first woolen-mill in the county, it having a carding and cotton-gin. In 1865 he located where he now lives, and built a woolen factory. He also carries on his farming interest in connection with the factory. He is conservative in politics, voting for principle rather than for party, and he and Mrs. Eastwood have for many years been church members.

Dr. Samuel C. Edmunds, a leading physician and surgeon of this part of the State, was born December 23, 1831, in Warren County, Ky., and is a son of John J. and Sallie (Martin) Edmunds. The father was born in Amherst County, Va., October 19, 1805, and removed to Warren County, Ky., at the age of five. There he lived until 1842, when he moved to Henry County, Tenn., and there remained until his death in 1848, having been a farmer all his life. The mother of our subject was also born in Amherst County, Va., in 1800, and died in 1870. Our subject was reared on a farm, received a practical education, and graduated in the medical department of the university of Louisville in March, 1856. He then began practicing at Cottage Grove, Henry Co., Tenn., continuing there until 1861, when he removed to Paris, and has since practiced his profession in this place with very great success. January 22, 1857, he married Drusilla Hardy, of Calloway Co., Ky. To them were born five children: Hinda, Sallie, Cora, William and Nellie. Politically Mr. Edmunds is a member of the Democratic party, and as a citizen is one of the leading men of the county.

Constantine Frazier, hardware merchant and prominent citizen of Paris, established his business in April, 1885, which he has continued up to the present time with commendable success. He was born in Henry County in 1854, and is one of a family of nine children, four of whom are living, viz.: D. W., of Calloway County, Ky.; Sarah J., who married E. B. Swan (deceased); H. E., of Dresden, and our subject. The father, Hon. Constantine Frazier, was born in East Tennessee in 1804, and received but a limited education. He came to Henry County with his parents when but a boy, and engaged in agricultural pursuits. At the age of twenty-five he married Mary E. Looney, who was also a native of East Tennessee, born about 1809, and who is still living in Paris. After his marriage Constantine settled two miles southeast of Paris, where he remained till his death in 1870. He was deputy sheriff for some years and served two terms as county court clerk. He was a member of the State Legislature at the opening of the late civil war, holding the office for several years. Our subject was reared under the parental roof and received a good business education at Paris. He began business for himself as a tiller of the soil and continued at this till 1880, when he engaged in the liquor business. In 1885 he came to Paris and established his present business. November 21, 1876, he married Nannie A. Covington, a native of Henry County, born in 1855, and the daughter of W. L. and Nannie Covington, natives of North Carolina. To our subject and wife were born three children: Lottie, Irma and Connie. Mr. Frazier is one of the most enterprising business men of Paris, and carries a stock of general hardware, stoves, tinware and agricultural implements, etc., to the value of about $5,000. He is a Democrat in politics and cast his first vote for S. J. Tilden. He is a member of the K. of H., and of the O. O. of H. He and wife are prominent members of the Christian Church. Mr. Frazier is the owner of eighty-five acres of valuable land apart from the old home farm. He has also a good residence in a very desirable locality of Paris.

M. H. Freeman was born in Lunenburg County, Va., September 20,

1833, and is one of eight children born to John C. and Eliza (Hurt) Freeman, both native Virginians. They were married in that State, and came to Henry County, Tenn., in 1839, locating near the present site of Cottage Grove, where John C. followed agricultural pursuits till his death in 1864. The mother followed him in 1873. Our subject remained with his parents till he reached his majority, and then was united in marriage to Margaret F. Julian. He was engaged in tilling the soil until the breaking out of the war, when he formed Company K, of Forrest's Twentieth Tennessee Confederate Cavalry, and with this served as captain until the close of the war. He then continued farming till 1876, and was then appointed deputy sheriff of this county. After serving four years he was then elected sheriff, which office he still occupies, serving his third term at the present. To his marriage above referred to eleven children were born, only five of whom are now living: Mary Alice (Mrs. Barton), Lena (Mrs. Foster), Beulah J., James M. and Maggie. Mr. Freeman is a member of the Masonic fraternity.

Thomas C. Fryer, a leading attorney of Paris, was born January 29, 1829, in Guilford County, N. C., and is a son of John Fryer, who immigrated to Henry County, Tenn., in the spring of 1838 and who was a farmer by occupation. He died in October, 1842. The mother, Martha (Landreth) Fryer, was also a native of Guilford County, N. C. Our subject was reared on a farm and received a practical education. He followed agricultural pursuits for some time before the war and also read law. About 1866 he was licensed to practice law, and has resided in Paris engaged in that profession ever since. He is also farming by proxy, owning a farm of 370 acres besides other lands. January 27, 1853, he married Ann McCullough, a daughter of Alexander McCullough, a farmer of this county. Mrs. Fryer died in November, 1879, leaving these children: Robert N., William L., Thomas L., John H. and George L. January 1, 1882, Mr. Fryer married Mrs. Alice Beadles of this county, but a native of Kentucky. One daughter, Lilian, has blessed this union. Mr. Fryer is a member of the Democratic party and he and all the family are members of the Cumberland Presbyterian Church. He is an enterprising and influential public spirited citizen of the county, and patronizes all institutions of benevolence, charity, morality and religion.

S. J. Grable, resident of Henry was born in January, 1818, in Kentucky, and is a son of Samuel A. and Mary (Morrison) Grable, natives of Kentucky and Pennsylvania, respectively. The father was born about 1780 and the mother about 1783. Our subject was a descendant of Dutch-Irish stock, was reared on the farm and received a rather limited education. At the age of twenty-one he engaged to travel in the interest of a firm in New York in the sale of clocks and continued at this about three years, at the expiration of which time he began trading in stocks. In 1836 he engaged in the mill business, but soon left that and farmed for seven or eight years. He was also in the merchandise business till 1859 when he came to Henry County, Tenn., and has been a resident of the State up to the present time. In June, 1835, he married Louisa J. Gordon and had five children: Mary J. (Mrs. J. M. Milan), Virgie Lee, Nervy (Mrs. William Owenby) and two others (deceased). Mrs. Grable died in 1846. She was a noble Christian woman and her loss was deeply felt. Our subject has been a successful man and is now in easy circumstances. He is a Mason, a Democrat in politics and a member of the Cumberland Presbyterian Church.

Capt. W. D. Hallum, a native of Tennessee, was born January 23, 1830, and is a son of Morris and Nancy (Marshall) Hallum, natives respectively of North Carolina and Virginia. The father was born January 5, 1785, immigrated to Tennessee at a very early date, when the State was in its infancy, and here died January 17, 1858. The mother was born January 26, 1779, and died October 12, 1859. The Captain's grandfather Hallum was a native of North Carolina, and his grandfather Marshall a native of Virginia. Their parents were originally from England, and consequently our subject is of English descent. At the age of sixteen he enlisted in the Mexican war in the Second Tennessee Infantry, Maury's company, was out about six months, when he was discharged on account of ill health. He remained with his father till twenty-one years of age, when he engaged in farming for himself, and this continued up to the time of the late war. He then organized a company in Henry County, and joined the Fifth Tennessee Infantry, Travis' regiment. He started with his command from Union City, went to Columbus, Ky., and while there was made provost-marshal. At New Madrid, Mo., he was shot through the neck, which disabled him from active duty for about six weeks. He then joined his command at Corinth, Miss., and was again wounded, shot through the left arm. He received still another wound at Athens, Ala., but at the end of six weeks was again ready for duty. At the close of the war he returned home and engaged in farming, in connection with the real estate business. In 1867 he engaged in the merchandise business and sold goods at three or four different towns till 1876, when he began farming and has continued this up to the present time. January, 1850, he married Delia Barham, and this union resulted in the birth of six children: Mollie, Clinton, Frankie, Susan, William and Katie. Mr. Hallum is an unswerving Democrat in politics.

Green D. Hancock, blacksmith, at Paris, was born in Henry County, in 1843, and is one of eight children, two of whom are living. His father, Henry Hancock, was born in North Carolina in 1803, and was of English lineage. He immigrated to Wilson County with his parents when but a boy, and at the age of twenty-five married Priscilla Hancock, a native of Wilson County, born about 1807. After their marriage they came to Henry County, but soon returned to Wilson County. Here they remained till 1851, when he removed to Stewart County. In early life he had run a shoe factory in Lebanon, but abandoned that and engaged in farming, which he continued the remainder of his life. He died about 1853. The mother died about 1850. Our subject being left an orphan at an early age, found parental care with his eldest brother, James W., with whom he remained till eighteen years of age. He received a fair education principally at Cherry Valley, in Wilson County. May, 1861, he enlisted in Company A, First Tennessee Cavalry and served during the entire war, without receiving a wound or being captured. He then returned home and resumed his blacksmithing. January 3, 1874, he married Rachel J., daughter of Thomas Howell, of Stewart County, and has five children, four now living: Evan W., Harry D., Vera Edna and Nettie Anna. In 1875 Mr. Hancock came to Paris and continued his business at this place. In 1882 he, in company with Ewing McVay, established a wagon and carriage manufactory at the corner of Market and Blair Streets. The firm is now known as Hancock & McVay, and is one of the most successful enterprises of the kind in the city. In politics Mr. Hancock is a Democrat and cast his first presidential vote for Horatio Seymour. He is a member of the K. of H., and he and wife are members of the Methodist Episcopal Church South.

Preston G. Haynes was born March 14, 1814 in Robertson County, Tenn., and is a son of Thomas Haynes, a native of Virginia, who imigrated to Tennessee, at a very early date and settled in Robertson County. Our subject's paternal grandfather was a native of Scotland and he together with two of his sons were Revolutionary soldiers. His maternal grandfather, Samuel Gilbert, was also a Revolutionary soldier and a native of Erin's Green Isle. Preston remained with his father till nineteen years of age after which he began clerking in a merchandise establishment but owing to failing health was obliged to resign. He worked on a farm till the beginning of the Mexican war, when he organized a company which he conducted to New Orleans and committed to Capt. James M. Scantlin. He was immediately detailed as recruiting officer, and April, 1847, he was appointed first lieutenant of Company G, Fourteenth Tennessee Infantry, by James K. Polk. At the close of the war he returned home and for three years had very poor health. In 1852 he was appointed deputy sheriff, which office he filled for a period of four years. In 1858 he was elected to fill the office of sheriff and occupied this position till the breaking out of the late war. He was also engaged in merchandising at that time, but closed out his business about 1860 and engaged in agricultural pursuits, which he has continued to the present time. Previous to this, in 1838, he served the people six years as magistrate and was re-elected in 1844 and has served from that time to the present, with the exception of the time he was in the Mexican war and also during the late war. He came to this county in 1819 and camped the first night after crossing the Tennessee River within thirty yards of the place where he now resides. February 12, 1834, he married Minerva Hayes and this union resulted in the birth of ten children. Those living are John P., Martha J., wife of N. J. Barham, and Minerva E., wife of B. J. Allen. Mr. Haynes is a member of the Cumberland Presbyterian Church and a Democrat in politics.

William H. Hudson was born December 4, 1829, in St. Johnsbury, Vt., in which State he was reared and educated. In 1853 he moved to Loudon, Tenn., and there worked at the railroad business, having charge of a gang of track layers. He remained there three years and then went to Memphis, where he continued his business and undertook contracting, laying track by contract on the road from Humboldt to Clarksville, Tenn. During the war he was engaged in manufacturing cotton yarn, purchasing the Blanton mills in Henry County, Tenn., which were erected in 1857 by J. W. Blanton. Mr. Hudson continued in this business till the close of 1867 when he went to St. Louis and engaged in a wholesale grocery and manufacturing tobacco. Although he did not move there he conducted the business at that place about six years and also engaged in merchandising at Paris for two years during that time. He was instrumental in establishing the Commercial Bank of Paris, being one of its first stockholders, and is now president of the same, also the largest stockholder. At Big Sandy, in Benton County, he has been merchandising since 1878 and is now operating an extensive stove factory there in connection with his son. He was married December 27, 1864, to Miss Mary M. Wygul of Benton County; this union resulted in the birth of five children; only one, Charles P., is now living. Mr. and Mrs. Hudson are members of the Methodist Episcopal Church South. Politically Mr. Hudson is a Republican. He is one of the most thrifty business men of the county, and a highly respected citizen.

Henry A. Humphreys, farmer, was born in Henry County, Tenn., in 1839, and is a son of Henry and Susanna (Paschal) Humphreys. The father was born in North Carolina in 1802, received a very limited education, married in his native State and came to Henry County about 1825, being among the very early settlers of that region. He died in 1881. Mrs. Humphreys was born in North Carolina in 1804, and is still living on the old home farm in the Thirteenth District. Henry A. was reared at home and educated in the common schools of Henry County, but afterward attended two years in Murray, Ky. He taught school for several years, and November, 1861, enlisted in Company G, First Tennessee Cavalry, as a Confederate soldier. He remained in the service till the final surrender, participating in all the engagements in which his command took part and escaped without a wound. After returning from the war he engaged in mercantile pursuits for about a year. January, 1868, he married Mrs. Malinda Dumas, a native of Henry County, born in 1837, and the daughter of James and Isabella Walker. To Mr. and Mrs. Humphreys were born seven children, four living: Maud, Jennie, Lillie and Fisher. Mr. Humphreys has since resided in his present home, and is now the owner of 550 acres of valuable land. In politics he is a Democrat, and his first presidential vote was for John C. Breckenridge in 1860.

Prof. T. H. M. Hunter was born in Marshall County, a son of Elihu W. and Susan (Wilson) Hunter. The mother died when our subject was young and he was reared by an uncle, receiving a good education at the Cumberland University, from which institution he graduated in the class of 1863. He enlisted in Company C, Eleventh Tennessee Cavalry, and served nearly three years. After returning from the war he entered upon the profession of teaching in his native county, continuing there until 1872, when he became professor of mathematics in Bethel College, McKenzie, Tenn., for three years, since which time he has been at Paris connected with the Paris Male High School, which afterward became the Paris public school, and of which he is now the principal. He was three years of this time not connected with these schools, but was in Texas. In 1870 he married Elia Baker, once connected with the schools at Columbia and at Winchester. One son was born to this union, and was only two years of age when he died. The mother died in 1877, and in 1880 Prof. Hunter wedded Bettie Atkins, daughter of Gen. J. D. C. Atkins, and the fruit of this union was one child, a son, named Atkins. Mr. and Mrs. Hunter are members of the Cumberland Presbyterian Church, and Mr. Hunter, besides school-teaching, is engaged in agricultural pursuits.

William A. and Sol. Jones, farmers and stock dealers, and sons of Thomas and Louisa H. (Terrell) Jones, were born in Benton County,

Tenn, the former in 1827 and the latter in 1834. There were seven children in the family, only three of whom are now living. The father was born in North Carolina in 1804, and was of Welsh ancestry. He received a limited education, and immigrated to Hickman County, Tenn., when about seventeen years of age with his father, Solomon Jones, who went there at a very early time, when the country was a vast wilderness abounding in wild animals, and who died about 1841. Thomas was married about 1824, and soon after removed to Benton County, settling on a large farm one mile west of Camden, where, in April, 1840, Mrs. Jones died. She was a native of Wake County, N. C., born 1806. In 1842 Thomas Jones married Mary Ann Smalley, and to them were born six children, all living. In 1859 Mr. Jones removed to Texas and there died in 1863. He was a man of considerable ability, and was sheriff of Benton County six years. Our subjects were reared at home and received their education at Camden. In 1856 W. A. was elected circuit court clerk of Benton County, and in 1860 was elected county court clerk. The following year he enlisted in Company A, of which he was made captain, and at the reorganization of a battalion, which became the Fifty-fifth Tennessee, he was elected lieutenant-colonel, and held this position during the remainder of service. He was captured at Island No. 10 April, 1862, was taken to Columbus, Ohio, and from there to Johnson's Island, near Sandusky, Ohio, where he was exchanged in September of the same year. He returned home in 1865, and resigned his position as county court clerk, but in 1866 he was again elected circuit court clerk, which position he held for four years. He then spent about five years in the mercantile business, after which he organized a stock store at Camden, which is still in a flourishing condition, and the first of the kind in the State. In 1872 he purchased 200 acres of land two miles west of Paris. Both brothers own 330 acres of good productive land; in fact, as good land as there is to be found in the county. May, 1861, Sol. Jones enlisted in the Confederate Army, Company C, Fifth Tennessee, and in October of the same year was transferred to his brother's company, and upon W. A.'s promotion to lieutenant-colonel, Sol. was made captain of the company. He was captured at Island No. 10, but was soon exchanged, when he rejoined his command and was re-elected captain, which position he held during the remainder of the service. He was in many of the principal battles and surrendered under Gen. Johnston. He returned home, and April 11, 1867, married Mary A. Atkins, daughter of John and Mary S. Atkins, half sister of Hon. J. D. C. Atkins, of Paris. He then settled on the farm, on which he still resides. Mrs. Jones died January 13, 1868, a devout member of the Methodist Episcopal Church

South. In politics W. A. and Sol. are both Democrats, and are ardent advocates of prohibition. The former cast his first presidential vote for Franklin Pierce and the latter for James Buchanan.

Charles M. Kennerly, farmer, was born in Floyd County, Va., April 16, 1844, and is a son of John W. and Martha (Ross) Kennerly. The father was a native of Virginia, born in 1806, was reared, married and remained in Virginia until 1850, when he came to Henry County, and here died in 1875. The mother was born in Patrick County, Va., in 1819, and died February, 1877. Our subject was reared under the parental roof and educated in the district schools of Henry County. October 30, 1876, he married S. A., daughter of Dr. J. H. Travis, of Henry County, Tennessee. She was born October 4, 1848, and by her marriage became the mother of four children: Carrie V., Charles, Joseph and Mattie Eliza. Mr. Kennerly now resides at the old home place where his father first located. He has 600 acres of good land situated ten miles due north of Paris. In 1872 he began merchandising at Conyersville, and this continued for six years, since which time he has devoted himself exclusively to his farm. He is a Democrat in politics and believes in national prohibition; a Mason and a member of the Methodist Episcopal Church. November 16, 1861, he enlisted in Company D, Forty-sixth Tennessee Infantry, and participated in these battles: Island No. 10; Atlanta, Ga.; Franklin, Tenn.; Jacksonville, Miss., and other minor engagements. He was captured at Island No. 10, and was taken to Camp Douglas, where he was confined five months. He was again captured and remained a prisoner until the close of the war.

Bank of Henry, established March 15, 1886; capital stock $100,000, $50,000 paid up; S. A. Champion, president; A. B. Lamb, cashier. Hon. A. B. Lamb, the cashier, was born in Paris, Tenn., October 28, 1859, and is the son of Hon. Benjamin F. Lamb, who was an attorney at Paris. The father was a native of Mississippi, born 1820, and when but a boy came to Paris, where he was reared. He entered upon his profession at this place, which he continued up to the time of his death. He was a member of the lower house of the Legislature of Tennessee a part of one term. In 1845 he married Henrietta Cooney, who still survives him. He was a very successful practitioner, always attending strictly to his profession. He died in 1868. Our subject was reared in Paris and received a practical education in its schools. He attended the law department of Vanderbilt University five months, and in 1881 was admitted to the bar. He then began practicing and continued this until he engaged in his present business. He was elected mayor of Paris in 1882, serving one year and was joint representative of Weakley and Henry

Counties, in the lower house of the Legislature in 1885-86. November 4, 1885, he married Minnie L. Caldwell, daughter of James Caldwell, of Texas. He is a Democrat in politics and he and wife are members of the Christian Church.

D. M. Lankford was born October, 1825, in Tennessee, and is a son of Henry and Sarah (Hamilton) Lankford, natives of Tennessee. The father was born October 27, 1800, and died May, 1874. The mother was born February, 1806, and died January 31, 1883. Our subject's maternal grandfather, James Hamilton, was born May 1, 1757, in North Carolina, and died about 1831 or 1832, in this State. His maternal grandmother was also a native of North Carolina and was within sound of the battle of Bunker's Hill when it was fought. D. M. worked on the farm till he was twenty years of age, at which time he engaged in tilling the soil on his own responsibility, and has continued that occupation up to the present time. In 1861 he entered the Confederate Army in Company H, Forty-sixth Tennessee Infantry, and at the re-organization our subject was elected orderly sergeant, which position he held till the surrender of his regiment on April 8, 1862. He was lodged in prison at Camp Butler, Ill., where he remained about six months, and was then exchanged at Vicksburg, September, 1862. On account of ill health he was discharged, but was conscripted December, 1863, and joined the Fifteenth Tennessee Mounted Infantry. He remained with his command till June 10, 1864, at which time he was wounded in the right breast, and now carries the ball. At the close of the war he again engaged in farming and has been quite successful in this occupation. He has been married twice, the first time February 14, 1847, to Ann Eliza Reed, who died July 29, 1865, leaving eight children: John H., Sidney C., Thomas J., James M., Theresa A. (Mrs. John B. Brummitt), Perina Jane (Mrs. William W. Routon), Sarah M. and Anna S. April 10, 1867, Mr. Lankford married his second wife, Maria C. Cable, and this union resulted in the birth of three children: Robert H., William E. and Adolphus. He is a Democrat in politics and an elder in the Cumberland Presbyterian Church.

William H. Lasater, lumberman and prominent citizen of Paris, was born in Wilson County, Tenn., in 1838, and is one of nine children, five of whom are living, born to Calvin and Martha (Goldston) Lasater. The father was born in Wilson County in 1817, educated at Lebanon University, and was a farmer by occupation. He was married in 1837, and in 1852 came to Henry County, settling in the Fourteenth District, where he remained till 1860. He then removed to Obion County, and continued farming till 1865, when he returned to Henry County, locating in the

Seventh District. He died here in January, 1876, a devout member of the Christian Church. The mother of our subject was born in Wilson County in 1820, and is now living on the old farm in the Seventh District. Our subject remained at home till he reached his majority, and received a good common-school education. He farmed for about eight years, and the following eight years was engaged in manufacturing tobacco five and a half miles east of Paris. He then went to Texas, and at the end of a year returned to his native county. He bought a saw-mill, which he ran about three years, when W. H. Hudson entered as a partner, and they introduced the manufacturing of staves for two years. In 1885 Mr. Lasater sold his interest to Mr. Hudson, and he, in company with M. H. Freeman, purchased a planing-mill in the south part of the city, where their present business is located. This is the only establishment of the kind in the city, and is doing a flourishing business. The firm is familiarly known as Freeman, Lasater & Co. May 8, 1857, Mr. Lasater married Nannie Hart, a native of Henry County, born in 1838, and the daughter of George and Catharine Hart. By this union our subject became the father of ten children, eight living: Laura (Mrs. George P. Lee), Rufus William, Nannie, Novella, Jesse, Herbert, John and Haford. Our subject was formerly a Whig, and cast his first presidential vote for John Bell; he is now a Democrat, a member of the Masonic fraternity, K. of H., K. of P., and he and wife are members of the Missionary Baptist Church, he being a deacon of the same.

John L. Lemonds, the genial clerk of the Henry County Court, was born October 6, 1837, near the Kentucky line, in Henry County. He is a son of Robert and Eleanor H. (Martin) Lemonds, who were natives of North Carolina, but were reared in Henry County. The father was a blacksmith in early life, and was surveyor of his county for many years. For three and a half years previous to his death, which occurred September 25, 1855, he was clerk of the county court. He was an elder in the Presbyterian Church, and was much esteemed by his many friends. He was in fair financial circumstances. His wife died December 9, 1869. She was a member of the Methodist Episcopal Church. Our subject was reared on his father's farm, and at the age of twenty years was appointed deputy county clerk for two years. He then enlisted in Company C, Fifth Tennessee Infantry, and served four years and ten days. He was shot in the arm at Murfreesboro, and at Peach Tree Creek, Ga., was wounded in the right shoulder. October 4, 1865, he married Margaret E. McCorkle, and to them was born one son, Robert J., who is now eleven years of age. Both Mr. and Mrs. Lemonds are members of the Methodist Episcopal Church South, and he is a Democrat, politically. In August, 1878, he was elected county court clerk, and in August, 1886, was elected to his third term. He was deputy clerk of the circuit court from 1865 to 1867, and was trustee from 1872 to 1876. He has been a farmer since 1869, and now owns about eighty-five acres of land near town.

H. H. Lovelace, farmer and extensive breeder of thoroughbred trotting horses and short-horn cattle, was born in Halifax County, Va., in 1833, and is one of a family of four children, all living: James R., of Martin, Weakley County; Ann E. (Mrs. C. N. Lovelace), H. H. and Susan J. (Mrs. T. M. Farmer), deceased. The father, Nat. M. Lovelace, was a native of Halifax County, Va., born in 1804, and was of English descent. About 1825 he married Ann E. Carleton, and removing to Weakley County in 1838, resumed his farming. He led an active and industrious life, and died about 1876, a much esteemed citizen. Mrs. Lovelace was born in Virginia, in King and Queen County, and died about 1873. Our subject was reared under the parental roof, and educated at the common schools of Weakley County. In 1858 he entered the mercantile business at Como, where he continued till about 1874, except during the war. Since that time he has devoted his attention exclusively to farming. He is the owner of 285 acres of land in this county, and of a third interest in 600 acres in Weakley County. The home farm of 110 acres is very fine and valuable land, under a high state of cultivation. Mr. Lovelace is a man of fine financial and good business capacity, and is a good citizen. He is one of the stockholders and electors of the Bank of Paris, and also of Martin. He is one of the stockholders in the co-operative store at Como. Soon after the war he was appointed by the State Legislature as commissioner of war claims for Henry County. May 1, 1861, he married Emma E., daughter of T. H. and Matilda Foster, of Weakley County. Emma E. was born in Weakley County, Tenn., in 1844. Our subject is a Republican in politics, and cast his first presidential vote for Millard Fillmore in 1856. He and wife are members of the Missionary Baptist Church.

J. W. Mathis, Esq., a resident of Henry, Tenn., was born April 1, 1842, in this county. His father, Josiah Mathis, was a native of Kentucky, and died in this county December 24, 1863. The mother was a native of this State, and died about 1846. Our subject remained on the farm assisting his father up to the time of the latter's death, when he assumed the responsibility of the family till 1879, after which he engaged in agricultural pursuits for himself. He was elected magistrate August, 1882, and at present is occupying that position. December 28, 1869, he married L. A. Wallace, of this county, and the fruits of this union were six children: Clark M., Mary H., John A., James J., Edward S. (who died in 1882) and Emerson E. Mr. Mathis' educational advantages, owing to circumstances, were rather limited, but he has always strongly advocated the cause and manifested a willingness to aid all enterprises pertaining to the advancement of education. He is a Mason, a member of the Agricultural Wheel, and a Republican in politics.

G. T. Morris, M. D., is a dealer in dry goods, ladies' and gents' furnishing goods, clothing, hats, caps, boots and shoes, established his business March 13, 1886, in Paris. He established a general store at Big Sandy, Benton County, in 1872 and carries a stock of $4,000 and does an annual business of $12,000. He has a $10,000 stock at this place and does a leading business. He was born at Camden, Tenn., January 30, 1851, and is a son of W. P. Morris, an extensive merchant and prominent citizen of Benton County. Our subject was reared in his native town and received a practical academic education. He graduated from the medical department of the university of Tennessee (now Vanderbilt) in February, 1872, and immediately afterward engaged in merchandising at Big Sandy and also engaged in practicing medicine for six months. September 3, 1874, he married Blanch Beasley, a daughter of Daniel E. Beasley, now a farmer of this county. Four children were born to our subject and wife: Elbert E., Granville T., Jr., Claudie L., and Minnie. Mr. Morris has been a member of the Methodist Episcopal Church South since thirteen years of age. He is a conservative Democrat in politics and is one of the most successful and thrifty merchants in this part of the State.

Dr. W. T. McClarin, a successful practitioner at Elkhorn, Tenn., was born at Carthage, Smith Co., Tenn., December 6, 1846; son of Charles and N. (Bradley) McClarin. The father was a native of the Emerald Isle born August 15, 1818, and came to America with his parents when a youth, locating in Smith County. He died May 12, 1851. The mother was born in Sumner County, Tenn., in 1818 and is now residing with her son Dr. W. T. Our subject received his education in the Smith County schools and afterward attended Conyersville Academy, Henry County. He then entered the office of Drs. Bradley & Bomar of that place and read medicine for two years, after which he attended a course of lectures at the medical department of the University of Nashville in 1865-66. In 1871 he married Laura Weldon, a native of Henry County, Tenn., born February 15, 1854, and the daughter of Dr. A. J. Weldon of Paris Landing. To this union were born seven children: Charles J., George C., William H., Henry B., Oswald Gross, Bertha L. and Annie Myrtle. After completing his medical education Dr. McClarin began practicing medicine and has continued that business up to the present time with evident success, as his many patients now living can testify. He is a member of the Masonic fraternity and has been master of the lodge at Elkhorn for some years. He is a K. of H. and a member of the Henry County Medical Society and of the West Tennessee Medical Association. He is a Democrat in politics and he and wife are members of the Cumberland Presbyterian Church.

T. C. McNeill, proprietor of the drug and book store, established his present business November 1, 1865, and has continued very successfully to the present time, carrying a large stock and having one of the best appearing stores of the kind in the State. He was born December 9, 1830, in Carroll County, Tenn., and is a son of William L. and Rachel (Clark) McNeill. The father was a native of North Carolina, was married in that State and came to Carroll County in the early settlement. He followed mercantile pursuits, and died in Carroll County. Our subject received a fair education at various schools, and at the age of thirteen began clerking in the mercantile trade at Huntingdon. At the end of five or six years he entered the literary department of the University of Michigan, at Ann Harbor, and graduated from that institution in 1857. He also graduated from the chemical and pharmaceutical department of that university in 1858. He was then professor of natural history in Andrew College, Trenton, Tenn., one year, after which he attended one course of medical lectures at Ann Harbor, and graduated from the University of Pennsylvania, Philadelphia (medical department), in 1860. After practicing a short time he was made surgeon of Russell's Twentieth Regiment Tennessee Cavalry, and served until the surrender. Returning from the war he continued practicing until November 1, 1865, when he began his present business. February 22, 1862, he married Lucy E. Randle, of Trenton, Tenn. He is a member of the Democratic party, and one of the county's most respected citizens.

N. W. McNeill is a native of Carroll County, Tenn., born in November 1827. His father was born in North Carolina and died in Tennessee about 1836, after having lived here about ten years. His mother, Rachel B. Clark, was a native of North Carolina. Our subject remained on the farm until twenty-three years of age, when he entered Kentucky Military Institute, and graduated in the year 1853. He then engaged in civil engineering, which he continued up to the late war. He was also division engineer of the Memphis branch of the Louisville & Nashville Railroad. In September, 1863, he entered Russell's regiment, Bell's brigade, Company B, and was first lieutenant of the same. He was neither captured nor wounded during the time he was in the service. At the close of the war he returned home and has been engaged successfully in farming ever since. February 14, 1858, he married Bettie Covington of Carroll County, who died in July, 1869, leaving one child, Charley. Mr. McNeill in December, 1872, married Susie Covington, of Henry County. This union resulted in the birth of two children; Addison Lee and Mattie Eva. Our subject is one of the substantial men of Henry County, being worth about $20,000, which sum he has amassed since the late war. Previous to the war Mr. McNeill was an old line Whig, but is now a Democrat in politics.

I. A. McSwain, physician and farmer of the Eighteenth District, was born where he now lives December, 1845, and is one of nine children, three of whom are living, born to David and B. (Randle) McSwain, both natives of North Carolina, the former born in 1802 and the latter in 1807. The father was a farmer by occupation, and magistrate of the Eighteenth District for about twenty-five years, being well known throughout the county. He died September 5, 1867. The mother is now living with her son, Dr. I. A., and is seventy-nine years of age; is quite spry and has reasonably good health. Our subject received his education mostly at Bethel Academy, and when a young man read medicine with Dr. Weldon, at Buchanan, for two years. He then entered the medical department of the University of Louisville, where he completed his studies in 1867. He then located at Buchanan and has remained there ever since, with the exception of two years that he spent at McKenzie. In 1868 he married Maggie, a native of Henry County, born August 20, 1852, and the daughter of Isaac and Jane Dale, and to this union were born seven children: Willie, Eddie, Horace, Lillie, Prentice, Marvin and Rubie. In connection with his professional work, the Doctor superintends his fine farm and is succeeding well in both profession and occupation. He is a member of the West Tennessee Medical Association and the medical association of the county. He is a Democrat in politics, a Mason, a Knight of Honor, and he and his wife and both of the eldest children are members of the Methodist Episcopal Church.

W. T. Nance, farmer, was born in Holmes County, Miss., February 1, 1842, son of W. F. and Elizabeth (Hill) Nance. The father was born in North Carolina April 7, 1814, came to Tennessee when seventeen years of age and located in Rutherford County, but afterward came to Henry County where he was married. Shortly afterward he removed to Mississippi and here remained till 1842, when he again returned to Henry County, where he has since remained. He is a farmer by occupation. The mother was born in Tennessee in 1807 and died about 1850. Our subject was reared at home and received his education in the common schools. He subsequently attended New Boston Academy. January 2, 1868, he married M. E. Upchurch, a native of Henry County, born May 30, 1850, and this union resulted in the birth of five children: James F., C. T., Elizabeth, Ella and May A. After marriage Mr. Nance located near where he now resides. He owns 316 acres of very desirable land, and is one of the county's best citizens. November 24, 1861, he enlisted in Company D, Forty-sixth Tennessee Infantry, and participated in many of the principal battles. At Island No. 10 his regiment was captured but he escaped and returned home, where he remained a short time. His command was in the rear of Grant when he took Vicksburg, and was in many battles opposing Sherman's march toward Atlanta. He was in the bloody battle of Franklin, and while at Nashville was taken prisoner and conveyed to Ohio, remained there till February, 1865, when he was discharged, and soon after returned home. He is a Democrat in politics.

Richard H. Ogburn, farmer and breeder of Jersey cattle, was born in Montgomery County, Tenn., in 1840, and is one of a family of nine children, six of whom are living. The father, John Ogburn, was born in Virginia about 1798 and was of Scotch-Irish extraction. He received a common-school education, and emigrated to Montgomery County with his parents when but a child. When about thirty years of age he married Caroline, a native of North Carolina, born in 1808, and the daughter of William Hunt. She is now living in Montgomery County. Mr. Ogburn was a man of good business ability and at the time of his death was tobacco inspector at Clarksville. He was a prominent member of the Methodist Episcopal Church South, and died in 1854. Our subject received a good common-school and business education, and when about eighteen years of age entered a mercantile house at Clarksville and acted as clerk for one year. He then purchased the stock and engaged in the business on his own responsibility till 1860, when he sold his stock. In June, 1861, he went to Mississippi, and during the same year joined Company A, First Kentucky Cavalry, Confederate Army, and at the end of one year's service was mustered out, after which, owing to ill health, he did not rejoin the ranks. For some time after the war he engaged in mercantile pursuits at Lafayette, Ky., and then returned to his old home and resumed his farming. January 6, 1871, he married Ellen J., daughter of Gen. James T. and Jane B. (Tharp) Dunlap, of Nashville. He was at that time living in Montgomery County tilling the soil, where he now owns two fine farms of 400 and 500 acres each. In 1877 he came to Paris and purchased a residence half a mile east of town, where he has since resided. He is extensively engaged in the breeding of registered Jersey cattle, and this is the most extensive enterprise of the kind in Henry County. For the past two years Mr. Ogburn has been connected with the Paris Rolling Mills. In politics he is a Democrat, and cast his first presidential vote for H. Seymour. He is a Mason and he and his wife are members of the Methodist Episcopal Church South. Mrs. Ogburn was born in Henry County in 1847.

Edward B. Parker, of Paris, junior member of the firm of Dobbins & Parker, manufacturers of barrel heading, flour, and dealers in cotton and tobacco, became a member in 1878. At that time they dealt in flour, cotton and tobacco, but in 1885 they added the machinery for the manufacture of barrel heading. Mr. Parker was born in Louisville, Ky., in 1843, and is a son of Lester L. and Martha (Jewell) Parker. The father was a native of New York, born in 1814 and of English descent. He was a steamboat engineer in early life, but spent the latter part of his days in tilling the soil. At the time of his marriage he was living in Louisville, Ky., and in 1870 he moved to Floyd County, Ind., bought property and located near Greenville, where he remained till his career ended in 1874. The mother of our subject was born in Jefferson County, Ky., in 1821 and died in 1850. They had seven children only two of whom are living: Miss R. A., and E. B., our subject. He was reared at home and received his education in the schools of Louisville, Ky. At the age of eighteen he began clerking in a dry goods store at Clarksville, Tenn., where he remained two years. In 1865 he came to Paris, established a general store, and carried on business for four years. During his career as a merchant he was also engaged in speculating in cotton and tobacco, and after selling his store he continued in the latter business. In 1876 he erected a cotton-gin and tobacco ware-room, and in 1878 he and Mr. Dobbins became partners. They handle on an average from 100 to 500 bales of cotton, 75 to 200 hogsheads of tobacco per year, and 2,000 sets of barrel heading per day. In February, 1870, Mr. Parker married Bell Matthewson, a native of Paris, Tenn., born in 1847, and the daughter of Dr. J. J. Matthewson. They have one child, Edward B., Jr. Mr. Parker is one of the leading business men of Paris, and has been for the past ten years. In politics he is conservative, voting for principle and not for party. He and family are members of the Methodist Episcopal Church.

James W. Porter, grocer at Paris, entered the business on his own responsibility, January, 1875, in company with E. P. Bomar, the firm being known as Bomar & Porter, till about 1878, when Mr. Bomar retired and E. M. Russell was taken in as partner. At the end of two years Mr. Russell sold his interest to W. C. Nance, and he in about one year retired, and since that time Mr. Porter has continued the business alone with good success. He carries a stock to the value of about $2,500, being one of the best grocery houses in the city. He is a son of Nathaniel and Eveline Porter, natives of Tennessee. The father was born in Nashville in 1812, and was of English extraction. He came to Paris when quite small and lived with his uncle. In 1836 he married and became the father of twelve children, seven of whom are now living. He settled ten miles east of Paris, where he owned a large farm, and where he passed the remainder of his days. He was a man of considerable prominence, being magistrate for a long time, and chairman of the county court. He was the first man to represent Henry County in the State Legislature after the war. He died in 1866. The mother was born in 1818, and died in 1875. Our subject was born in Henry County, Tenn., in 1851, and received a good common-school education in that county, and subsequently attended Eastman College at Poughkeepsie, N. Y. He began clerking at the age of nineteen which he continued for some time. In November, 1876, he married Nellie Thornton, a native of Georgia, born in 1858, and the daughter of DeWitt and Clementine Thornton. To our subject and wife were born two children: James T. and Nell. In 1877 he erected a fine brick residence on Wood Street in which he has since resided. He is also the owner of considerable real estate in Nashville. He is a Democrat in politics, and cast his first presidential vote for Horace Greeley. He is a member of the K. of H., and he and wife are members of the Methodist Episcopal Church South.

William M. Rowe, farmer of the Fourth District and son of Adam and Mary (Sewell) Rowe, was born in the house in which he now resides in 1842 and is one of eleven children. The father was born in Muhlenburg County, Ky., in 1797 and being left an orphan at an early age, received no advantages for an education. He came to Henry County in the spring of 1820 and purchased the land on which our subject now resides. On September 17 of the same year he married a neighbor girl, the ceremony taking place under a small oak tree on his plantation, and is still standing and has grown to a mammoth oak. This was the first marriage in what is now Henry County. It was before the county was organized when the county business was transacted at Dover, in Stewart County, that being the place where he obtained his license. He continued to remain on the same farm till his career ended, March 25, 1883. He was one of the sturdy and prominent farmers in the vicinity, and a Christian gentleman. He served as a soldier in the war of 1812 and was under Gen. Jackson's command at the time of the battle of New Orleans. Mrs. Rowe was a native of Muhlenburg County, Ky., also, born in 1802 and died in 1857. Our subject was reared under the parental roof and educated at the common schools of the neighborhood. In November, 1862, he enlisted in Company G, Seventh Tennessee Cavalry, Confederate Army, where he remained till April, 1863, when he was taken sick and returned home. In December, 1863, he was captured while at home and soon after was taken to Camp Morton, Ind., where he remained about two months, after which he was taken to Ft. Delaware. In April, 1865, he was released and returned home after an absence of about thirteen months of hardship and suffering. In November 28, 1862, he married Mrs. Nancy E. Rowe, a native of Wilson County, born in 1834, and the daughter of Gilbert and Rebecca Young. Since his marriage our subject has resided on the homestead, and is now the owner of 300 acres of excellent land seven miles north of Paris. Mr. Rowe is a man of industry and frugality. He is one of the county's best citizens. In politics he is a Democrat and cast his first presidential vote for H. Seymour. He and wife are worthy members of the Missionary Baptist Church.

J. M. Rushing, a native of Benton County, Tenn., was born May 22, 1836, son of Robert Rushing, a native of North Carolina, and one of the early pioneers of the State, who died in Benton County in 1854. Our subject received a fair education, and assisted his mother on the farm till he was about twenty-two years of age. He then engaged in the merchandise business, which he carried on in connection with his farming up to the time of the late war. In May, 1861, he enlisted in Company G, Seventh Tennessee Cavalry, Confederate Army, and served till the latter part of the war, when he was discharged on account of ill health. After his return home he engaged in the same business that had occupied his attention previous to the war, and has been quite successful. He soon sold his interest in the merchandise business and afterward engaged in the general produce and stock business, shipping all of the principal crops raised in the county, viz.: cotton, tobacco, etc., and has made it quite a success. He now owns one of the finest farms in this community—about 700 acres, all well improved. In March, 1861, Mr. Rushing married N. E. Diggs, who died June 6, 1876, leaving four children: J. Oscar; B. W., attorney at law at Barnum, Tex.; Bobbie H. and Lillie. December 23, 1877, Mr. Rushing married Sue M. Beasley, and the fruits of this union were two children: Nannie M. and a boy unnamed. Mr. Rushing is a Mason, a member of the Cumberland Presbyterian Church, and a Democrat in politics.

Barney Speight, one of the most extensive farmers and stock dealers of the Eleventh District, also breeder of thoroughbred horses, was born in Henry County in 1851, and is one of five children, only two now living. The father, John M. Speight, was born in North Carolina about 1820, came to Henry County when about eighteeen years of age, and about 1843 married Lila S. Beman. They had five children. After her death he married Patsey Barton, and to this union were born two children. She died, and John M. took for his third wife Maria Coley and by her became the father of six children. He settled and remained in the Eleventh District till his death, which occurred in 1885. He was a Baptist minister by profession, and followed this calling the last twelve years of his life, doing a noble work for the Christian cause. Our subject remained with his parents until he was twenty-four years of age, receiving a fair education at Cottage Grove. January 20, 1876, he married Rebecca P. Shell, daughter of William Shell, and this union resulted in the birth of three children—only two now living: Barney H. and Lida L. Mrs. Speight died on January 23, 1880, and in May, 1882, Mr. Speight married Mrs. Betty Dumas, a native of Henry County, born in 1846, and the daughter of Howard Street. To this union were born two children: Willie Wain and Harris Lovelace. Mr. Speight is now living on a fine farm of 300 acres, and is a man of good business management and a successful farmer. He is a man of considerable information, having served as constable of the Twelfth District for a period of four years. He is a Democrat in politics, and cast his first presidential vote for S. J. Tilden.

Dr. James G. Stark, physician and surgeon of the Third District, was born in Henry County in 1852, son of Thomas C. and Winnie G. (Humphreys) Stark, both natives of Tennessee. The father was born about 1819, educated in the common schools, and when a young man came to Henry County, where he was married about 1840. He was a farmer and resident of Henry County till 1855, when he removed to Calloway County, Ky., resumed his farming, and is still residing there. Mrs. Stark was born about 1825 and is still living, and is a member of the Primitive Baptist Church. The Doctor remained with his parents till he reached his majority, and received his education in the common schools of Calloway County, Ky. In 1876 he began the study of medicine under Dr. J. P. Humphreys, of Calloway County, Ky., and continued here till the fall of 1876, when he entered the medical department of the university of Louisville, Ky., during the years 1877 and 1878. In the fall of 1878 he returned to college and graduated in 1879. Immediately afterward he came to Henry County and settled in the Third District, where he has since continued his practice with commendable success. He has an extensive and lucrative practice, and is fast becoming one of the leading physicians of Henry County. October 28, 1877, he wedded Emma J. Dumas, a native of Henry County, born January 13, 1859, and the daughter of Franklin F. and Malinda I. Dumas, natives of Tennessee. Three children were born to our subject and wife—two living—Homer, Thomas F. (deceased) and Helen. The Doctor is now living on a farm of sixty acres, all in a high state of cultivation. In politics he is a Democrat, and cast his first presidential vote for S. J. Tilden in 1876.

J. J. Sweatt, farmer of the Twenty-second District of Henry County, was born in Warren County, Tenn., in 1819, and is one of thirteen children, six now living, born to Virtue and Elizabeth (Cox) Sweatt. The father was born in Maryland, in 1782, and moved with his parents to North Carolina, at an early day; he remained there until after his marriage when he emigrated to Tennessee, and located in Warren County, being one of the very first settlers. In 1837 he came to Henry County, where he remained until his career ended in 1859. The mother was born in North Carolina in 1795 and died in 1883. Our subject was reared at home and received his education in the schools of Warren County. In 1839 he married Sarah Edwards, a native of Wilson County, Tenn., born in 1822, and they have five children: Mary (Mrs. James Bratton), Martha T. (Mrs. J. L. Turner), America Florentine (Mrs. J. P. Lamb), F. V. and G. H. Mr. Sweatt learned the carpenter trade when a boy and followed it exclusively until the breaking out of the war. In 1860 he located where he now resides, three miles east of Conyersville, on 320 acres of desirable land, and is one of the county's best farmers. He is a Democrat in politics, a Mason, and he and wife and entire family are members of the Christian Church.

John C. Sweeney, a prominent member of the Henry County bar, was born June 22, 1849, near Paris, and is a son of James and Elizabeth (Barbee) Sweeney, natives of Virginia, and North Carolina, respectively. The father was born in 1813, was a farmer and brick mason, and a member of the first company of Confederate troops raised in Arkansas. He was discharged in 1862, and died in the same year from disease contracted in the service. The mother was born in 1819 and died in 1858, at the age of thirty-nine years. Our subject inherits Irish blood from his paternal grandparents, and Scotch blood from the maternal side. He was reared on a farm and worked also in a brickyard; his educational advantages were quite limited, and in 1859 all the family moved to Arkansas (the father and a brother died there). In 1865 John C., returned to Paris, entirely dependent upon his own resources. He worked at manual labor for his earnings, and thus attended school (not more than nine months altogether). After clerking in the Carter

House for one year, and four more years in a drug store, in March, 1873, he began studying law, having accumulated by thrift and economy about $800. In 1875 he was admitted to the bar. and has continued to practice very successfully. Upon entering the practice he invested his last dollar in a law library. He now owns a one-half interest in the Commercial Bank building, and his law office is the most commodious in the city. He is a member of the town board, and was treasurer for some time. March 1, 1886, he was employed by the Louisville & Nashville Railroad as a claim agent of the Memphis branch, and now in connection with that duty still practices his profession. December 23, 1879, he married Mattie Bomar of this county; three sons are the fruits of this union: Samuel, Bomar and John. Mr. Sweeney is a Democrat in politics, and is regarded as an enterprising and respected citizen of Paris.

Stacker J. Taylor, a leading criminal lawyer of this part of the State, was born October 9, 1842, in Davidson County, Tenn., and is a son of Dr. N. C. Taylor, a native of Rhode Island. The father removed to Nashville with his mother when seven years of age, and grew to manhood there. He commenced the practice of medicine at that place, but soon removed to Charlotte, Dickson Co., Tenn., where he married Matilda Farrar, the mother of our subject; he then removed to Lagrange Furnace. In the late war he was assistant surgeon of the army of western Virginia, and died at Warm Springs Hospital, West Virginia, in 1861. The mother is still living in Tennessee. Our subject was reared in his native county; in 1855 he entered Cumberland University and graduated from the law department in 1860, taking also a scientific course; he then entered Company C, Fourteenth Regiment Tennessee Infantry, and remained in the service until discharged for disability, caused by erysipelas, in 1863. After returning home he was arrested by the Federals, and imprisoned at Ft. Donelson for six months, was then paroled and went to Kentucky, and taught in Canton Academy, Trigg County, Ky., until the close of the war. He then went to St. Louis, and was traveling correspondent for the St. Louis *Times* for some time. He then located in Paris, January 1, 1872, where he has ever since remained in the practice of law, with very great success, ranking among the first criminal lawyers in the State. He was married February 22, 1872, to Emma Ledbetter, of Murfreesboro, daughter of Maj. William Ledbetter, of that place. Two children have been born to this union: Stacker J. and Kate L. Mr. Taylor and wife are members of the Methodist Episcopal Church South. He is a member of the K. of H., a Democrat in politics, and takes an active interest in the political affairs of the State, but adheres strictly to his profession. As a citizen he stands very high in all circles.

Hon. Jasper N. Thomason, a prominent member of the Henry County bar, was born March 15, 1832, in that county fourteen miles west of Paris and is a son of Richard L. and Elizabeth (Smith) Thomason. The father was a native of North Carolina, born in 1801, and a farmer by occupation. In 1815 he immigrated to Stewart County, Tenn., and from there to this county in 1818, where he passed the remainder of his days. The mother was born in North Carolina the same year as her husband. They were married in 1820 and reared a family of nine children. Our subject grew to manhood on the farm and graduated from the law department of Cumberland University in 1855. He has ever since attended strictly to business and enjoys good success. He was a member of the State Legislature in 1883–84. In 1857 he married Sarah F. McCampbell, daughter of Andrew McCampbell, late chancellor of this district. By this union seven children were born, all of whom are living. The mother of these children died January 25, 1883, and June 8, 1886, Mr. Thomason married Frances Harvey of Greenville, Miss. The children are Andrew M., attorney in Gainesville, Tex.; James R., practicing law with his father; Charles H., John B., Sarah E., Mary L. and Jasper N., Jr. Mr. Thomason is a Democrat in politics and an active member of his party. He is a prominent citizen and a member of the Cumberland Presbyterian Church. Mrs. Thomason is a member of the Episcopal Church.

James M. Todd, merchant at Cottage Grove, was born in that town in 1845 and was one of three of the first settlers of the town. The father, Moses Todd, was born in Wake County, N. C., in 1806 and was married July 30, 1829, to Penelope Bowden, a native of North Carolina, born in 1809. They came to Cottage Grove in the same year and purchased a large tract of land on which he farmed till 1852 when he entered the mercantile business at Cottage Grove, being the first merchant of the place, also the first tobacco dealer. He was one of the most popular men of the vicinity in his day and was for a short time magistrate of the Eleventh District. Mrs. Todd died August 14, 1858, and in 1859 Mr. Todd took for his second wife Z. C. Watson, *nee* Wilson. The father died August 26, 1874. Our subject grew to manhood under the parental roof and received his education principally at Caledonia College. In August, 1861, he enlisted in the Confederate Army, Company G, Fifth Tennessee Infantry but was soon discharged on account of age. He remained at home till November, 1863, when he entered the cavalry, and when reorganized was in the Sixteenth Tennessee, as sergeant-major of the regiment. He remained in the service during the remainder of the war on Col. A. N. Wilson's staff, and after returning home farmed for some time. He then engaged in the mercantile business for the next ten years, when his health failed and he then engaged in the tobacco trade. He is now engaged in the merchandise business, carrying a stock to the value of about $2,500. He is a man of fine business capacity, is a successful merchant and a good salesman. April 5, 1864, he married Mary Ellen Watson, a native of Kentucky born in August, 1846, and the daughter of Stewart and Zorena Watson. To our subject and wife were born eight children: Zorena Penelope (Mrs. P. W. Odom), Moses, Virgie, Mary, Birtie, Jimmie, Alby and Willie Grace. Mr. Todd is a Democrat in politics and cast his first presidential vote for H. Seymour. He is a member of the Masonic fraternity, and he and wife are active and long standing members of the Missionary Baptist Church. Mr. Todd is now in business in company with his son-in-law, P. W. Odom.

Dr. Edward A. Travis, physician and surgeon at Como, was born in McClellan County, Tex., in 1860, and is one of five children, four of whom are living, born to Ludson W. and Sophia (Crump) Travis. The father was born in Henry County in 1825, and was of English extraction. He was a farmer and at the age of twenty-two was married. In 1859 he went to Texas, enlisted in the Confederate Army in 1861 under Gen. Beauford and died at Alexandria, La., in 1863, while in the service. Mrs. Travis was a native of England born in 1832. About 1838 she came to the United States and died here August 24, 1886. She was a member of the Methodist Episcopal Church South and a kind parent. The Doctor remained with his mother till nineteen years of age. Previous to this, in 1866, he and his mother came to Henry County, Tenn., and here our subject received a common-school education. In 1878 he entered the medical department of the University of Louisville, Ky., and graduated from this institution in 1880, after which he immediately began practicing at Crawford's Mill, Henry County. In 1883 he came to Como and has since continued his extensive and lucrative practice with renewed success. October 26, 1885, he married Lillie Wilcox, daughter of John and Margaret Wilcox. Our subject is a man of industry and enterprise. He is a Democrat in politics and cast his first presidential vote for Grover Cleveland. He is a member of the I. O. O. F. and he and wife are both prominent members of the Cumberland Presbyterian Church. Mrs. Travis was born in Calloway County, Ky., in 1864.

Albert G. Trevathan, a prominent citizen and business man of Paris, is a son of Henry and Mary (Ingg) Trevathan, and is one of a family of thirteen children, three of whom are living. The father was born in North Carolina in 1806, and was of Scotch ancestry. He received but a limited education and at the age of twenty married, after which, in 1834, he came to Henry County, and settled near Paris. He was a farmer, and died in 1884; was one of the very early pioneers of Henry County. He was a just man and was noted for his generosity, integrity and industry. Mrs. Trevathan was born in Virginia in 1808, and died in 1846. She had a fair education and was much esteemed. Our subject was born near Paris, Tenn., in 1837, received a good literary and business education at Paris, and attended one term in the law department of the Cumberland University at Lebanon, was admitted to the bar in 1859, and soon began the practice of his chosen profession. In 1861, at the breaking out of the war, he enlisted in Company I, Fifth Tennessee Infantry, Confederate States Army, and in the early part of 1862 was promoted to second lieutenant, which position he held with distinction till the spring of 1863, when he was compelled to resign on account of ill health. At the end of about four months, having sufficiently recovered his health, he then entered Gen. Forrest's command in the Fifteenth Tennessee Cavalry, with which he remained during the remainder of hostilities, taking an active part in all the battles in which his command was engaged. In January, 1865, he married Martha F. Yowell, daughter of J. M. and H. A. Yowell, of Holly Springs, Miss. This union resulted in the birth of three children: Jesse, Harry A. and Mattie Clyde. The first four years of his married life were spent in Mississippi tilling the soil. He then returned to Paris and entered the mercantile business, which he continued for about six years with evident success. He abandoned his business in 1875, and became engaged in politics. That he might more universally and firmly lay his political opinions before the public, he established the *Paris Gazette*, of which he was editor for two years, after which he reentered the mercantile business. In 1883 he was appointed by Gov. Bate one of the State railroad tax assessors, of which body he was made chairman. This position he still holds to the entire satisfaction of the public. In 1884 he entered as one of the proprietors of the Paris Roller Mills and has since continued the business. Mr. Trevathan was born on a farm, but not liking farm life obtained permission from his father at the early age of eleven to start upon the voyage of life for himself. At the age of sixteen he had a good knowledge of the English language, which he obtained by his own efforts. His indefatigable will has brought him success in all his undertakings. He is of a very prolific ancestry, all of whom have made industry and morality their distinct characteristics. In politics he is a life-long Democrat, and cast his first presidential vote for J. C. Breckinridge. Mrs. Trevathan was born in Marshall County, Tenn., in 1842, and is a member of the Christian Church.

G. H. Trevathan, dealer in drugs and books, established his business in 1872 and carries a stock of $4,000 to $7,000. He has a good and lucrative business, one of the leading in the place. He was born in 1846 within one mile of Paris, where he was reared. In 1865 at the age of sixteen he began clerking in a drug store and continued to do so till 1872 when he engaged in his present business. The parents came to this county from North Carolina about 1834, where the father followed agricultural pursuits successfully. He was a man of moderate means and one of the county's most respected citizens. He died in 1884 and the mother previous to this, in 1846. Our subject is an unswerving Democrat in politics but takes no active interest in political affairs.

Miles F. Tyler, farmer and stock dealer of the Third District and a son of John and Elizabeth (Holt) Tyler, was born in Virginia in 1829, and is an only child. The father was a native of North Carolina born in 1802 and his father Reuben Tyler was a native of Virginia and served as a soldier in the war for independence. John was reared in North Carolina and in 1827 married and settled in Virginia where, in 1837, Mrs. Tyler died. In 1839 he married Rebecca Fields and they had three children, only one now living. Mr. Tyler's second wife died in 1844 and in 1849 he wedded Elizabeth Waters, who died in 1854. In 1849 or 1850 he came to Henry County and settled in the Third District, where he resumed farming. He was a man of judgment and served six years as magistrate of his district. He died in 1864. Our subject remained with his father till his death, receiving his education in the common schools of North Carolina. December, 1861, he enlisted in the Confederate Army in Company F, Forty-sixth Tennessee Infantry, as second lieutenant and after the capture of Island No. 10, returned home. He was not permitted to again rejoin the ranks and so resigned his commission. Previous to the war, in 1852, he married Susanna Chance, daughter of Rev. Thomas and Sarah Chance; they had three children (all deceased). Mrs. Tyler died in 1857 and in 1864 our subject married Laura Olive, a native of Henry County, born in 1841 and the daughter of Leroy and Harriet Olive. By this union our subject became the father of six children: James A., M. E., Edwin H., Horace M., Hattie U. and Miss Willie Lee. For five years Mr. Tyler lived in the Fifth District; was a tenant for one year; since that time he has been in the Third District, settling in 1865 on his present farm which consists of 500 acres; he has besides this 145 acres near there. In 1876 he was elected to the office of magistrate and held this for six years. In politics he was formerly a Whig and cast his first presidential vote for M. Fillmore in 1856. He and wife are both active members of the Methodist Episcopal Church South.

Rev. Robert L. Veazey, farmer and minister of the Eleventh District, and a son of Fielding and Mary T. (Bowden) Veazey, was born in Granville County, N. C., December 31, 1820. The father was a native of North Carolina, born about 1792, received a fair education and was a farmer and mechanic. At the age of twenty-six he married, and in 1821 emigrated to Carroll County. At the end of two years he came to Henry County, settling in the Eleventh District, and here remained till his career ended in 1829. He was a soldier in the war of 1812. Mrs. Veazey was born in Granville County, N. C., in 1794, and died about 1877, a devout member of the Primitive Baptist Church. Our subject was reared principally by his mother. He being the eldest son the main support of the family depended upon him, thus depriving him of the advantages of an education. This he made up to some extent by close study in after life. November 23, 1843, he married Caroline B. Bowden, and five children were born to this union (all deceased). Mrs. Veazey died September 30, 1861, and May 29, 1862, Mr. Veazey married Ann E. Pierce, a native of North Carolina, born in 1825, and a devout member of the Primitive Baptist Church. They have two children: Mary Jane and Robert L. In 1851 Mr. Veazey entered the mercantile business at New Boston, which he continued with good success till the breaking out of the Rebellion, when he sustained a loss of about $10,000. He then farmed as a tenant for several years, and in 1867 purchased 140 acres in the Eleventh District, where he has resided ever since. He is one of the oldest residents of the county, having lived here sixty-three years. In May, 1843, he identified himself with the Primitive Baptist Church at Walnut Fork Church, and has since continued an unswerving and active member of that organization. In September, 1862, he was ordained to enter the ministry, and has had the pastoral charge of the Walnut Fork and other churches for nearly ten years, and of one church for eighteen years. He has been a faithful worker in his high calling and has done a noble work in advancing the Christian religion. He is a life-long Democrat and cast his first presidential vote for James K. Polk.

Pleasant C. Wade, farmer, and son of Robert A. and Mary (Callicott) Wade, was born in Randolph County, N. C., in 1819, and is one of twelve children, only two of whom are living. The father was a native of Virginia, born in Halifax County of that State in 1763. He received a good common education and taught school for several years. At the age of twenty-three he married, and soon after went to Randolph County, N. C., where he remained till 1823, after which he came to Henry County and settled in the Third District for seven years. He was one of the very early settlers, and died in October, 1832. Mrs. Wade was born in Prince Edward County, Va., in 1776, and died in 1848. Our subject received his education at Spring Hill Seminary; worked on the farm till he was twenty-six years of age, when he was married, January 2, 1845, to Mary Ann H. Robinson, a native of Maury County, born April 16, 1820, and the daughter of James S. and Malinda G. Robinson, natives, respectively, of North Carolina and Kentucky. To our subject and wife were born five children: Isadora, Malinda Alabama, Robert J., Thomas R. and Pleasant A. Mr. Wade soon after marriage settled near his present home, in 1847, and is now the owner of about 270 acres in the home farm. In 1868 he was elected to fill an unexpired term as magistrate, and has been three times re-elected to the same office which he has held to the entire satisfaction of the public. He is a Democrat in politics and cast his first presidential vote for M. Van Buren, in 1840. He has been a Mason since 1852, and since the war (1865) has passed the Royal Arch Degree. Mr. and Mrs. Wade are worthy members of the Primitive Baptist Church.

V. B. Walker, a prominent citizen and farmer of the Sixteenth District, was born in North Carolina, March 21, 1827, and is one of a family of twelve children, born to the union of James and Elizabeth (Edwards) Walker, natives, respectively, of North Carolina and Virginia. The father was a teacher and a farmer by profession. Our subject was reared by his uncle, John S. Walker of Decatur County, and received his education in that county. December 12, 1854, he married Louisa Kendall, a native of Henry County, born October 1, 1838, and the daughter of Eli Kendall. Mrs. Walker died October 12, 1878, leaving a family of nine children, seven of whom lived to be grown, and six of whom are now living: Robert J. (deceased), Elizabeth (Mrs. R. M. Blackemore), Jarratt, Kate (Mrs. Ed. Wynns), Joe, Lola P. and Alexander C. In 1849 Mr. Walker went to Kentucky, where he remained till 1852, engaged in the tobacco business. He then came to Henry County, located where he now resides and was engaged in the tobacco business until 1869. He manufactured plug tobacco and of such quality that many times he won the prize for its excellence. Mr. Walker is now an extensive farmer, owning as much as 800 acres in Henry County, and besides has two sections of land in Mississippi. He is well known and much esteemed by all his acquaintances both as a citizen and neighbor. He was postmaster at Mt. Vista from 1852 to 1857, and at the present time is deputy county surveyor. He is a Democrat in politics and took a great interest in his State and county affairs during the late war. He is a man who has read a great deal and has made a careful study of all the great subjects both of political and religious ethics. In religion, he is liberal to the fullest extent, being a humanitarian.

A. J. Weldon, a prominent physician, was born in Marshall County, Tenn., in 1831, and is one of ten children, three of whom are living, born to W. B. and Lillian (Cook) Weldon. The father was a native of Franklin County, N. C., born in 1787, and was married in his native State, where he remained till 1827, after which he came to Tennessee and located in Marshall County. In 1841 he came to Henry County, and here remained till his career ended in 1847. He was sheriff of his native county for four years previous to 1827. The mother was also a native of North Carolina, born 1793, and died in December, 1876. Our subject was reared under the parental roof and received his education in Henry County. He began teaching school at the age of sixteen and followed this occupation for a number of years, and at the same time added to his mental stock of learning by studying all his spare moments during this time, and afterward he read medicine with Dr. John Londis for two years. He then took a course of lectures at Louisville, Ky., and in 1859-60 took a course at the Jefferson Medical College at Philadelphia, where he graduated in the spring of the latter year. He then located at Buchanan and began the practice of his chosen profession. In 1868 he moved to Paris Landing, where he still resides and practices medicine. Previous to this, in 1852, he married Sarah McSwain, a native of Tennessee, born 1831, and the daughter of David McSwain. Mrs. Weldon died in 1864, leaving three children: Laura (Mrs. Dr. W. T. McClarin), W. E. and Thomas J. In 1868 he married Virginia Chenoweth, a native of Indiana, born in December, 1849, and the daughter of Richard Chenoweth. They have five children by this union: Ida, Robley D., John D., Stella and Mary. In 1866 the Doctor began the mercantile business at Paris Landing, which he still continues. He also built a cotton-gin and engaged extensively in growing and dealing in cotton till 1880. He has for some years bought, raised and dealt extensively in cotton, and has at the home place 2,400 acres of valuable land, much of which is under a fine state of cultivation. The Doctor has an extensive practice and is one of the best physicians in the county. He is a member of the American Medical Association and also of the State Medical Association. In 1880 he built a mill and began manufacturing lumber, shingles and staves. In 1884 he lost the mill by fire, together with machinery and a large amount of lumber. Recently he has rebuilt and now has the business in good running order. He has also for many years been engaged extensively in raising stock. He is a Democrat in politics and since twenty-one years of age has been a Mason. He is also a member of the K. of H.

W. E. Weldon, a member of the firm of the Chickasaw mills, and traveling salesman for Rainwater, Booger & Co., wholesale merchants at

St. Louis, was born in Henry County in 1855, and is a son of Dr. A. J. Weldon, of Paris Landing. Our subject received his early education in the schools near home, but subsequently graduated at the Military Institute in Murray, Ky. In May, 1881, he married Bettie M., a native of Henry County, born in 1861, and the daughter of Nathaniel and Maria Currier. To our subject and wife were born two children: Sallie and Louisa. Previous to moving to Chickasaw Mills Mr. Weldon was engaged for five years in the mercantile business at Paris Landing, where he was quite successful. He is a man of fine business qualifications and a thorough gentleman. He is a member of the K. of H., and one of the county's best citizens.

Fitzgerald Williams, one of seven children born to Isaac B. and Adeline (Fitzgerald) Williams, was born March 29, 1842. The father was born in Sumner County, Tenn., near Fountain Head, April 13, 1812, and came to Henry County when a boy. His own father being dead, he lived with his stepfather, Capt. James Greer, for a few years, and then clerked in a mercantile establishment and read law. He was licensed to practice law, and entered the profession at Paris in 1835. About 1845 he was elected attorney-general of this judicial circuit, and in 1854 was elected chancellor of this division, but resigned in 1860 to resume practice. He was stricken with paralysis in the summer of 1861 and disabled, but in 1865 resumed practice, and while in an argument in chancery court in 1869 he was again stricken, and lingered in the clasp of this nervous affection till February 1, 1871, when he passed from earth, honored as an able lawyer and one of the ablest chancellors in the State, as well as a highly honored citizen. He was appointed by Gov. Harris during the war to make a settlement between Tennessee and the other Confederate States, but could not attend on account of ill health. He was appointed Confederate tax collector of Tennessee, but declined. In 1863 he was commissioned circuit judge of the circuit. The mother of our subject was the oldest daughter of Judge William Fitzgerald, who was from 1845 to 1861 judge of this circuit, and was one of the ablest and most polished men of this part of Tennessee. It was he who (in 1851) defeated Davey Crockett for Congress, in which body he served one term. He was in the Tennessee Legislature prior to that time, and was attorney-general for several years. He died in 1864 from a stroke of paralysis. Our subject was born in Paris, and received a good practical and classical education at that place. In 1861 he enlisted in the Confederate Army as second lieutenant of Company F, One Hundred and Fifty-fourth Senior Tennessee Regiment, which was the first company that entered the service. He was afterward elected first lieutenant, and remained in the service until the close of the war. He was wounded at Franklin. Returning from the war he resumed the reading of law, which he had pursued eighteen months before. In 1870 he was admitted to the bar, and has ever since continued to practice with evident success. He has adhered strictly to his profession, and does not mingle much in political affairs.

Alex. Wilson, farmer and prominent citizen of the Third District, was born in Trigg County, Ky., 1832, and is a son of William and Dosia (Daniel) Wilson. The father was born about 1808 and is of Scotch-Irish ancestry. He immigrated to Trigg County, Ky., with his parents when but a boy, grew to manhood, and was married in that county when about twenty-five years of age. In 1849 he removed to Arkansas, but while on business back to Kentucky, he was taken sick and died in 1852. Mrs. Wilson was born in Trigg County, Ky., where she died in the prime of life. Our subject remained with his father till his death, and was educated in the common schools of Trigg County, Ky. In April, 1856, he married Elizabeth Dawson and they had one child, Elizabeth D. (Mrs. A. Dawson). Mrs. Wilson died in February, 1865, and December 28 of the same year Mr. Wilson married Mrs. Mary Ann (Willis) Caldwell, a native of Henry County, born in 1835, and a member of the Methodist Episcopal Church South. She had two sons by her former marriage: R. D. and William M. By her marriage to our subject she became the mother of eight children: James A., Quitman L., Emma I., Etta and Ella (twins), Mary S., Minnie and Miss Sammie. Mr. Wilson remained in Trigg County till 1860, when he removed to Graves County, Ky., and in 1878 from there to Henry County, settling on the farm where he now resides. This consists of about 200 acres of good productive land, well cultivated and well improved. In April, 1864, Mr. Wilson enlisted in Company E, Third Tennessee Mounted Infantry, Confederate Army, and took part in several severe battles, was wounded at Harrisburg and rendered unfit for active service but did not return home till the final surrender. He is a Democrat in politics and cast his first presidential vote for James Buchanan. He is a Mason and a member of the Reformed Church.

Thomas R. Wilson, M. D., physician and surgeon of Cottage Grove, was born in Wilson County, Tenn., in 1844, and is one of nine children, only one of whom is living. The father, John R. Wilson, was born in 1800, and was of Scotch-Irish ancestry. His parents were natives of North Carolina, and settled in Wilson County at a very early day. John R. received a practical education and at the age of twenty-three married Mary Donaldson. He was a farmer and held the office of magistrate for a long time. He died in 1858. Mrs. Wilson was born in

Wilson County about 1803, and died about 1850. Our subject received his education at Silver Spring and at String Town in Wilson County. In November, 1863, he entered the Confederate Army in Company K, Sixteenth Tennessee Cavalry, as orderly sergeant, and participated in nearly all the battles in which his command was engaged. At the close of the war he returned home, and in January, 1867, began the study of medicine under his brother, Dr. A. R. Wilson, of Cottage Grove and in the fall of the same year entered the medical department of the Tennessee University, where he graduated in 1869. In 1871 he commenced practicing medicine at Como, where he remained two years. He then removed to Cottage Grove where he has continued practicing with evident success, as his many patients now living can testify. He is also running a store of general merchandise in connection with his practice. In January, 1878, he married Henrietta V. Freeman, a native of Henry County, Tenn., born in 1848, and the daughter of J. C. and Eliza Freeman. They have four children: Mary Eliza, Robert Howard, Alfred Bluford and Nellie. In politics the Doctor is a Democrat and cast his first vote for Horace Greeley in 1872. He is a member of the Masonic fraternity and he and wife are members of the Methodist Episcopal Church South.

William T. Wrather, dealer in general hardware, agricultural implements, groceries, etc., established his present business in 1877, in company with T. B. Ellison, with whom he remained till 1884, when Mr. Ellison retired. Since that time Mr. Wrather has continued the business alone with evident success. He is carrying a stock to the value of about $6,000, and his is one of the most flourishing business enterprises in the city. His father, William B., was born in Rutherford County, Tenn., of Welsh origin. About 1846 he married Mary Kellow, by whom he had one child. About 1847 he removed to Arkansas, where he resumed his farming, and died in 1848. The family soon after returned to Rutherford County, where Mrs. Wrather married H. H. Ozment. They afterward removed to Arkansas, where Mrs. Ozment died in 1884. Our subject was born in Rutherford County, Tenn., in 1847, was reared principally by his mother, and educated mostly in the common schools of Henry County. In 1871 he began clerking in a mercantile house, where he remained till about 1876. He then engaged in the business on his own responsibility at Crossland, Ky., and here remained one year, after which he came to Paris and engaged in his present business. September, 1874, he married Kate Matthewson, a native of Murray, Ky., born in 1854, and the daughter of Daniel and Gabriella Matthewson. Mr. Wrather has accumulated his property by his own efforts, and is a man of good business and financial ability. He is the owner of some real estate in Paris. In politics he is a Democrat, and cast his first presidential vote for H. Seymour in 1868. He and wife are members of the Cumberland Presbyterian Church.

C. N. Wright, now a resident and practitioner of this place, was born March 13, 1851, in Carroll County, Tenn. He grew to manhood on the farm, and at the age of eighteen began the study of medicine under Dr. Wright, of Huntingdon, Tenn. In 1870 he entered the medical university of Nashville (old school), and graduated from that institution in the spring of 1873, after which he located at this place and began practicing his profession with evident success up to the present date. He is a self-made man, and has accumulated his property since 1872, and is now in good circumstances, notwithstanding the fact that he has labored under many disadvantages. His educational advantages were very limited, but by hard study and work he has fitted himself for the enviable position he now holds. He is also a man of good social standing, and is respected by all. In politics he is a Democrat.

Iverson M. Wrinkle, produce dealer and prominent citizen of Cottage Grove, was born in McNairy County, Tenn., in 1840, and is one of nine children, eight of whom are living. The father, Morgan Wrinkle, was born in Bradley County, Tenn., in 1812, and was of Irish extraction. He received but a limited education, and when a young man went to Hardin County, where he was married; by this union one child was born. Mrs. Wrinkle soon after died, and in 1836 he married Cloann Smith; both were at that time living in McNairy County, where Mrs. Wrinkle was burned to death about 1858. In 1860 Mr. Wrinkle married Gensey McGarety, who died about 1881, and in 1882 he married Mrs. Elizabeth Finley. Soon after his last marriage they removed to Henderson, in Chester County, and are living a retired life. Our subject was educated at the common schools of McNairy County. In 1863 he entered the army as one of the "boys in gray," by enlisting in Company F, Twenty-first Tennessee Cavalry, under Gen. Forrest, and took an active part in all the battles in which his command was engaged; was severely wounded by bushwhackers, in the latter part of 1864, which rendered him unfit for duty. April 30, 1865, he returned home and was married to Mrs. Clemmie J. Brown (nee Bowden), a native of Cottage Grove, Tenn., born January 20, 1845. The fruits of this union were four children, three living: Eurah Ann, Ola Jane, Iva Josephine (who died March 11, 1881), and Estella D., who was born February 9, 1882. Mr. Wrinkle spent the first year of his married life in Kentucky, after which he returned to Cottage Grove and farmed for three years; he then entered a mercantile house and acted as clerk until 1874, when he began the business on his own responsibility, and this continued until 1886, with complete success. He had very little of this world's goods to start in life with, but he has accumulated a fine property, and now owns 120 acres of good land and a good residence in town. In politics Mr. Wrinkle is a Democrat and cast his first presidential vote for Horace Greeley. He is a member of the Golden Cross and he and wife are active members of the Missionary Baptist Church.

William G. Wynns, farmer and leading citizen, was born in Stewart County, Tenn., in 1844, and is one of a family of two children, only our subject living. The father, William G., was born in North Carolina, in 1810, and immigrated to Stewart County with his parents when he was but a boy. He was reared at home and received a good common and business education, mostly at Paris. When eighteen years of age he clerked in a mercantile establishment at Dover, and about 1836 began the business on his own responsibility. In September, 1838, he married S. Eveline Atkins, of Dover, a native of Stewart County, born in 1824, and the daughter of Henry L. and Sallie (Stell) Atkins. Mr. Wynns led an active, industrious life and died in 1845. Our subject received his education principally in the common schools, and finished at Caledonia College. In September, 1864, he enlisted in the Confederate Army, under Capt. William Hawkins, in Forrest's cavalry, and was wounded near Columbia, Tenn. This rendered him unfit for further duty, but he did not return to his home until near the final surrender. He taught school for some time, and in 1873–74 was engaged in the mercantile business at Paris, which he had to discontinue on account of ill health. He traveled for some time, and in 1880 he purchased eighty-four acres of land near Paris, on which he and his mother now reside. He is a Democrat in politics and cast his first presidential vote for Horatio Seymour. He and mother are worthy members of the Methodist Episcopal Church South.

BENTON COUNTY.

Aaron Arnold, proprietor of the Arnold Hotel, of Camden, Tenn., and a native of Benton County, same State, was born June 7, 1832, son of Wyly and Sally Arnold, natives of North Carolina and Mississippi, respectively. The father came to Benton County at an early day and followed farming on Beaver Dam Creek until his death in 1860. Our subject was reared to manhood on the farm, and secured but a limited education in the county schools. He followed agricultural pursuits till 1868, when he moved to Camden and engaged in the saloon business. He built his hotel and has followed that occupation in connection with the saloon business up to the present time. He has the leading traveling trade, and keep a first class hostelry. In 1853 he married Josephine Hawley, of Mississippi, and to them were born five children: Dora (Mrs. John D. McAuley), Cora Cordelia (Mrs. John Rives), Wyly, Bettie and Pearl. The Judge, as he is familiarly known, is an ardent and stanch Republican in politics, although he was formerly a Democrat. He is a member of the K. of H., and is one of the county's best citizens.

J. A. Barnes, farmer, was born near where he now resides in the Eighth District, in 1828, and is a son of Charles and Elizabeth (Wyatt) Barnes. The father was a native of South Carolina, born in 1795, and of German lineage. When young he left his native State, and immigrated to Stewart County, Tenn., where he lived at the time of his marriage in 1818. He soon moved to Henry County, and in 1828 came to Benton County and bought 200 acres in the Eighth District, where he remained until his career ended. He died in 1844. His wife was a native of North Carolina, and was of Irish-German extraction. She died in 1868. Our subject was reared at home, and received but a limited education, not attending school more than two months during his entire life. In 1855 he married Mary E. Byrn, a native of Davidson County, Tenn., born in 1832, and the daughter of Stephen and Mary Byrn. The marriage of our subject resulted in the birth of four children: James H., John P., Thomas E. and Edmond B. Mr. Barnes now owns upward of 350 acres, and is one of Benton County's well-to-do farmers. In politics he has been a stanch Democrat, casting his first presidential vote for Franklin Pierce in 1852.

Silas W. Bullock, postmaster of Big Sandy, Tenn., and a native of Benton County, of this State, was born August 13, 1851, son of Obidiah and Penelope (Nobles) Bullock, both natives of North Carolina. The father came to Tennessee in 1838 or 1839, locating the first year in Dyer County, then located on the river, near Point Mason, Benton County, and followed farming until his death, December 25, 1885. Our subject was reared to manhood on a farm, and securing but a limited English education, at the age of twenty-two he came to Big Sandy and engaged in the retail liquor business two years, and then accepted a position as clerk with William Caraway, where he continued two years. He then spent one year prospecting in Texas and Arkansas, after which he returned to Big Sandy and followed the carpenter's trade until 1881, when he resumed his clerkship with Mr. Caraway, and has remained with him ever since. January, 1886, he engaged in the drug business in Big Sandy with Geo. W. Cantrell, and now has a half interest in the business. March, 1886, he was made postmaster, which position he has since held, having a deputy in the office. Mr. Bullock married his present wife, who was Miss Dora Rushing, February 18, 1886. He lost his first wife by death. He is a Democrat in politics, a Master Mason, and is justly recognized as one among the popular and reliable business men and citizens of Benton County.

William Caraway was born in Smith County, Tenn., May 14, 1836; was reared on a farm; removed to West Tennessee at the age of six years. In 1858 he engaged in the mercantile business in Benton County, one-half a mile from the present town of Big Sandy, where he continued successfully till the Louisville & Nashville Railroad was built, when he moved to a point 400 yards below the station. He assisted largely in building up the town, and has conducted a large mercantile business here ever since. He has been engaged in the saw-mill business for the last five years; also owns and runs a cotton-gin in town. He is a Republican in politics, a Mason, and a member of the Methodist Episcopal Church South.

Travis Davidson, attorney at law of Camden, and ex-register of Benton County, was born in Perry County, Tenn., December 4, 1856, son of L. Berry and Mary J. (Langley) Davidson, natives respectively of Kentucky and Tennessee. Our subject's grandfather, William Davidson, came to Tennessee from Virginia early in the present century, and located in Davidson County, but later moved to Kentucky, where our subject's father was born and reared. L. B. came to Tennessee about sixty years ago, and located in Perry County, where he married and reared a family of nine children, two sons and three daughters now living. He died there December 20, 1860. The mother still survives him. Our subject, Travis, left Perry County at the age of fifteen, and grew to manhood on the farm in this county. He secured a good literary education, and by his own efforts prepared himself for teaching. He followed this profession until 1882, when he was elected register of the county. During his term of office he studied law, and in April, 1885, was admitted to the Benton County bar. From that time to the present he has been actively engaged in his profession, having also served his term of four years as magistrate. In July, 1886, he was elected mayor of Camden, and now fills this position. August 6, 1884, he married Lucy B. Hughes, of McKenzie, Tenn., and to them was born one child, Daisy. Mr. Davidson is a true and unswerving Democrat in politics. He is a member of the O. O. of H., and he and wife are members of the Cumberland Presbyterian Church, of which he is deacon. He is clerk of the session and superintendent of the Sunday-school, and is one of the county's best citizens. He was constable of the Second District from 1880 to 1882, and has been a regular correspondent for the Nashville *Union* since that paper started. Mrs. Davidson is a native of Carroll County, Tenn., and a daughter of William and Virginia (Gaines) Hughes. She was reared in Carroll County and attended McKenzie and later Bethel College, from which she graduated. She studied art four years, which she has made a profession, making a specialty of landscape painting in oil, in which she has gained much well merited popularity.

John H. Farmer, magistrate of the Fifth District of Benton County, and a resident of Camden, was born June 22, 1822, on Sulphur Creek, Benton Co., Tenn. He is the son of George W. and Catherine (Harmon) Farmer. The father was born in Orange County, N. C., in 1795. In 1798 he, in company with his father and sister Catherine, left his native State and immigrated to Robertson County, Tenn. They remained there till 1809 or 1810, when they moved to Humphreys County, and from there to Benton County in 1819. They located on Sulphur Creek, where they lived quite a number of years, and afterward moved to Harmon Creek. The father was a soldier in the war of 1812, and assisted in fighting the Creek Indians. He drew a pension for quite a number of years for services rendered in the war. He died in 1876. His wife, Catherine Harmon, was a native of Middle Tennessee, and died in 1843. Her father, Adam Harmon, was one of the pioneer settlers of Benton County, Harmon Creek being named in his honor. Our subject was reared at home, receiving his education in the country schools and at Camden. At the age of twenty he left home, and in 1851 became a resident of Camden. The following year he was elected constable. He also flatboated on the Mississippi River, making forty-three trips in all, and for twelve years was engaged in merchandising in Camden, at the same time looking after the interests of his farm. In 1859 he was elected sheriff of Benton County, and served the people in that capacity for four years. During the late war he was in the service for about seven months under Gen. Chalmers. In 1865 Mr. Farmer was elected justice of the peace of the Fifth District, and at the same time was elected as chairman of the county court. From 1865 to the present, with the exception of one term, Mr. Farmer has been magistrate, and for many years was chairman of the county court, thus forcibly illustrating his popularity among the people. For over twenty years he has adjusted his neighbors' difficulties with judicial fairness. November 27, 1854, he married Martha Jane Atchison, a native of Henry County, Tenn., born November 11, 1830. She died

April 14, 1866. Mr. Farmer is the owner of 900 acres of land, and is one of the substantial citizens of the county. He is a Republican in politics, casting his first vote for Lewis Cass in 1848.

A. J. Farmer, attorney at law of Camden, was born February 22, 1846, in Benton County, Tenn., son of Ichabod and Martha (Davidson) Farmer. The father was a native of Benton County, Tenn., born in 1819, and his father, George W. Farmer, was a native of Orange County, North Carolina, and at a very early date immigrated to Middle Tennessee, locating in Humphreys County. In 1819 he came to Benton County and located in the Seventh District, on the Tennessee River. Ichabod was living in Benton County at the time of his marriage, and after that event he settled in the Seventh District, but afterward moved to the Fifth District, where he passed the remainder of his days. He was a successful farmer, owning upward of 1,900 acres. He died in 1885. He represented Benton and Humphreys Counties in the lower branch of the General Assembly of Tennessee one term. The mother of our subject was born in Dickson County, Tenn., and died at her home in Benton County in August, 1864. They had four children, only two of whom are living at the present time: Keziah (Mrs. L. E. Davis) and our subject. He was reared at home, and received his early education in the schools of his native county. During the great civil war he enlisted in the Confederate Army in July, 1864, in Company A, Fifty-fifth Regiment Tennessee Infantry. He fought at Peach Tree, Ga., and Atlanta, and in the last named battle was unwell, and at the surrender was captured and taken to the hospital. He was soon sent to Nashville, and from there home. In 1867 he began teaching, and taught one term. December 25, of the same year, he married Tennessee Hall, a native of Benton County, Tenn., This marriage resulted in the birth of eight children: William I., Florence E., Thomas N., Vernon A., Mattie, Eunice, Myrtle and Carrie. In 1874 Mr. Farmer became a resident of Camden and began the practice of law, at which he has since continued. For the past three years Mr. Farmer and S. W. Hawkins, of Huntingdon, have been law partners. Our subject was reared on a farm, and most of his life work has been spent in looking after the interest of the same. He now owns 600 acres, and is one of the solid business men of Camden. He is conservative in politics, but is in principle a Democrat, voting for principle and not for party. He cast his first vote for Horace Greeley in 1872. He and wife are members of the Cumberland Presbyterian Church.

Green B. Greer, clerk and master of the Benton County Chancery Court, and a native of the county, was born January 21, 1840, son of Hezekiah and Mary (Wyatt) Greer, natives of Tennessee. Our subject's grandfather, James Greer, came to Benton County, Tenn., with his family about 1816 or 1818, and here Hezekiah grew to manhood, married and reared a family of seven children, two of whom are dead. He followed farming successfully in his day, principally in Benton County, although he lived for a short time in Henry and Carroll Counties. He died in March, 1862, in his fifty-seventh year. Green B. Greer was reared and educated in this county, spending his early days on the farm. During the great civil war he enlisted in October, 1861, in Company A, Fifty-fifth Confederate Tennessee Infantry, serving first as a non-commissioned officer, and after the reorganization was elected first lieutenant of his company. He served in this capacity until wounded in the left leg at Atlanta, and was not again able to enter the service. During service he was captured at Island No. 10, and held a prisoner of war five months in Northern prisons. After the war he followed teaching and farming in the Sixth District (his home) until January, 1871, when he accepted the position of clerk and master of the chancery court under Chancellor Nixon. He has served long and faithfully in this most important office, which he holds at the present time. Mr. Greer has been a life-long Democrat in politics, and as such began his public career in August, 1870, by making the race for county court clerk, but was defeated by a small majority, along with eight other aspirants to the office. September 12, 1866, he married Elizabeth McGill, who died January 15, 1873, leaving three children, all now living: Jesse H., Robert S. and Lena. By his second marriage, with Ada Haley in 1876, he has three living children: Alma, Clarice and Nixon. Mrs. Greer died September 2, 1884, and in 1885 Mr. Greer married his present wife, Mary S. Haley. He is a Mason, a member of the Agricultural Wheel of this State, and he and wife are members of the Methodist Episcopal Church South. He is one of Benton County's most enterprising men and an efficient and trustworthy public official.

Dr. Adam M. Hawley, of Big Sandy, Tenn., was born in Sullivan County, of that State, December 10, 1847, and is a son of William and Sarah (Holt) Hawley, both natives of East Tennessee. It was in this part of Tennessee, that our subject grew to manhood, received an ordinary English education and at the age of sixteen began the study of medicine with a view to make it a profession, but soon relinquished it to enter the Confederate Army. He served from October, 1863, to April, 1865, with Company F, Fifty-ninth Regiment Tennessee Mounted Infantry. At the close of the war he resumed his medical studies, and at the same time farmed some in Washington County, Va. His medical preceptor in Virginia was Dr. W. F. Barr, and in East Tennessee was Dr. R. H.

Young, both eminent practitioners. In 1867 he came to West Tennessee, and practiced medicine in Henry County with Dr. J. W. Pritchell for about nine years. He practiced sixteen months in southeast Missouri, and in 1881 came to Big Sandy where he has since resided, engaged successfully in the practice of his profession. In 1871 he married Nannie W. Melton, of Henry County, and to them was born one child, Lula C. The Doctor is a Democrat in politics, is an enterprising and reliable citizen and a medical practitioner of experience and ability.

J. M. Holladay & Bro. began the mercantile trade at Mount Carmel, Benton Co., Tenn., April 28, 1873, and have since continued as a firm at the same place. Their stock of goods, one of the largest and best carried in the county, consists of dry goods, boots and shoes, hats, caps, notions, etc., groceries, drugs, queens, glass and hardware, and the business is conducted in two buildings, one for the dry goods, etc., and the other for the groceries, etc. John M., the senior member of the firm, was born August 22, 1840. The father, Geo. W., was a native of Smith County, and came to Carroll County when young, met and married Catharine Crider, the mother of our subjects; they spent the balance of their lives in that county. The father was justice of the peace twelve years, deputy sheriff four years, and sheriff of the county six years. John M. remained with his parents till the commencement of the war, and then enlisted in the Fifty-fifth Tennessee Confederate Infantry, at the organization of which he was elected third lieutenant, and served till captured at Island No. 10. When his regiment was reorganized at Jackson, Miss., he was elected second lieutenant, which command he held till the cessation of hostilities. July 28, 1864, he lost an arm at Atlanta, Ga., but still retained his command. At the close of the war he returned to Carroll County, where he remained about two years, then came to Benton County, locating at his present residence in 1867. On October 13, 1869, he married Rachel R. B. Mathews, a native of Benton County, by which union two sons and two daughters have been born, one daughter being deceased. He is member of the Cumberland Presbyterian Church and K. of H. S. W., the junior member of the firm, was born December 25, 1842, and remained with his parents till the commencement of the war, when he enlisted in the same regiment with his brother, and served as a private throughout the war. He then returned to Carroll County and remained till 1868, then came also to Benton County, farming till the establishment of business with his brother at Mt. Carmel. December 26, 1872, he married Cordelia Wood, by which union seven children have been born, one son and four daughters still living. He is a member of the F. & A. M.

William T. Hubbs, M. D., of Camden, Tenn., was born in Fulton County, Ky., December 23, 1849; son of William and Charlotte (Curlin) Hubbs, both natives of Tennessee. William T. removed to Obion County, Tenn., with his parents when but an infant, and was reared to manhood in that county. He secured a fair literary education and at the age of nineteen began the study of medicine with a view to making it a profession. In 1872 he graduated from the medical department of the University of Louisville, Ky., and began to practice in Obion County. In 1874 he removed to Johnsonville, Tenn., and in 1877 went to Texas, where he remained till 1878. In July of that year he came to Camden where he has since resided, engaged successfully in the practice of his profession. He conducted a drug business here for about a year during 1881-82. In October, 1885, he engaged in the dry goods and general merchandise business, in which he has continued to the present time with good success. The Doctor married his present wife in 1879; she was a Miss Emma Hill of Benton County. He lost one wife by death and has no issue by either marriage. He is an unswerving Democrat in politics, a reliable business man and a medical practitioner of experience and ability.

J. H. Hudson, farmer of the Eighth District, was born in 1834 in Windham County, Vt., a son of Holman and Clara (Oaks) Hudson. The mother was of Scotch descent and born in Vermont, where she died in 1840. The father again married. He was of English origin and passed the most of his life in Vermont where he died in 1864 at about the age of sixty years. J. H. Hudson was but six years old at the time of his mother's death and at an early age was cast upon the world to care for himself. In 1862 he enlisted in the United States Army in Company E, Sixth Iowa Cavalry. His principal duty was on the frontier of the West battling with the Indians for about three years. In December, 1865, Mr. Hudson came to Benton County, West Tenn., and April 11, 1868, he married Miss Elizabeth Wygul, daughter of Elbert Wygul. Mrs. Hudson is a native of Benton County, born in 1838. They are the parents of three children, named Carlos N., Wm. E. and Oaks J. Mr. Hudson is one of the enterprising and successful farmers of Benton County, and now owns 570 acres of good land, well improved. In 1886 he erected a good frame dwelling house and barn and has added other improvements to his property. He is a Democrat in politics, a member of the Masonic fraternity, Lodge No. 290, of Big Sandy, and he and wife belong to the Methodist Episcopal Church South.

Jo. G. Hudson, merchant of Camden, Tenn., and a native of Kentucky was born near Glasgow, Ky., September 7, 1837, son of James G. and Margaret (Stayton) Hudson, natives respectively of Tennessee and Kentucky.

The father spent the greater part of his life in Henry County, Tenn., removing to this county in 1859, and followed farming near Camden until his death in February, 1885. Jo. G. was raised on the farm and received a limited education. In 1861 he enlisted in Company C, Fifth Regiment Tennessee Confederate Infantry, serving as private and noncommissioned officer in the late war until the surrender. After the war he followed farming until 1880 when in March he came to Camden and engaged in the saloon business. In March, 1881, he engaged in the dry goods, grocery and general merchandise business, in which he has continued to the present time under the firm name of J. G. Hudson & Co. July 9, 1886, his store was made the Agricultural Wheel store of Camden. Mr. Hudson has been very successful in his business adventures, carrying a large and select stock of goods, and controls a large trade in the city and county especially among the members of the Agricultural Wheel. In 1867 he married Elmira N. Bell, who died in 1876. They had two children both deceased. On April 15, 1884, he married Mrs. Mary (Barfield) Wyly of Humphreys County, and by this union had one child, John James. Mr. Hudson is independent in politics. He is a Master Mason, a member of the K. of H., and is justly recognized as one among the enterprising and successful business men of Camden.

F. G. Hudson, M. D., who resides about five miles from Camden was born in this county in 1838, and is a son of Albert J. and Jemimah M. (Rushing) Hudson. The father was a descendant of the English explorer, Henry Hudson, and was born in the year 1818 in Humphreys County, Middle Tenn., and in a few years his father, Dorsey P., came to Benton County. He was a very influential citizen and was clerk of the various courts for many years. Albert J. lived in Benton County at the time of his marriage and afterward located in the Fifth District where he resided a number of years, then moved to the Sixth District where he died in 1884. His wife, Jemimah, was a native of Benton County born in 1823 or 1824. She is yet living and resides on the old home place. Our subject, Dr. F. G. Hudson, is one of three children living of the nine born to his parents. He received his literary education in the common schools of Benton County and worked on the farm of his parents until twenty-one years of age, when he commenced the study of his chosen profession under his uncle, Dr. Joseph U. Hudson. In 1864 he enlisted in Company H, Fifty-fifth Regiment Tennessee Infantry, and actively engaged in the battles of New Hope Church, Ga., Atlanta, Jonesboro, Franklin, Nashville and many others. During the time he was not in active battle he was on detached service acting as surgeon. In 1865 Dr. Hudson entered upon the regular practice of his profession and November 17, 1867, married Miss Frances R. Combs, who is a native of North Carolina. They are the parents of five children, named Dorsey G., Susan Stella, Eula Lee, Elihu and Charles M. Dr. Hudson is a Democrat in politics, a member of the Masonic fraternity (Chapter Lodge, No. 64, and Blue Lodge, No. 179) of Camden, and he and wife are members of the Methodist Episcopal Church.

Joseph E. Jones, attorney-general of the Twelfth Judicial Circuit of Tennessee, and a native of Carroll County, same State, was born October 29, 1857, son of Thomas E. and Sarah Jones, both native Virginians and both now deceased. The father came to Tennessee in 1852, located at Huntingdon, where he followed farming principally, and was mayor of the town a number of years; he died there September 19, 1885. Our subject was reared to manhood in his native county, securing an academical education in the Huntingdon schools. At the age of eighteen he began the study of law, with a view of making it a profession, and entered in 1876 the office of Hawkins & Townes, where he remained two years. December, 1878, he came to Camden and was admitted to the Benton County bar, after which he entered regularly in the practice of his profession and has remained here to the present time, having acquired a prominent and leading position among the lawyers of West Tennessee. Mr. Jones has been an active and unswerving Democrat in his political views, and as such was elected to the office of attorney-general in August, 1884. He has discharged the duties of this important office in an efficient and highly satisfactory manner. November 16, 1881, he married Ella Hill, of Benton County, and they have two children: Harry E. and Cecil Hill. Mr. Jones was for years mayor of Camden and is recognized by all as an excellent citizen and legal practitioner of decided ability. In 1886 he declined to make the race for the State Legislature, although petitioned by several hundred of the leading citizens. He and wife are members of the Cumberland Presbyterian Church, in which he has been an elder since 1874.

John B. Lindsey, hotel-keeper, of Big Sandy, and a native of Benton Co., was born September 17, 1835, son of Edward and Levicy (Rumley) Lindsey, natives respectively of North Carolina and Tenn. The father, who was a well known and successful farmer, spent a long and useful life in this county, dying upon his farm, one mile east of Big Sandy, in 1872. John B. was reared on a farm, securing a limited education. He has followed farming successfully to the present time, owning at present a good farm near town. In 1871 he built the first business house in Big Sandy, and conducted a family grocery business here for six years. He also during this time built his present residence and began keeping a public house and has conducted the only hotel business here up to the present time. January 12, 1873, he married his second and present wife, who was Miss Mary L. Rushing. They have three children: Minnie May, Eddie and John Sherman. Mr. Lindsey is a stanch Republican in his political views; was not a participant in the late war, but was a Union man. He is a Mason, himself and wife are Missionary Baptists, and he is justly recognized as one among the reliable and successful business men and citizens of Benton County.

Samuel Lockhart, miller and farmer of the Eighth District, was born in Stewart County (now Houston), Tenn., in 1822, and is the son of Samuel and Nancy (Hornberger) Lockhart. The father was of English extraction and a native of North Carolina. He came to Tennessee in his youth, and at the time of his marriage was living in Stewart County, where he passed the remainder of his life. He was twice married and had sixteen children. He died about 1858. The mother, Nancy (Hornberger) Lockhart, was born in Stewart County, Tenn., and was of Dutch extraction; she died about 1838, leaving nine children who lived to be grown, but only four of whom are now living. Our subject grew up and received his education in Stewart County. August 27, 1848, he married Mary Ann Pitt, a native of Stewart County, born December 25, 1822, and the daughter of Wyley Pitt. To our subject and wife were born seven children: Andrew J., Thomas M., Sophrona A. (Mrs. W. F. Snyder), Martha A. (Mrs. N. McNiel), William Z., Mary J. (Mrs. Thomas Rushing) and Sarah E. In 1849 Mr. Lockhart came to Benton County and bought 200 acres in the Eighth District of Rushing Creek, where he located and began clearing and tilling the soil. In 1872 he purchased a saw-mill and grist-mill of Hudson & Thomas. In 1873 he erected and added a wool machine and in 1881 attached a cotton-gin. From that time to the present, Mr. Lockhart has run the combined machines, meeting with good success. Owing to advanced age Mr. Lockhart desires to dispose of his valuable mills and retire to quiet life. Mr. Lockhart lost his wife April 22, 1882, and in 1883 he married Mrs. Amanda (Shilling) Baker, daughter of Jacob Shilling. Our subject is a Democrat but was a Whig previous to the war. He cast his first vote for Henry Clay, in 1844. He is a Mason and a member of the Cumberland Presbyterian Church. Mrs. Lockhart is a member of the Methodist Episcopal Church South.

John C. McDaniel was born in Lincoln County, Tenn., March 2, 1811, son of John and Mary (White) McDaniel, natives respectively of Virginia and Kentucky. John C. removed to Alabama with his family when quite young, and was reared to manhood in that State on a farm. He came to this county with his parents about 1820, and has resided here ever since, engaged in farming principally and has also conducted mercantile and tobacco business in Camden. He ran a tobacco factory here before the war, and was an old time Whig before that event—since then he has been a Democrat in politics. In 1865 he was elected county trustee, serving one term of two years, and was a magistrate in the First District six years. In 1831 he married Martha White, who died the following year leaving one daughter now living, Martha, the wife of J. D. Fry, of Harris Station, Obion County. By the second marriage with Harriett Menzies, he has two living children: Archibald G. and William Neal. The second wife died in 1852, and later he married his present wife, Olivia Fry, and they have nine children: John C., Millard F., Michael Alonzo, Wiley, Eugene, Mary (the widow of Oliver Black), Beulah, Beta and Sarah. Mr. McDaniel is a Royal Arch Mason and a member of the Methodist Episcopal Church.

Archibald G. McDaniel, ex-clerk of the circuit court at Camden, Tenn., was born in Benton County, January 9, 1851. He was raised on a farm in this county, securing an ordinary English schooling. In 1873 he began mercantile life as a clerk and continued but one year when he followed farming and school-teaching until 1878. He was then elected clerk of the Benton County Circuit Court, serving one term of four years. He was re-elected in 1882 and has served faithfully and efficiently to the present time. April 4, 1877, he married Miss Melvina B. Kelly of this county, and they have three children: Anna, Ora and Wm. Thomas. Mr. McDaniel is a Democrat in politics, a Mason and a member of the Agricultural Wheel. Himself and wife are members of the Methodist Episcopal Church.

Gilbert McKenzie, farmer and old resident of District No. 8, was born in Houston County, Tenn. (then Stewart County), in 1820, and is one of a family of ten children born to Malcolm and Nancy (Beaton) McKenzie. The father was of Scotch origin and a native of North Carolina, born in 1774. He was a farmer by occupation, and about 1810 left his native State and immigrated to what is now Houston County. He married here and located near where Erin now is. In 1824 he came to Benton County and settled in the Eighth District. He died in 1834. His wife, Nancy (Beaton) McKenzie, was a native of North Carolina and died about 1870. Our subject has been a resident of Benton County since he was four years of age. He remained with his mother till twenty-six years of age and in 1846 married Easter Pitt, a native of Stewart (now Houston) County, Tenn., born 1820, and the daughter of Arthur Pitt. To our subject and wife were born seven children: Catherine (Mrs. W. J.

Cooper), Nancy (Mrs. B. F. Peeler), John P., Caroline (Mrs. D. W. Stockdale), Jethro, Martha A. and Easter. When about twenty-one years of age our subject entered forty acres in District No. 8, where he located after marriage and where he has always resided. He now owns 2,700 acres and is a well-to-do farmer. He is one of the county's oldest citizens and is highly esteemed for his honesty and integrity. In politics he is a Republican, casting his first vote for Henry Clay in 1844. Mr. McKenzie lost his wife December 13, 1882, since which time his daughters, Martha and Easter, have been keeping house for him. Mr. McKenzie is a member of the Cumberland Presbyterian Church.

Hon. William P. Morris, a prominent and well known business man and citizen of Camden, Tenn., was born in Sumner County, Tenn., January 12, 1817; son of Isaac and Elizabeth (Brown) Morris, both natives of North Carolina. The parents married in North Carolina and came to Tennessee as early as 1810. In 1820 they removed from Sumner to Dickson County, and in 1822 to Henderson County. The father died while on a visit in Carroll County, in 1826. Our subject attained years of manhood on the farm and secured a limited education in the log schoolhouse of that early day, undergoing many of the hardships incident to pioneer life. At the age of seventeen he began the mercantile life as clerk in Perryville, Tenn., where he continued over two years. He then repaired to a farm in Decatur County, and from there to Benton County in 1841, locating two miles north of Camden on a farm. In March, 1843, he was elected clerk of Benton County Court, and removed to Camden where he served in the clerk's office nine years. In 1850 he engaged in the mercantile business at Camden in the building he is now occupying, and has remained in the business continuously up to the present time. In politics Mr. Morris was originally an old line Whig but since the war he has been a firm and unswerving Democrat. In 1861 he was elected to the State Senate during the memorable session of 1861–62. Again in 1879 he represented his district in an able manner in the State Senate serving with honor and distinction, also in the House of Representatives in 1883–84. Mr. Morris was not a participant in the war and was strongly opposed to secession, but after the State seceded his sympathies were enlisted with the South from a conscientious sense of duty and right. Mr. Morris has been one of the few very successful business men of Benton County. He started here with little or no capital, but by industry, close application to business and strict integrity has accumulated a very handsome competency. The war caused him great loss of property as it did many others, but he has recovered almost wholly from its ravages. July 2, 1838, he married Elvira Jane Johnson, a native of Perry County, Tenn., and to this union were born these children: John Pitts, of Fulton, Ky.; Dr. Granville T. of Paris, Tenn.; Adelaide the wife of W. F. Maiden; Louisa C., wife of William Carraway, of Big Sandy Tenn.; Virgil F.; Leehentz, wife of Joshua Bowles of this county, and William L. of Big Sandy. Mr. Morris is a Master Mason, and he and wife are members of the Methodist Episcopal Church South. He has always taken an active and leading interest in all public and private enterprises that tended to the welfare of the town and county, in which he has been a highly successful and respected citizen for almost half a century.

Dr. James M. Moses, of Big Sandy, Tenn., and a native of Benton County, was born July 1, 1853, at Camden; son of James M. and Mary (Wyly) Moses, natives, respectively, of Humphreys and Benton Counties, Tenn. The father, who was one of the leading and prominent medical practitioners of Benton County, practiced his profession successfully at Camden until his death in 1860. He was a student of old Dr. Marable, of Humphreys County. Our subject was reared to manhood in Camden, securing an ordinary English education, and at the age of twenty-five years began the study of medicine under Dr. R. B. Travis of Camden. Attended lectures at Nashville in 1881-82 in the medical department of the University of Tennessee. He then began practicing at Camden and in May, 1883, came to Big Sandy and has remained exclusively in practice of his profession to the present time, having met with good and well deserved success. October, 1875, he married Miss Ida Hill, of Camden, and to them were born two children: Nellie and James Hill. The Doctor is strictly independent in his political views although formerly a Democrat. Himself and wife are members of the Presbyterian Church and he is justly recognized as one among the enterprising and reliable citizens of Benton County and a medical practitioner of experience and decided ability.

Alexander C. McRae, county court clerk of Benton County, Tenn., and a native of the same county, was born February 4, 1843, son of Alexander and Lavina (Rumbly) McRae, natives, respectively, of North Carolina and West Tennessee. The father, who was born in 1786, came to Tennessee when a young man, about the beginning of the present century, locating on the river near where Point Mason now is, and later removed to Sugar Creek where he reared his family of two children by his first wife, and later married our subject's mother, by whom he had ten children, nine of whom are still living. He followed farming successfully in this county until his death August, 1877. The subject of this sketch was reared and educated in Benton County. In 1861 he enlisted in Company A, Fifty-fifth Regiment Tennessee Infantry Confederate Army, and served as private until the close of the Rebellion. He was wounded in the arm at Atlanta from which he still suffers on account of gangrene. After the war he followed farming near Big Sandy and also followed carpentering, assisting largely in building up the town. In 1878 he was elected county court clerk and removed to Camden where he has since resided. He has held this office continuously by re-election up to the present time, and is now serving on the third term, having discharged the duties of this most important public trust in a faithful, efficient manner. January 1, 1868, he married Lenora Ann Brown, a native of Madison County, Tenn., and has five children: William E., Ida A., Anins D., Marvin C. and Herman. Mr. McRae is, and always has been a firm and unswerving Democrat in his politscal views. He is a Mason and I. O. O. F. and himself and wife are members of the Methodist Episcopal Church South. He is one of the public-spirited and enterprising citizens of Benton County and a justly popular official. He has been a local preacher in the Methodist Church South since 1871 and has given a great deal of time and means to the promotion of the cause of Christianity.

H. R. Pierce, farmer and old resident of District No. 7, was born in 1836 in Benton County, Tenn., and is the son of John and Rachel (Ross) Pierce. The father was a native of North Carolina, born in 1801 and of English-German descent. In 1819 he left his native State and came to Benton County, Tenn., erected a log cabin, cleared an acre of ground, went to Kentucky to get married and then returned to his western home. It is said that Mr. Pierce erected one of the first houses west of the Tennessee River. He died in 1862. His wife, Rachel Ross, was born in the State of Kentucky on the Cumberland River in 1806. She was of Irish origin and died in 1871. They had ten children, five of whom are living. Our subject was reared at home and received his education in the common schools of Benton County. At the age of twenty-two he left the parental roof and December 10, 1857, he married Nancy J. Stockdale, a native of Benton County born 1836, and the daughter of Dennis and Christia Stockdale. To our subject and wife were born eight children: Mary C. (Mrs. H. A. Phifer), James F., Martha (Mrs. H. Melton), Rachel A., John W., Henry H., Roena B. and Victoria C. Mr. Pierce has resided in his native county since his birth. In 1861 he located where he now resides on a fine farm of 283 acres. In politics he has been a life-long Democrat and in August, 1876, he was elected magistrate of the Seventh District and from that date to the present has adjusted his neighbors' difficulties with judicial fairness. He has been a

Mason since 1855 and he and wife and six children are members of the Methodist Episcopal Church South. Mr. Pierce has been a member of that church since he was thirteen years of age and has been a class-leader in the same for twenty-eight years.

Uriah A. Potts, clerk in the mercantile establishment of William Caraway, Big Sandy, was born in Davie County, N. C., February 9, 1861, and is a son of William S. Potts, a former citizen of the Eighth District of Benton County (see sketch of father). Uriah came to this county with his parents in 1869, was reared here on a farm and secured a good English education in the academical department of the Big Sandy school. He prepared himself for teaching, which profession he followed for four years in this county. In January, 1884, he accepted a clerkship with Dr. T. Morris, where he remained a year. He then entered the employ of Mr. Caraway, where he has remained ever since. He is a Master Mason and a member of the Sons of Temperance. He is a Democrat, a member of the Methodist Episcopal Church and an estimable young man.

H. Rushing, commission merchant and farmer at Point Mason, was born in 1825 in Benton County, Tenn., son of Robert and Lively (Webb) Rushing. The father was a native of North Carolina, was of Welsh origin and in 1824 left his native State and immigrated to Benton County, W. Tenn. He located on Rushing Creek, it being named after his brother Able and his cousins, Willis and Dennis Rushing, who had settled here as early as 1818. Robert was one of the pioneer settlers and was quite successful as a tiller of the soil, owning upward of 800 acres. He died in 1854, aged about sixty-four. His wife, Lively Webb, was a native of South Carolina; she died in 1866 about seventy-six years of age. Our subject received his education in the country schools and at Camden. He remained with his parents till thirty-one years of age. In 1855 he located at Point Mason and engaged in his present business. In April of the same year he married Elizabeth Lashley, a native of Benton County, Tenn., born March, 1835, and the daughter of Anderson and Eliza Lashley. To our subject and wife were born six children: Robert, Horace, Eliza (Mrs. Goodlin), Lillie, Lucy and Lizzie. Mr. Rushing has lived at Point Mason for the past thirty-six years, where he has been actively engaged in merchandising and superintending his large farm. In 1870 he erected a two-story brick store-room at a cost of $3,000. Mr. Rushing is the possessor of upward of 5,500 acres and is the largest land holder in Benton County. In politics he has been a life-long Democrat, casting his first vote for Lewis Cass in 1848. He is a member of the Masonic fraternity, Camden Lodge, and also a member of the Methodist Episcopal Church South. Mrs. Rushing is a member of the Presbyterian Church.

W. C. Rushing, farmer of the Eighth District, was born in Benton County in 1826, and is one of a family of ten children born to Willis and Mary (Rasberry) Rushing. The father was of Welsh origin, born in Anderson County, N. C., about the year 1790, and was a farmer by occupation. In 1818 he immigrated to Benton County, W. Tenn., and entered 80 acres of land in the Fifth District, where he located and passed the remainder of his days. Rushing Creek was named for him, his brother Dennis and his cousin, Able Rushing. At the time of his death which occurred in 1855, he owned 1,000 acres of good land. His wife, Mary, was a native of North Carolina, and died in 1862 at about the age of sixty-five years. W. C. Rushing was reared at home, receiving his education in Benton County, and making his home with his parents until he was twenty-five years of age. In 1855 he married Miss Sophiah Rushing, a daughter of Robert Rushing, born in 1834 and a native of Benton County. They have twelve children: Dora, wife of Silas Bullock; Robert W., Lee, Walter, John, Ida, Etta, Sophiah, Rachel, Holden, Nat and Finis. Mr. Rushing has always been a resident of Benton County, and during the many years has proven to be a man of honesty and integrity. By his energy, industry and good management he now owns upward of 1,000 acres of land and has a good home well improved. He is a life-long Democrat, casting his first vote for Lewis Cass in 1848. Mr. Rushing is a member of the Masonic fraternity, Lodge No. 179 of Camden, and he and wife are influential members of the Cumberland Presbyterian Church.

Alexander H. Smith, M. D., was born August 17, 1841, in Lauderdale County, Ala., and is the oldest of a family of seven children born to John A. and Margaret C. (Wood) Smith, of which our subject, one brother and two sisters are the only surviving members. The father was born in Wake County, N. C., came to Nashville when young and here remained several years. He then went to Florence, Ala., about 1839, and from 1840 to 1850 was interested in the stage and mail line from Nashville to Florence, via Boliver, Jackson, etc. At Florence he met and married the mother of our subject. She was of English and Welsh extraction. The parents of our subject were citizens of Florence and there died in 1864 and 1865 respectively. The father was engaged in the mercantile trade there for several years, and at the breaking out of the war was postmaster of the town. Our subject remained with his parents till the beginning of hostilities between the North and South, when he enlisted in the Sixteenth Alabama Confederate Infantry, with which he served thoughout the war. He then engaged in the drug trade at Florence till 1868. He attended session 1868–69 of the medical department of the University of Louisville, and located at Patriot Landing, Perry County, where he followed his chosen profession till 1875, at which date he located at his present residence in Benton County, near Sugartree Postoffice, Decatur County, and has since enjoyed a lucrative practice. March 2, 1870, he married Isabel Vise, a native of Perry County, by which union three sons and four daughters have been born, all but one son still living. Mrs. Smith is a member of the Methodist Church and Mr. Smith of the Cumberland Presbyterian Church and also of the F. & A. M. Politically he is identified with the Democratic party.

James M. Spencer, farmer, was born November 14, 1827, in Maury County, Tenn., and is one of a family of six children born to Frederick and Ellen (Wheat) Spencer, our subject, two brothers, and two sisters being the surviving members. The father was a native of North Carolina, came to Maury County when young, married there, then moved to Hickman County about 1830 and resided there till his death, 1837. The mother reared the family there, and moved to Perry County, 1853, where her death occurred in 1870. Our subject remained at home till twenty-three years old, then married Mary Williams, a native of Smith County, and followed farming in Perry County till 1884, at which date he moved to Benton County locating at his present residence, a farm of 270 acres, four miles south of Camden. He served in Cox's Regiment from 1863 till the evacuation of Shelbyville, then returned home and has since continued farming. To the marriage above referred to, four sons and five daughters have been born, four sons and three daughters still living. Mr. Spencer and family are members of the Methodist Church, and politically he is a Democrat.

Jeremiah Thompson, merchant of Camden, Tenn., and a native of Benton County, of that State, was born April 2, 1839; son of William and Penelope (Holland) Thompson, natives respectively of Virginia and North Carolina. The parents both came to Tennessee in their youthful days, at the beginning of the present century. They married in Dickson County and came to Benton County a year later. The father followed agricultural pursuits until his death in 1842. The mother is still living at the advanced age of eighty-nine. Our subject grew to manhood on the farm and secured but a limited education in boyhood. He farmed until 1877 when he came to Camden and engaged in mercantile business in the present firm of McDaniel & Thompson. He has contributed largely to the success of this well known and leading firm in Benton County. June 2, 1882, he married Frances Cowell of this city. He has seven living children by his former marriage with Emily J. Thompson (now deceased). Our subject is a stanch Republican in politics, was not a participant in the late war, but was a firm supporter of the Union. He is a Master Mason and held the office of deputy sheriff of Benton County in 1868–69.

Robert B. Travis, M. D., of Camden, is a native of Henry County, Tenn., born May 18, 1832, and a son of Silas and Virginia (Caruthers) Travis, both natives of North Carolina. They came to Tennessee as early as, or before, 1825, locating first in Middle Tennessee, and some four years later removed to Henry County, where they died. The Doctor was reared to manhood on a farm in his native county, and received an academical education. In 1854 he began the study of medicine, and attended Memphis Medical College one course of lectures. He began practicing in Missouri where he continued two years; he then entered a drug establishment at Lake Providence, La., and studied chemistry and pharmacy, after which he accepted a position as professor of languages in Carroll Institute of that city two terms; later he held a similar position in Conyersville (Tenn.) High School. November, 1856, he came to Camden, was in charge of the academy ten months, when he attended a course of medical lectures at Memphis, Tenn. He then engaged in the practice of medicine which he has continued to the present time. He conducted the Benton *Banner* two years and later established the Camden *Herald* in company with E. M. Travis, which they conducted eighteen months. Dr. Travis has been twice married. In November, 1858, he married Mary J. Gillespie, who died April 26, 1860, leaving one child, James V. February 10, 1861, he married Sarah J. Cowell. They have three children: Charles N., Viola F. and Eugene E. The Doctor is a Democrat, a Mason and he as well as wife are members of the Methodist Episcopal Church South.

Christopher K. Wyly, a prominent and highly respected pioneer citizen of Camden, Tenn., was born in Sequatchie Valley, Tenn., February 2, 1807, and is a son of Harris K. and Arty (Taylor) Wyly, natives respectively of the Old Dominion State and Tennessee. The father came to Tennessee when a young man in the year 1790, and located at Jonesboro, Tenn., where he married. He followed mercantile persuits in Georgia a few years and spent twenty years or more in agricultural pursuits in Alabama. He died in East Tennessee about 1835. Our subject passed his youthful days in Alabama in securing a limited education in the primitive log schoolhouse of those early days. At the age of nineteen he came to Tennessee and located on the Tennessee River at Old Reynoldsburg, where he began life as a clerk in a mercantile establishment. In 1838 he came to Camden and engaged in the mercantile business for himself, and has devoted his entire life to that business ever since. Mr. Wyly has been one of the few very successful business men of Benton County. He started in life with but little if any capital, but by indomitable industry has succeeded in accumulating a handsome competency, notwithstanding the fact that he lost over $100,000 during the late war. Before the war Mr. Wyly was an old line Henry Clay Whig, and he was strongly opposed to the Rebellion, but after the State was voted out and the Union virtually dissolved, his sympathy and means were extended to the people of the South. In 1839 he married Lemira C. Pavatt, a sister of old Chancellor Stephen C. Pavatt. She died in March, 1876, and left these children: Harris K.; Carrie C., wife of J. S. Bartlett of Texas, and Eva G. Mr. Wyly is not a member of any fraternal or sectarian institution, but is a believer in the Christian religion. He is one of the county's most reliable and successful citizens.

Dr. J. R. Young, whose residence is eight miles northeast of Big Sandy, was born in Stewart County, Middle Tenn., in 1836, and is a son of Elisha and Sarah (Scarborough) Young. The father was born in Dickson County, Tenn., in 1803, and was of English extraction. He was a collier by trade and in connection did farming. At the time of his marriage he was living in Stewart County, and in 1844 he moved to Decatur County, W. Tenn., where he died February, 1845. His wife was born in Stewart County, Tenn., in 1813, and died in 1877. The subject of this sketch was reared at home and received his literary education in the common schools of Stewart and Benton Counties. At the age of fourteen he started out on life's rough road for himself. He worked for some time on the farm as a day laborer. In 1856 he came to Benton County, and soon commenced the study of medicine, his preceptor being Dr. P. B. Adams. He followed the Doctor's advice for nearly a year, and in 1858 engaged in the practice of his chosen profession. October 9, 1860, he married Jane Ross, and to them were born two children: David E. and Mary Jane (Mrs. B. F. Stockdale). Mrs. Young died in 1867, and November of the following year he married Nannie Askew, who bore him seven children: William W., Sallie, Vibella, Elbert and Gilbert (twins), Walter and Flora. The Doctor lost his second wife July 20, 1885, and May 26, 1886, he married Parlee (Wyatt) Metheny. He has been a resident of Benton County since 1856, and since 1858 he has constantly practiced his profession. He has also carried on his farming interests and has 600 acres of good land. In politics the Doctor is a Democrat, and cast his first vote for Breckinridge. He is a member of the Masonic fraternity, Big Sandy Lodge, No. 290, and he and wife are members of the Methodist Episcopal Church South, the Doctor being a member for the past thirty-eight years.

Prepared by:
Miss Karon Mac Smith, Nixon, Texas

Acton, John G. 832
Adams, C. D. 847
  George W. 847
  Fredonia 886
  G. J. 847+
  James A. 847
  Joseph M. 847
  Meads 847
  P. B., Dr. 954
  T. H. 847
  William 800
  William E. 847
Aden, Clinton 821, 824(2), 841, 888+
  Harvey E. 888
  Harvey F. 888
  John B. 888
  Mary L. 888
  S. B. 828
  Sheila 888
  Thomas B. 888
  William H. 888
Alexander, Adam R. 821
  Eva 889
  Jacob & Co. 827
  Marion, Dr. 889
  Mattie 889
  Ose F. 888+
  (Ose interlined)
Alexander & Barton 888
Algea, Grace E. 847
  James 847
  James A. 847
  Mary E. 847
  Peter 847
  W. W. 847+
Algee, J. B. 803
  R. H. 810
  Robert 804
Allen, Beverly A. 857/58
  Beverly S. 803(2), 858
  B. J. 907
  B. S. 806
  D. J. 836, 837
  Ella 869
  John 834
  John L. 804
  Littleton 816
  V. S. 803, 806
  W. J. F., Rev. 869
  Young W. 802
Allen, ___ 862
Allen & Dougherty 808
Anderson, Anna 890
  Charles B. 890
  Elizabeth 889
  Elizabeth L. 890
  John 821, 834(2), 889+
  Isaac 836
  Isaac, Capt. 844(2)
  Nellie 890
  Robert 889
  Robert A. 890
  Sallie 895
  (interlined)
  William 804
Arbuckle, Edward, Capt. 826
Arman & Lake 826
Arnold, Aaron 838, 935+
  Bettie 936
  Cora Cordelia 936
  Dora 936
  James 833
  John 838
  Josiah, Rev. 846(2)
  Pearl 937
  Sally 935
  William 804(2), 821, 824
  Willis 844

Arnold, Cont.
  Wyatt 833
  Wyly 833, 935
  Wyly #2 936
Arthur & Stevens 827
Ary, Daniel 815
Askew, J. 839
  Nannie 954
Aspy, Jack 801
Atchison, Martha Jane 938
  S. M. 836
Atkins, Bettie 891, 908
  Clintie 891
  Eldridge 824(2)
  Henry L. 935
  J. D. C. 821(4), 890+, 909
  J. D. C., Gen. 901, 908
  John 818, 890, 909
  John D. 891
  Mary A. 909
  Mary S. 909
  Mattie 891
  Sallie 901
  Sarah 891
  S. Eveline 935
Avery, George 847
Aycock, Robert 819
Ayers, R. W., Capt. 842, 843
  Samuel B. 824, 841
  Walter 841
Babb, Philip 816
Babbitt, H., Rev. 846
Baber, W. F. 836
Baker, Amanda (Shilling) 945
  Elia 908
  Mary E. 874
  Robert, Rev. 812, 831, 874
  T. H. 809, 839
Baldwin, Lewis, Rev. 830
Ballard, G. W., Lieut 843
  H. W. 826
Balmforth, J. 887
Banks, Thomas 801, 802
Barbee, Elizabeth 922
  T. O. 820
Barecroft, Daniel 800
  William 800
Barfield, Mary 943
Barger, J. S. 891+
  Sammie Eva 892
  W. O. 891
Barham, Delia 905
  N. J. 907
Barker, I. M. L. 806
  Zachary 833
Barnes, Charles 937
  Edmond B. 836
  J. A. 936+
  James H. 936
  John P. 936
  Thomas E. 936
  William 834
Barnett, John 822, 833
  Mansfield 834
Barr, W. F., Dr. 940
Bartlett, J. S. 954
Barton, Adolphas H. 892
  Benjamin J. 892
  C. C. 888
  Eldorado 892
  Hamilton H. 892
  J. Wade 892+
  Mary A. 892
  Mrs. 904
  Orion C. 892
  Patsy 921
  Scott W. 892
  A. O. 893
Bate, William B. 862

Bateman & Herrin 838
Beadles, Alice, Mrs. 904
Beard, Burrell 834, 836, 837(2)
  Richard, Rev. 831
Beasley, Blanch 914
  Daniel E. 914
  Sue 920
Beaton, Nancy 946
Beauchamp, Marietta 901
Beauford, Gen. 925
Beckerdite, L. M. 803
  L. W. 806
Belew, Ada 848
  Jacob 847
  James S. 848
  John G. 847+
  Ludie 848
  Martha 877
  Mettie 848
  Robert L. 848
  Thomas 807(2), 848
  William E. 848
Bell, A. 839
  D. D. 821
  Elmira N. 943
  John 879, 912
  Martha (?) 884
  Seth W., Dr. 807(2)
Bell-Everett Ticket 862
Bell, ___ 915
Bellow, James, Leiut 842(2)
Beman, Lila S. 921
Benjamin, Charles 833
Benton, A. 803
  David 833, 834
  Jesse 798
  Nathan 798
  Samuel 798, 833
  Thomas H. 798
  W. C. 836
Bethel, Green 797
Bibbs, John, Lieut. 844
Bigham, Mathews 803
  S. Y., Dr. 797
  William, Rev. 797, 813
Biles, Mary 896
Black, Caroline 884
  Oliver 946
Blackemore, R. M., Mrs. 929
Blair, Harriet 886
Blake, Bettie Lee 893
  Charley Waterfield 893
  Eugene 893
  James 893
  John J. 893+
  Luna 893
  Sallie 893
Blakemore, R. M. 820
Blanchard, Mary 852
Blanton, E. H. 828
  J. W. 907
  Maria L. 899
Blanton & James 827
Bledsoe, Jacob 801
  Yancey 803
Blount, Aquilie 849
  Frances Elizabeth 849
  Isaac 798, 848
  Isaac C. 849
  John G. 816, 848+
  Josephine 849
  Larcena 849
  Lovey 848
  Lovie L. 849
  Rosena 849
  Thomas 816
  Wiley W. 849
Blythe, Joseph 819

Bolton, C. A. 882
Bomac (?), Sarah E. 861
Bomar, Calvin 840
  E. P. 918
  James 820
  Mattie 923
  Reuben 814
  Robert J. 836
Bomar & Porter 918
Bond, James 821
Bone, John 800
Booth, Eliza 898
  John L. 822
Boucher, Joshua 832
Bowden, Caroline B. 928
  Clemmie J. 934
  Dr. 829
  Louisa A. 893
  Margaret 860
  Mary T. 928
  Penelope 924
Bowen, John C. 804
Bowles, Joshua 948
  Matthew C. 820
Bowlin, Frances 871
Boyd, Headley 829
  James 822
  John H. 802
Bradford, Alex. B. 805
  Crawford 815, 819
Bradley, A. L. 827
  Eliza 897
  N. 914
Bradley & Bomar, Drs. 914
Brady, C. J., Rev. 811
Bragg, Gen. 843(3)
Bramley, Dossie P. 849
  J. H. 849+
  J. P. 849
  S. D. (Smith) 849
Brandon, Mattie 898
  Minerva 898
  N., Col. 898
Brandon, ___ 841
Braswell, Jacob, Dr. 815
  O. F. 820, 827
  Sol. C. 824
Bratton, James, Mrs. 922
Breckenridge, John C. 890, 908, 926, 954
Brewer, Capt. 818
  David 836(4)
  E. 849
  H. C. 806
  Keziah A. 849
  Lewis 833, 834(2)
  Nicholas 833
  Scott, Rev. 846
  Sterling 799, 800, 818
Briant, Aaron R. 850
  Albert D. 850
  Alfred 849+
  Capt. 862
  David B. 850
  Gardner M. (Ca.) 850
  Reuben 849/50
  Reuben A. 850
  Sarah A. 850
  Thomas J. 850
  William H. 850
Bricken, Morgan 816
Bridges, H. T. 807
  Willis, Rev. 812
Brigham, Mathis 805
Britt, John 866
  Sophia 866
Broach, Berry 823
  J. H., Mrs. Dr. 900
  S. S. 821
Brooks, G. K., Dr. 828
  Michael 816
  T. B. 803
Brown, Araby 815

Brown, Cont.
  B. C. 824
  Benjamin C. 820, 821, 824
  Clemmie J., Mrs. 934
  Elizabeth 947
  Henry H. 803
  Henry M. 821
  H. H. 802
  Isabella W. 890
  J. A. 827
  James S. 824
  J. B. 824
  John 800, 815, 827
  John C. 839
  Leonora Ann 949
  Louisa M. 888
  Milton 806(2), 821
  S. A. 802
Brown, ___ 862
Browne, Albert Gentry 894
  George H. 894+
  William 894
Browne & Co. 894
Browning, Benjamin, Rev. 846
  Jacob, Rev. 830, 846
Brownlow, Gov. 805, 841
Bruce, Amos 836
  Barney, Mrs. 849
  C. J., Mrs. 849
  D. A. 836
  D. A., Lieut. 844(2)
  Mrs. 828
Brummitt, John B., Mrs. 911
Bryant, A. D. 851+
  Alfred 802(3), 851
  Alfred, Capt. 807
  Cullen 814
Buchanan, E. 894
  James 898, 910, 932
  J. W. 894
  President 829
  Sallie E. 894
  Thomas 894
Bullock, Joe H. & Co. 827
  Obidiah 936
  Silas 951
  Silas W. 936+
Bullock & Cantrell 839
Bunch, B. B. 821
  B. B. Capt. 826
  Bryan 822
  Henry M. 811
Bunn, M. 807
Burradelle, Elizabeth 883
Burrow, Banks 851
  Banks W. 800, 801, 802
  George H. 852
  Harriett E. 852
  John J. 851+
  N. B. 806
  N. B., Lieut. 806
  Reuben, Rev. 797, 813
Burton, Samuel H. 834, 837
  Thomas H. 837
Busby, ___ 829
Busey, Edward 805 (2)
  Frances W. 859
Butler, Joshua 798
Byers, C. R. P. 809
Byrn, J. P. 839
  Mary 936
  Mary E. 936
  Stephen 936
Cable, Maria C. 911
Cage, J. H. W. 810
Caldwell, Albert B. 895
  Alice 895, 896
  James 815, 895
  Juliett 896
  Mary 895
  Mary Ann (Willis), Mrs. 932
  Mary R. 895
  Minerva 895

Caldwell, Cont.
  Minnie L. 911
  O. B., Lieut. 842
  R. D. 896, 932
  R. D., Col. 815, 817
  Robert D. 896
  Robert D., Col. 895
  R. P. 821
  Samuel H., Dr. 895
  S. H., Dr. 895+
  William H. 896
  William M. 932
  Yancy Quitman 895
Callicott, Mary 928
Camp, George 834
  Henry C. 846
  H. K., Leiut. 843, 844
Campbell, Alexander 888
  Daniel 816
Canon, A. H. 852
  E. M. 852+
  Emma E. 852
  J. M. 852
  John 852+
  R. F. 852
  T. W., Rev. 852
Cantrell, George 937
Caraway, William 839(2), 936(2), 937+, 939(2), 948, 950(2)
Cardwell, A. M. 803
  A. W. 826
Carleton, Ann E. 913
Carnal, Fannie L. 853
  James E. 853
  Joshua 853
  Lizzie P. 853
  M. DeWitt 853+
  Martha D. 853
  William 853
Carnes, Irwin B. 837, 846
  James B. 834
Carraway, William 840
Carroll, Gov. 800
Carson, Ann E. 855
  Mary 900
  William H. 853
  William M. 853+
Carter, Alice Ray 896
  John M. 827
  Landon 816
  May F. 896
  W. A. 828
  William L. 896(2)
  William L., Jr. 896+
  W. L. 825
Carter & James 896
Carter & Priest 808
Caruthers, Virginia 953
Cary, Aaron 822
Cashon, Elam 797
Cass, Lewis 893, 900, 939, 951
Castile, J. M. 836(2)
Castlione, Jos. 816
Cavitt, Josiah 815
  Joseph 816
Chalmers, James K. 804
  W. P. 810
Champion, S. A. 821, 824, 910+
Chance, Sarah 927
  Susannah 927
  Thomas, Rev. 927
Chappell, Edwin B., Rev. (B.A.) 812
  E. R., Rev. 860
Chase, L. B. 821
Cheek, Ethridge & Co. 810
Chenoweth, Richard 930
  Virginia 930
Cherry, Albert G. 897 (2)
  L. 897+

Cherry, Cont.
  Lafayette 897
Cherry & Purath 897
Childress, J. R. 836
  L. 839
Churchwell, A. R. B. 807
Clark, David 798
  J. J. 810
  John, Col. 874
  John R. 802
  Julia B. 883
  Kelly 810
  L. W., Capt. 807
  Rachel B. 874, 915(2)
Clark & Morrison 808
Clay, Henry 849, 851, 954
Clements, Calvin 871
  Cynthia 871
  Mary E. 871
Clendening, Mary H. 854
  Robert 854
Cockrill, Granville LaForce 859
  John 860
  Sallie Louise 859
Cockrill, ___ 860
Coffman, Isaac 897
  John M. 897
  Wm. M. 897+
Cole, Jesse 798
  J. T. W. 827, 828
  Richard 798
  R. P. 824
Coley, Maria 921
Collins, R. D. 819
  Robert, Rev. 846
Combs, Frances R. 944
  J. H. 842
Connell, Walter 805
Conway, Capt. 888
  T. H. 826
  Thomas H. 821
Conyer, Pack. 829
Conyers, James, Rev. 820
Cook, Alice A. 878
  J. C. 841
  John 878
  John W. 805, 824, 827, 828
  J. W. 834
  Lillian 930
Cooke, J. W. 824, 825
Cooley, Daisy 898
  Harry 898
  Henry 898
  Mamie 898
  Maurice 898
  Minerva 898
  Simeon W. 898+
  William 898
  William M. 898
Cooney, Henrietta 910
  T. 826
Cooper, Abner, Rev. 797, 813, 846
  A. E., Rev. 854+
  Eliza A. 854
  Isles 854
  J. P. 827
  Martha L. 854
  Mary A. 854
  Robert A. 854
  S. C. 854
  William F. 854
  W. J., Mrs. 947
Copeland, Solomon 821
Corbett, Amos 836
  Meredith 842(2)
  M. S., Capt. 842 (2)
  M. S., Rev. 846
  S., Captain 826
Cornell, E. M. 838(2)
Corum, J. M. 828
Cottingham, William 833
Couch, Rev. 830, 831
Coulter, J. M. 803(2)

Covington, Bettie 916
  Nannie 903
  Nannie A. 903
  Susie 916
  W. L. 903
Cowell, Frances 952
  Joseph 833
  Sarah J. 953
Cox, Elizabeth 922
  Green D. 855
  Henry, Mrs. 879
  James B., M. D. 855+
  Mary 876
Cox, ___ 952
Craig, James 833
Crawford, Mr. 874
Crider, Catharine 941
  John D. 865
  R. H. 797
  W. A. 797
Crittendon, Flora Elizabeth 868
Crockett, Alice 884
  Davey 931
  David 803, 804(2)
  David, Col. 821(2)
  John 797, 801(2), 808, 813
  John W. 821
  W. G. 797, 807, 813
Croff, Capt. (Federal) 826
Crossett, W. R., Mrs. 871
Croswell, J. R. 821
Cruise, David 824
Crump, Sophia 925
Crutcher, John H. 821
Crutchfield, Charles 816
  Delilah 889
  Thomas 821
Culp, Daniel 815, 819, 826
Cummins, H. F. 828
Cunningham, Amanda 880
  John 880
  Sarah A. 880
Curlin, Charlotte 942
Currier, Ann 899
  Bettie 899
  Bettie M. 931
  James C. 899
  John Nathaniel 899
  John T. 899+
  John T. & Co. 899
  Maria 931
  Maria, Mrs. 817
  Nathaniel 899, 931
Currier, Mann & Peters 817
Curtis, Alice 855
  Harriet Ella 855
  John 855
  John William 855
  Lillian Howard 855
  Mrs., Dr. 853
  Thomas C. 855
  W. E., Dr. 855+
Dale, Isaac 916
  Jane 916
  Maggie 916
Dalton, Timothy 818
Daniel, Dosia 932
Darwin, Mr. 828
Davidson, Daisy 937
  John W. 836, 840
  L. Berry 937(2)
  Martha 939
  Travis 836, 841, 937+
  William 937
  William W. 836
  W. W. 836
Davis, Arthur 831
  David 822
  L. E., Mrs. 838, 939
  Mahala 878
  Mary 895
  W. O. 802

Dawson, A., Mrs. 932
  Elizabeth 932
  Jonathan 805
  W. F. 827
DeBruce, John 839
Deloach, William 815
Demoss, Lewis 797, 804, 805
Denman, Mollie 880
Denney, B. A. 856+
  George 856
  James T. 856
  John D. 856
  Maggie M. 856
  Robert C. 856
Dickens, J. L., A. M., B. D. 856+
  John L., Rev. 812
  Robert G. 856
Dickerson, Malinda 876
Dickson, Elizabeth 852
Dickey, G. W. 856
  Mary M. 856
Diggs, H., Dr. 899
  Harriet Lee 893
  J. D. 900
  John H. 899
  Lula B. 900
  N. E. 920
  R. K. 900
  R. P. 820
  W. C. 820(2)
Dill, Martin 802
Dinwiddie, Callie C. 900
  Eliza Ellen 900
  J. A., Mrs. 900
  James 900
  James M. B. 900
  John N. 900
  J. R. B. 900+
  Mary M. 900
  Nancy Lee 900
  Priscilla Gordon 900
  Sarah H. 853
  Thomas B. 900
  William Floyd 900
Dinwiddie, ___ 816
Dinwiddie & Co. 900
Dixon, Joseph 804
Dobbins, Mr. 918
Dobbins & Parker 918
Doherty, John 837
  W. F., Col. 840
  Wm. F. 838
Donaldson, Mary 932
Doty, F. E. 827
Dougherty, James W. 806
  J. W. 806
  R. E. C. 797, 798, 800, 805
  Robert E. C. 803
  William 806
Douglass, Emma 901
  I. G. 901
  J. W. 901
  Loula 901
  Mary J. 901
  R. C. 901
  R. E. 900
  R. E., Jr. 901
  Sallie 901
  Thomas, Dr. 837
  W. J. 900
Dowdey, J. F. 839
Drain, J. W., Dr. 838
Driver, Sarah E. 875
  William 875
Dudley, Ambrose 797
Dumas, Betty, Mrs. 921
  Emma J. 922
  Franklin F. 922
  J. D. 826
  Louisa, Mrs. 859
  Malinda, Mrs. 908

Dumas, Cont.
　Malinda I. 922
Dunlap, Bethenia A. 901
　Ellen J. 917
　Hugh 902
　Hugh P. 901
　Hugh P., Mrs. 891
　Hugh W. 815, 822, 824
　H. W. 825
　James T. 821(2), 824, 902(2)
　James T., Gen. 917
　John 901
　John H. 824, 901(2)
　Marietta 901
　Richard W. 901
　Richard W., Rev. 901
　Ripley E. 902(2)
　Squire 826
　Susan E. 901
　W. A. 819, 901+
　William A. 825, 826, 901
　William C. 841
　Will C. 824
Dunlap & Bro. 827
Dunn, Sarah 853
Dunn & Crutchfield 827
Dupree, Sarah 895
Dupree, ___ 823
Eastwood, Abel 902
　Alice 902
　Hannah 902
　John 902
　Joseph 902
　Mary 902
　Richard 902
　Robert 902+
Edgar, Lewis M., Rev. 830
Edmonds, Mary A. 894
Edmonson, Reuben 859
Edmunds, Cora 803
　Hinda 903
　John J. 902
　Nellie 903
　Sallie 903
　Samuel C., Dr. 902+
　S. C., Dr. 828
　William 903
Edwards, Elizabeth 929
　Nancy 854
　Nathaniel 885
　Owen H. 821
　Sarah 922
　W. J. 885
Elkins, Alsey 818
Ellison, T. B. 933
Embry, Michael 816
Enloe, B. A. 803, 821
Enochs, Enoch 804, 805
Espey, James 871
Ethridge, Elijah 820(2)
　Emerson 821(3), 887
Evans, Joseph H. 832
Everett & Bullard 808
Falkner, Birdie 858
　Capt. 883
　E. 858+
　Elijah 802
　Elijah J. 858
　G. J. 858
　Joe 858
　Lula 858
　Nancy 858
　Wayne 858
Farabough, W. W. 825
Farmer, A. J. 836, 840, 939+
　Carrie 939
　Catharine 938
　Cave 837
　Eunice 939
　Florence E. 939
　George W. 833, 834, 938
　Ichabod 836, 939
　J. H. 837

Farmer, Cont.
　John H. 803, 836, 837,
　　938+
　Keziah 939
　Mattie 939
　Myrtle 939
　Thomas N. 939
　T. M., Mrs. 913
　Vernon A. 939
　William I. 939
Farrar, Matilda 923
Farris, John 826
Felt, Gertrude 868
　Mabel 868
　Minor 868
Fentress, James 799, 800, 818
Ferrell, George 854
Fields, Alexander 873
　Martha J. 873
　Rebecca 927
Fillmore, Millard 865, 927
Finley, Elizabeth, Mrs. 934
　J. 808
　N. E. 839
　Thomas 804
Fitzgerald, Adeline 931
　Edward, Capt. 825
　Edwin 824
　Judge 888
　William 821, 823, 824(3),
　　841
　William, Judge 931
Fleming, Samuel W. 830
Flowers, Green 834(2), 836,
　　844
Floyd, Austocia 866
Forrest, Jane, Mrs. 824
　Mr. 823
　Nathan Bedford, Gen. 826, 862,
　　876, 879, 926, 934, 935
　Shim 824
Foster, Emma E. 913
　Matilda 913
　Mrs. 904
　T. H. 913
Fowler, J. E. 826
Fox, Nathan 797
Francisco, Diana 861
Frazier, C. 827
　Connie 903
　Constantine 819, 820, 821,
　　822, 903+
　D. W. 903
　H. E. 903
　Irma 903
　Julian 821
　Lottie 903
　Sarah J. 903
Freeland, Allen, Mrs. 894
　A., Rev. Dr. 811
　Beulah J. 904
　Col. 873
　Eliza 933
　Henrietta V. 933
　J. C. 933
Freeman, H. V. 828
　James M. 904
　John C. 904
　Lena 904
　Maggie 904
　Mary Alice 904
　M. H. 820, 826, 903+, 912
Freeman, Lasater & Co. 827,
　　912
Frey, Michael 833
Frick, Elizabeth 874
Fry, "Bud" 842
　J. D. 946
　Olivia 946
Fryer, George L. 904
　John 904
　John H. 904
　Lilian 904

Fryer, Cont.
　Robert N. 904
　T. C. 825, 828
　Thomas C. 904
　Thomas L. 904
　T. L. 825
　William L. 904
Fuqua, Armon E. 847
　Joseph 847
　J. P. 847
　Mary 847, 888
　William, Mrs. 854
Gainer, James C. 819, 820(2)
　Jesse C. 822
Gaines, B. M. 807
　Virginia 938
Galbreath, L. W., A. M. 812
Gallion, Frank B. 896
　L. 896
　Sarah Alice 896
Gardner, Hester B. 864
　James N. 803
　John A. 821
Garfield, Gen. 874
　James A. 855
Garrett, Lewis, Jr. 832
　Miss 881
Gates, William 828
　W. W. 809
Gee, James H. 797, 801,
　　804, 805
Gibbs, George W. 805
Gilbert, A. G. 809
　Benjamin 858
　B. P. 806
　Elizabeth 868
　J. B. 869
　J. M. 797
　J. M., Sr. 858+
　Robert 797
　Samuel 906
　Samuel, Lieut. 842
Gilbert (Negro) 823
Gilbert, Stofle & Co. 882
Giles, M. C. 871
Gillespie, B. 824
　Berry 806
　David 797
　Mary J. 953
Gilliam, Devereaux 902
　Susanna 902
Gillum, R. M., Rev. 846
Goldston, Martha 91
Goldston & McGehee 827
Gooch, James, Capt. 879
Goodlin, Mrs. 950
Goodloe, A. Theodore, Rev.,
　　Dr. 89
Granville, M. A. 812, 859+
Gordon, Louisa J. 904
　Sallie Lee 900
　W. L. 836
Gossett, David A. 836
Grable, Mary J. 905
　Nervy 905
　Samuel A. 904
　S. J. 904+
　Virgie Lee 905
Grace, Capt. 818
Graham, Lewis 833
　R. M. 839
Graham & Grainger 839
Grainger, John 823
　R. A., Jr., Dr. 828
Grant, Gen. 917
　Pres. 876
Graves, Allen T., Rev. 812
　William H. 802
Gray, Catherine 891
　Thomas 803, 815, 818, 820
Greeley, Horace 896, 933,
　　935, 939
Green, Hezekiah 834

Green, Cont.
  John 798
Green, ___ 798
Greer, Alma 940
  A. P. 824
  Aquilla P. 824
  Bird 823
  Clarice 940
  David S. 825, 826
  David Searcy 815, 819
  Green B. 836, 843, 939+
  Hezekiah 939
  James 815(2), 819, 940
  James, Capt. 931
  Jesse H. 940
  Lena 940
  Nixon 940
  Robert S. 940
  W. J. 836
Grizzard, Edmund 808
  G. W. 808
  Mollie, Mrs. 808
  W. B. 802
  W. R. 803
Grizzard & Algee 809
Grove, E. W. 827
Guin, Edward 860
  R. D., Dr. 860+
Guthrie, James C. 820
  William, Rev. 846
Gwin, Edward 800, 802, 804, 805
  John 797, 800, 805, 808
  Mary 874
Hagler, J. L., Maj. 825
  Joel 814
  Willis T. 814
Haley, Ada 840
  Mary S. 940
  R. P. 836, 838
Haliburton, Samuel 834
Hall, A. B. 807
  A. C., Lieut. 844
  A. P. 893, 807
  A. R. 802, 808
  Archibald C. 804
  B. F., Lieut. 843
  E. P., Capt. 807
  Jesse D. 834
  Tennessee 939
  Thomas 808
  William H. 803
Hall & Sharp 837
Hallum, Clinton 905
  Frankie 905
  Katie 905
  Mollie 905
  Morris 905
  Susan 905
  W. D. 826
Hallum, W. D., Capt. 905+
  William 905
Hallum, ___ 905
Hamby, Robert J. 820
Haman, W. R. 838
Hamilton, Elizabeth 852(2)
  Ephraim 832
  James 911
  John C. 824(3)
  Joseph 807
  Lee, Rev. 846
  Sarah 911
  Thomas 797, 800, 852
  William 797, 858
Hampton, James 797
  Noah 849
  Winnie R. 849
Hancock, Evan W. 906
  General 894, 899
  Green D. 906+
  Henry 906
  Harry D. 906
  James W. 906

Hancock, Cont.
  Nettie Anna 906
  Priscilla 906
  Vera Edna 906
Hancock & McVay 906
Hankins, Samuel 819, 830(2)
Hanna, Erin 888
Harcourt, T. C., Dr. 901
Hardin, Obediah, Rev. 846
Harding, Obediah, Rev. 846
Harding, Henry 830
Harding, ___ 860
Hardy, Drusilla 903
  Mary Ann 892
Harman, Alex 815
Harmon, Adam 938
  Catherine 938(2)
Harris, George L. 802
  George W. D., Rev. 832(3), 846
  Gov. 931
  Isham G. 821(2), 824
  John W. 822
  Nancy 877
  Richmond S. 832
  William 797, 798
  William R. 824(3), 841
Harris, ___ 862
Harrison, Benjamin F. 802
  B. F. 803, 806
  J. H., Rev. (A.B.) 812
  William 803
Hart, Catharine 912
  George 912
  James 877
  Nannie 912
  Susan 877
  U. 877
Hartsfield, Andrew 814
Harvey, Emily 851
  Frances 924
Harwood, John W., Capt. 807
Haskell, Josuah 823, 824
  Joshua, Judge 805
  Wm. T., Col. 806
Hastings, A. E. 803(2)
  Andrew E., Dr. 861+
  John 861
  Guy M. 861
  Rufus B. 861
Hatley, Eli 836
Hawkins, A. G. 803(2), 806
  Albert G. 806, 824, 862+, 884
  Alonzo 806
  Alvin 806, 807(2), 813, 837, 840, 861+
  Alvin, Capt. 842
  Ashton W. 806
  A. W. 803
  A. W., Capt. 806, 807(2)
  A. W., Dr. 807, 809, 813
  Clarence M. 863
  Commillis 806
  E. M. (Wright) 887
  Hugh R. 864
  Isaac G. 864
  Isaac R. 82, 862, 863, 872
  Isaac R., Col. 806, 807(2)
  Isaac R., Lieut. 806
  J. C. 806
  John M. 861
  Jo. R. 841
  Joseph R. 806, 824
  Leslie O. 863
  L. L. 803, 806, 841
  L. L., Judge 805, 871, 887
  Lucien L. 824
  Prince A. 863
  Samuel 863
  Samuel W., Capt. 863+
  S. W. 806(3), 939
  Thomas A. 802

Hawkins, Cont.
  William H. 809
  W. H., Capt. 807
  William, Capt. 935
  William H. 864
Hawkins & Townes 944
Hawley, Adam M., Dr. 940+
  Josephine 936
  Lula C. 941
  Orrin, Lieut. 843
  R. M. 838(2)
  William 940
Hawthorne, Robert 834
  Robert H. 836
Hayes, Benjamin A. 832
  Minerva 907
Haynes, James, Rev. 830
  John P. 907
  Martha J. 907
  Minerva E. 906
  Preston G. 820, 906+
  Preston G., Capt. 825
  Thomas 906
Hays, Mary 867
  President 876
Haywood, Edward 837
  James 837
Head, J. J. 828
Head & Carter 827
Hearn, S. C. 821
  S. C., Rev. 828
Heggie, J. T., Lieut. 843
Henderson, James M. 803
  Mattie A., Mrs. 875
Hendricks, Samuel 808
  W. W., Rev. 811
Henry, T. A. 836, 840, 841
  William, Rev. 831
Hern, George 802
Herrin, Lemuel, Rev. 846
  W. R., 843
Hicks, A. J., Lieut. 844
  James 814, 821, 826
  John 820
Hill, Elizabeth 916
  Ella 944
  Emma 942
  Ida 948
  Joseph 820
  M. R. 803
Hilliard, Albert 864+
  Albert E. 864
  Arthur 864
  Elia 865
  Edie May 865
  Eliza 865
  Emma 865
  Fannie 865
  John B. 864
  Linnie E. 864
  Louisa Essie 865
  Minnie Lee 864
  Richard H. 864
  Rightmon 864
  Sebron J. 865
  Walter G. 864
  W. H. 864+
  William 864
  William S. 864
  W. J. 865
Hillsman, Mary A. 895
  Reddick 797, 798, 895
Hogg, Dr. 808
  James 834
Hoggard, Frances 881
Holaday, George W. 802
Holladay, C. 864
  Emily 864
  George 864
  George W. 941
  John M. 941+
  J. M. 836
  J. M. & Bro. 941

Holladay, Cont.
  S. W. 941+
Holland, Benjamin 833
  Penelope 952
  R. S. 820
  Spearman 820, 821
Hollowell, George 836, 844
  George, Rev. 846
Holsapple & Hutchins 828
Holt, Elizabeth 927
  Sarah 940
  William 822
Honnell, Peter 804(2)
Hooten, Jasper, Lieut. 844(2)
Hoover, Jacob 821
Horn, Mahala P. 878
Hornberger, Nancy 945
Horton, John 821
  William 797
House, Everett 822
  George 818
  John 818
  John B. 815
Howard, James 816
  J. S., Rev. (A.M.) 811
Howard & Pearce 827
Howard & Powell 827
Howell, Rachel J. 906
  Thomas 906
Hubbard, Josiah 806
Hubbs, William 833, 834, 845, 942
  William T., M. D. 942+
  W. T. 838
  W. T., Dr. 838
Hudson, A. J. 839
  Albert J. 943
  Carlos N. 943
  Charles M. 944
  Charles P. 907
  Dorsey G. 944
  Dorsey P. 833, 834(2), 836(2), 943
  D. P. 844
  Ed., Lieut 842
  Elihu 944
  Eula Lee 944
  F. G., M. D. 943+
  G. W. L. 836
  Henry 943
  Holman 942
  Isaac M. 824
  James G. 836(2), 942
  J. G. & Co. 943
  J. H. 942+
  Jo. G. 942+
  John James 943
  Joseph G. 838
  Joseph U., Dr. 943
  Oaks J. 942
  Susan Stella 944
  W. H. 912
  William E. 942
  William H. 907+
Hudson & Son 839
Hughes, Lucy B. 937
  Robert 804, 805
  William 938
Humble, Benjamin 866
  George 865
  G. W. 802, 865+
  G. W., Judge 805, 813
  Jacob 865
Humphreys, Fisher 908
  Henry 815, 907
  Henry A. 907+
  Jennie 908
  J. P., Dr. 921
  Lillie 908
  Maud 908
  Winnie G. 921
Hunt, Mimucan 800
  Minucan & Co. 798

Hunt, Cont.
  Thomas 800
  Thomas, Dr. 798
  William 917
Hunter, Atkins 908
  Elihu 908
  F. F., Mrs. Prof. 891
  T. H. M., Prof. 908+
Huntsman, Adam 821
Hurst, W. J. 821
Hurt, Eliza 904
  Graville C. 803
  James, Rev. 797, 813
  Robert, Rev. 797, 813
  W. J. 822
Ingg, Mary 925
Ingman, Sarah 880
Ingram, James 806
  Samuel 797, 800, 801, 802, 804(2), 808
Irby, H. C., Capt. 812
  Jane 847
Jackson, Andrew 852
  John 834
James, ___ 862
Jamison, Robert 804
Janes, W. M. 821, 825, 896
Jeffrey, James 838
Jennings, Dudley S. 818
  Thomas 806
Jewell, Martha 918
Johnson, Abner 818
  A. J. 853
  Andrew 824, 862
  Annetta D. 866
  Cave 821
  Cordila 865
  Dora 866
  Elvira Jane 947
  Felix, Rev. Dr. 811
  Frank 808
  Gen. 860
  James 866
  James Clarence 866
  James M. 865
  Johanna 882
  John F. 834
  Joseph A. 802
  J. P. 865
  Louisa E. 865
  Martha 853
  Nnaommaah 884
  Rev. 812
  R. J. 850
  Tilman 859
  William 866+
Johnson & Vancleave 827
Johnston, Gen. 909
Jones, Annie 866
  B. B. 866
  B. F. 866+
  Calvin 806, 824
  C. C. 866
  Cecil Hill 944
  C. F. 866
  David 827
  Delany 864
  Harry E. 944
  James 818, 821
  J. H. 866
  John 866
  Joseph E. 841(2), 944+
  Laura 866
  L. M. 807
  Mary C. 866
  Miss 865
  R. L. 866
  R. R. 866
  Sarah 944
  S. L. 866
  Sol. 908+
  Solomon 909
  Solomon, Capt. 843

Jones, Cont.
  T. F. 827
  Thomas 833, 836, 908, 909
  Thomas E. 944
  W. B. 866
  William 814
  William A. 836(2), 908+
  William A., Capt. 843
Jordan, Archibald, Lieut. 842
  M. D. L. 803(2)
Joyner, Thomas 832(2)
Julian, Margaret F. 904
Justice, Allen, Rev. 846
Keaton, Beatrice 867
  C. W. 867
  Elizabeth 867
  Ella 867
  Emma 867
  J. H. 867+
  John D. 867
  Laura A. 867
  Mary 867
Leach, Sallie 867
Kellow, Mary 933
Kelly, Melvina B. 946
Kelough, John 804
Kelsey, George R. 844
Kemp, G. A. 843
Kendall, Eli 929
  Louisa 929
Kennerly, Carrie V. 910
  Charles 910
  Charles M. 910
  John W. 910
  Joseph 910
  Mattie Eliza 910
Key, Thomas L., Mrs. 879
Kilbreath, John 834
Killebrew, Rebecca 892
Kilmer, Adam, M. D. 867+
  Daniel 867
King, Clinton, Capt. 807
  Col. (CSA) 827
  William M. 837
  Winnie R., Mrs. 849
King, ___ 834
Kirk, W. G. 836
Kirkland, Levi 845
Komez, John 805
Kuykendall, Jesse 815, 816
Kyle, Barney C. 868
  Emma D. 868
  James D. 868
  John S. 868
  Mora 868
  Robert B. 868
  Robert G. 868+
  William M. 868
Lacy, Amos H. 818
  Capt. 818
Lake, Armer & Co. 808
Lamb, A. B. 910+
  Benjamin F. 824, 910
  Charlie B. 901
  J. J. 821, 824
  J. P., Mrs. 922
Landreth, Martha 904
Langley, Mary J. 937
Lankford, Adolphus 911
  Anna S. 911
  D. M. 911+
  Henry 911
  James M. 911
  John H. 911
  Perina Jane 911
  Robert H. 911
  Sarah M. 911
  Sidney C. 911
  Theresa A. 911
  Thomas J. 911
  William E. 911
Lannon, W. D. 824
Lasater, Calvin 911

Lasater, Cont.
  Haford 912
  Jesse 912
  Herbert 912
  John 912
  Laura 912
  Nannie 912
  Novella 912
  Rufus William 912
  W. H. 828
  William H. 911+
Lashlee, Anderson 837(3), 845/6
  George, Lieut. 842
  John P. 836
  J. P. 836
  Lewis 837
Lashlie, A. P. 838
  Cynthia 872
Lashley, Anderson 950
  Eliza 950
  Elizabeth 950
Latimer, James 802
Lauderdale, Capt. 826
Lawhon, F. E. 868
  H. C. 809, 868+
Lawler, Aaron, Capt. 844
Larence, John 815
  R. J. 836
Laws, Dudley S., M.D. 869+
  George 869+
  Hiram 869
  James 869
  James, Rev. 831
  John 869
Leach, Abner 867
  J. F. 802
  J. F. & Co. 808
  Martha M. 867
League, H. H., Maj. 827
Ledbetter, Emma 923
  William Maj. 923
Lee, George P., Mrs. 912
Lee, James 833
  Levi B., Rev. 846
Lee Bros. 808
Leeper, James 818, 820
Legg, William 873
Lehon, E. W., Rev. 887
  Sallie 887
Lemonds, David 815
  J. B. 827
  J. L. 820, 821
  John L. 912+
  Robert 821, 912
  Robert J. 912
Lewis, David 833
  J. W. 821, 825
Liggin, Peter 818, 821
Lightfoot, B. H. 836(2)
  Henry 830
  Wilson 805
Liles, M. Rev. 811
Lilly, Thomas T. 814
Lincoln, A. 872, 886
Linderman, Henry, Lieut. 842
Lindsey, Eddie 945
  Edward 944
  J. B. 839(3)
  John B. 944
  John Sherman 945
  Minnie May 945
Lipe, Aaron 810
Lockhart, Andrew J. 945
  Martha A. 945
  Mary J. 945
  Samuel 945+
  Samuel Sr. 945
  Sarah E. 945
  Sophrona A. 945
  Thomas M. 945
  William Z. 945
Lomaner, John 833

Londis, John, Dr. 930
Long, M. 826
Longacre, J. S. 821
Longford, Angeline 902
Longmire, Margaret 885
Looney, Harriet 855
  J. D., Dr. 855, 900
  J. W. 819
  Martha E. 900
  Mary E. 903
Love, John D. 803, 821(2)
  S. C. 820
  Thomas 821
  William Lieut. 843
Lovelace, Ann E. 913
  C. N., Mrs. 913
  H. H. 913+
  James R. 913
  Nat. M. 913
  Susan J. 913
Lowenstein, B. & Bro. 827
Lubin, B. 827
Lynch, Edward W. 834
Lyons, General 889
  Mr. 816
McAnulty, Mrs. 828
McAuley, E. M., Dr. 838
  J. D. 838
  John, Mrs. Dr. 936
  William M. 836
McBride, John 804
McCall, Andrew 870
  Caledonia 886
  Emma J. 871
  Fannie J. 871
  Frances 886
  George T. 809, 871
  G. W. 806
  Henry, Dr. 870, 871, 886
  J. A. 821
  James H. 871
  J. C. R. 802
  Joseph W., M.D. 870+
  J. W., Dr. 855
  Lenora J. 871
  W. A., Dr. 855
McCampbell, Andrew 806, 824(4), 924
  Benjamin B. 803, 805
  J. H. 821
  Judge 888
  Sarah F. 924
McCauley, Elizabeth 881
McClarin, Annie Myrtle 914
  Bertha L. 914
  Charles 914
  Charles J. 914
  George C. 914
  Henry B. 914
  Oswald Gross 914
  William H. 914
  W. T., Dr. 914+
  W. T., Mrs. Dr. 930
McClary, James A. 800
  Samuel A. 800
McClellan, Capt. 844
McCorkle, Lewis 815
  Margaret E. 912
  Samuel 804, 805, 815, 819, 827
McCorry, ___ 862
McCracken, Joseph 802, 808(2), 872+
  Jo. & Co. 858
  Licurgus 872
  Linnie 872
  Robert 872
  R. P. 806
  William 872
McCracken & Co. 872
McCray & Co. 873
McCollum, A. C. H. 871
  C. C. 871(2)

McCollum, Cont.
  D. A. 871
  E. C. 871
  Hugh L. 871
  J. C. 871+
  Jo. 871
  Lucus B. 871
  M. I. 871
  M. L. D. 871
  R. G. 871
  S. F. 871
McCulloh, Aaron 871/2
McCullough, Alexander 904
  Ann 904
  R. W. 827
McDade, P. W. 839
McDaniel, A. G. 836
  A. G. & Bro. 838
  Anna 946
  Archibald C. 946+
  Archibald G. 946
  Beta 946
  Beulah 946
  Eugene 946
  George 833
  J. C. 836, 837
  John 945
  John C. 945+
  Martha 946
  Mary 946
  Michael Alonzo 946
  Millard F. 947
  Ora 946
  Sarah 946
  Wiley 946
  William Neal 946
  William Thomas 946
McDaniel & Thompson 952
McDonald, B. W., Rev. Dr. 811
  McDowell, Gracie 874
  J. L. Rev. 874
  M. S. 874
McElyea, Daniel 845
  D. F. 836, 837
  F. A. 836
  F. G. & F. A. 838
  Lindsey 839
McEwen, Bettie 872
McFarland, Edward J. 820, 821
  E. J. 827
  James W. 832
McFarland & Aycock 827
McGarety, Gensey 934
McGee, James P. 829
McGill, Arthur 874
  Elizabeth 940
  E. T. 873, 886
  Gracie M. 874
  H. D., M.D. 873+
  Maggie May 874
McGowan, Samuel 818, 820
  Samuel, Rev. 819, 830
McIver, Duncan 803
McKee, John 800
McKelvy, J. W., Mrs. 852
McKenzie, Amelia 858
  Caroline 947
  Catherine 946
  Easter 947
  Gilbert 946+
  James M. 809
  Jethro 947
  John 798
  John P. 947
  Malcomb 836
  Malcolm 946
  M. A. Q. 804
  Martha A. 947
  Nancy 947
  W. L. 836
McKenzie & McClintock 809
McKernan, John 806

McKinney, G. W., Mrs. Dr. 878
  J. R. 803
  Mary 849
  Ralph 849
  S. A. 849
McKissick, Lewis D. 824
McKnight, J. H., Rev. 846
McLemore, Abraham 870
  John C. 826
  Martha 870
  Pernelia 870
McMackin, David 874+
  Eli A. 875
  James 874
  James William 875
  Mary A. 875
  Nancy E. 875(2)
McMeans, James R. 803, 804, 821
McNeal, A. C. & Co. 808
  J. C. 808
McNeill, A. C. 872, 874+
  Addison Lee 916
  Addison W. 874
  C. & F. W. 827
  Charley 916
  George H. 874
  James 874
  Kate 874
  Maggie E. 874
  Mattie Eva 916
  N. W. 915+
  Robert B. 874
  T. C. 827, 915+
  William L. 874(2), 915
McNeill Bros. 827
McNiel, N., Mrs. 945
McNutt, Samuel, Rev. 813
McRae, A. C. 836, 839
  Alexander 948
  Alexander C. 948+
  Anins 949
  Herman 949
  Ida A. 949
  Marvin C. 949
  William E. 949
McSwain, David 916, 930
  Eddie 916
  Horace 916
  I. A., Dr. 916+
  Lillie 916
  Marvin 916
  Prentice 916
  Rubie 916
  Sarah 930
  Willie 916
McTyeire, Bishop 832
McVale, Hezekiah 804
McVay, Ewing 906
Mackey, James, Rev. 831
Madden, Samuel 846
Madison, J. J. 820
Maiden, W. F. 948
Manly, Hamilton F. 814
  John 819
  John, Rev. 814, 830, 831
  Martha 899
  Richard 814
  Sarah 890
  William 829
Manning, Alfred 870(2)
  B. 870
  Beulah 870
  Lucy 870
  Mike 870
  Pernelia 870
  T. B. 870+
  Thomas Edward 870
  William 870
Marable, Dr. 948
Marberry, John 818, 822
Markham, Daniel 838
Marshall, David 797

Marshall, Cont.
  Nancy 905
  W. A. 807, 810
Marshall, ___ 905
Martin, Eleanor H. 912
  George W. 821(2)
  J. L. 897
  J. M. 803, 807
  John 804
  John G. 810
  M. A. 824
  Mary, Mrs. 878
  Miranda 868
  Mortimer A. 841
  Sallie 902
  Zoe 861
Mason, Daniel 834
Massey, William 822
Mathews, Rachel R. B. 941
Mathewson, Ann, Mrs. 899
Mathis, Clark M. 914
  Edward S. 914
  Emerson E. 914
  James J. 914
  John A. 914
  Josiah 913
  J. W. 913+
  Mary H. 914
Matlock, "Cos" 833
Matthews, John, Lieut. 842(2)
Matthewson, Bell 918
  Daniel 933
  Gabriella 933
  J. J., Dr. 918
  Kate 933
Maury, Abram 800, 818
Maxwell, John 815
Mayne, H. 827
Meals, Sarah 873
Mebane, Elizabeth 872
  Harris B. 872+
  Lon F. 873
  Maranza D. 873
  Margaret 866
  Mattie S. 873
  Newton H. 873
  Pitt 873
  Sarah E. 873
  Vandela 873
  W. E. 802
  William 872
  Wright 807
  Yancy 873
Mebane, Elbow & Covington 809
Meeheny, Peter 822
Melton, H., Mrs. 949
  Joseph 834
  Meritt 836
  Merritt, Rev. 846
  Nannie W. 941
  P. M. 840
  "Si" 834
Menzies, Harriett 946
Metheny, Parlee (Wyatt) 954
Milam, Irene 864
Milan, J. M., Mrs. 905
Miller, James 829
  John A. 807
  Pleasant M. (Chancellor) 805
  Preston A., Rev. (A.M.) 812
  Samuel, Mrs. 895
Millikin, Amos 815, 818
Mills, Mary 885
Milton, P. M., Capt. 843
Mimms, M. 833
Mitchell, A. H. 836(2), 843, 844
  B. G., Rev. 828
  Miss 848
  Scott 848
Mitchum, Emily, Mrs. 895
  Mrs. 890

Mizell, Hardy 815
Moiden, W. F. 840
  W. F. & Co. 839
Moise, Mr. 828
Montgomery, John 805
Moore, A. R. 875
  A. W. 875
  David 805
  Dennis V. 875
  Eliza B. 875
  George W. 820(2)
  James A. 875
  J. D. 875+
  Mary 866
  Mary A. 875
  Nancy 875
  Olivia A. 887
  Robert S. 875
  Sarah 866
  Stephen H. 875
  William, Col. 887
  Yancy 866
Moore, ___ 875 (grandmother)
Moore, & Wilson 827
Morgan, Theophilus 805
Morris, Adelaide 948
  A. J. 838
  Claudie L. 914
  Elbert E. 914
  Granville T., Dr. 948
  Granville T., Jr. 914
  G. T. 827, 839(2)
  G. T., M. D. 914+
  Isaac 947
  John P. 836(2)
  John Pitts 948
  Leehentz 948
  Louisa C. 948
  Minnie 914
  T., Dr. 950
  Virgil F. 948
  W. D. 895
  William L. 948
  William P. 947+
  W. P. 836(2), 837, 838(2), 914
  W. P., Lieut. 842
Morrison, Mary 904
Moses, G. T. 840
  James, Dr. 837
  James M., Dr. 948+
  James M., Sr. 948
  James Hill 948
  Nellie 948
Mullinix, Pleasant 834(2)
Murray, Charles H. 876
  Eddie 876
  G. W., Gen. 875+
  H. F., Capt. 806
  James W., Rev. 876
  Joseph 876
  Robert 797, 801, 803, 808, 821, 874
  Robert M., Dr. 876
  Sarah W. 874
  W. W. 806, 891
Myrick, John W. 806
Nance, C. T. 917
  Elizabeth 917
  Ella 917
  J. A. 827
  James F. 917
  Mary A. 917
  W. C. 918
  W. F. 916
  W. T. 916+
Napier, Alonzo, Capt. 843
Neely, Andrew 798, 802
  H. L., Lieut. 807
  James M. 802
  John, Capt. 807
  John S. 798, 800
Neely, ___ 861

Nesbit, Nathan 797, 800, 801,
   804, 805
   Wilson 797
Nesbitt, Jane 865
New, William S. 801
Newland, John A. 821/22
   William 822
Newsom, Green B. 876
   James 877
   N. C., Dr. 877
   W. R. 877
   W. R., M. D. 876+
Nicholson, Robert, Dr. 808
Nixon, Chancellor 940
Nobles, Penelope 936
   Simon 834
Noell, J. H. 802
Norman, Gabriel, Dr. 808
   John 802(2), 803(2)
Norton, H. G. 820
Nunnery, "Mira", Lieut. 843
Nutt, Thomas 821
Oaks, Clara 942
Odom, P. W. 925
   P. W., Mrs. 925
Ogburn, John 917
   Richard H. 917+
Olive, Harriet 927
   Laura 927
   Leroy 927
Olive & Loving 827
Oliver, Frank (Negro) 805
Organ, Sterling 820
Orr, F. A., Mrs. 827
Ott, Ellen A. 863
   Justinia M. 862
Owenby, William, Mrs. 905
Ozment, H. H. 933
Page, Martha 893
Palmer, Marcus 877
   (?) Martha Bell 884
   Nancy 884
   W. Albert 877+
   William 822, 877, 884
Paralee, Mrs. 893
Parker, Adaline 848
   Edward B. 918+
   Edward B., Jr. 918
   Elizabeth 879
   Hugh P. 901
   J. C. 879
   John 801
   J. P. & Co. 892
   Lester L. 918
   Lou 879
   P. E. 858
   P. E., Jr. 853
   R. A. 918
   Stephen 822
Parsons, P. K. 807
Parvatt, ___ 862
Paschall, Jesse 815
   Susanna 907
Pasture, Thomas A. 810
Pate, E. E. 802
   Stephen 798
Patterson, A. R. & R. 889
   W. S. 819
Patton, William 804
Pavatt, Lemira C. 954
   S. C. 836, 840
   Stephen C. 806(2), 954
Payne, Joseph 882
   Robert 832
Peacock, Susan 879
Pearce, Aaron 822
   Abner 818, 821
Peeler, B. F., Mrs. 947
Peeples, Benjamin 822, 842
   Benjamin, Rev. 812, 814, 822,
      830, 831
   Benjamin P. 831, 845
   John R. 831

Peeples, Cont.
   Samuel 831
   Thomas 831
   William 831
Perkins, Ephraim 833, 834
Perry, Soloman 811
Peterson, ___ 829
Phifer, H. A., Mrs. 949
   John 834, 837
Philips, E. P. 858
Phillips, Amanda 879
   Charles F. 878+
   Charley (Negro) 805
   Claude 878(2)
   Edgar 878(2)
   James M. 878
   John W. 878
   Mahala P. 878
   Marina T. 878(2)
   Robert P. 878
   Rosalinda A. 878
   William 878
Pickett, William 837
Pickett & McDaniel 837
Pickett & Morris 837
Pierce, Ann E. 928
   E. A., Lieut. 843
   Franklin 866, 910
   Henry H. 949
   H. R. 949+
   James F. 949
   John 833, 949
   John W. 949
   Martha 949
   Mary C. 949
   Rachel A. 949
   Roena B. 949
   Victoria C. 949
   William 833
   W. R. 839
Pillow, J. B., Jr., Dr. 828
Pinson, Caroline 866
Pitt, Arthur 946
   Easter 946
   Mary Ann 945
   Wyley 945
Polk, James K. 867, 906, 928
Pope, John 834
Porter, Dudley 891
   Elizabeth 891
   Eveline 919
   F. F., Dr. 828
   Horace, Gen. 887
   James D. 824(2), 841
   James D., Jr. 819
   James T. 919
   James W. 918+
   J. D. 821, 901
   J. D., Gov. 891
   J. D., Jr. 803
   J. H. 826
   John, Major 814
   John C. 820(2)
   J. W. 827
   Nathaniel 919
   Nell 919
   Richard, Col. 815, 827
   Sarah E., Mrs. 901
   Thomas K. 821
   W. B. 828
   William 814, 821
   William, Col. 891
   William N., Capt. 825
Potts, Uriah A. 950+
   William S. 950
Poyner, Peter 821(2)
Presson, A. C. 836(2)
   Allen C. 836, 844
   Isaac, Lieut. 843
   J. F. 836(2), 841
   L. H. 838
   William 844
Preston, J. F. 839

Priest, Jane 872
   Napoleon 806
Priest & Son 808
Priestley, C. P. 803, 808
   J. P. 806(2)
Prince, Frank (Negro) 805
   Ellen 863
Prince, Carson & Co. 810
Pritchard, Benjamin S. 879+
   B. S. 879
   Charles 879
   Jesse 879
   J. Homes 879
   Martha J. 879
   Sherad 879
   Susan 879
Pritchell, J. W., Dr. 941
Propst, A. G. 879+
   John H. 879
   Joseph 880
   Mary 880
   Nena 880
Privince, William H. 811
Puckett, S. W. 821
Purath, E. 897
Quigley, James B. 822
Quillin, David 836
Quin, Aletha M. 851
   S. R. 851
Raines, R. P. 862
Rainwater, Booger & Co. 930
Ralston, Polly G. 861
Ralstone, George H. 806
Ramsey, James S. 803
Randall, ___ 814
Randle, B. 916
   E. H., M. A. 812
   George D. 829
   John 831, 833
   John, Maj. 829
   John H. 818, 821
   Lucy E. 915
   Peyton 818
   Richard 831
   Thomas 831
   William 829
Rankin, S. F. 803
Rasberry, Mary 951
Ray, Cornelia 867
   James, Mrs. 895
   James W. 821(2)
Reavis, John 830
Reddick, Kenneth 821
Reed, Ann Eliza 911
   Capt. 818
   Elizabeth M. (see
      Dinwiddie) 854
Reid, Amelia 876
   Elizabeth 876
   H. R., Rev. 846
   Jesse 876
Revins & McAuley 838
Richardson, J., Lieut. 806
Ridgley, Daniel 880
   E. G. 802, 808, 809, 880+
   John D. 880
Ridley, Sarah A. 854
Risen, J. R., Squire 829
   J. V. 827
Rives, John, Mrs. 936
Roach, Ann 883
   B. N., Rev. 811
   Eliza J. 877
   Isaac J. 803(2)
   J. N., Rev. 877
   M. A., Mrs. 877
Robbins, Fannie 827
Roberson, Henry, Lieut. 843
Roberts, "Bit Nose Bill" 799
   Cynthia A. 878
   Gen. 863
   Isaac 798, 804
   James H. 832

Roberts, Cont.
  J. M., Mrs. 871
  Mark, R., Senator 800
  Moses 797
  Nancy 863
  R. W. 878
Robertson, Hy., Lieut 844
  James, Gen. 860
  Joel 822
  Mary 881
Robinson, James S. 929
  Malinda G. 929
  Mary Ann H. 929
  Miss 894
  William 804
Robison, David 805
Rodgers, Sion 802(2)
Rogers, Henry 804
  J. F. 803
  J. F. 803
  Mintie 875
  Samuel 797, 815
  Sarah A. 885
  Sion 800
  Vandela 873
  W. E. 827
  William 797, 798
Rose, Robert H. 806
Ross, Addie 882
  Adeline 882
  Jane 954
  Martha 910
  Rachel 949
  Thomas 797, 808
  W. R. 882
Rosser, James, Mrs. 849
  Paley, Mrs. 849
Routon, William W., Mrs. 911
Rowe, Adam 815, 919
  Nancy E., Mrs. 920
  William M. 919+
Ruff, Peter 819
  T. B., Mrs. 866
Rumbly, Lavina 948
Rumley, Levicy 944
  Widow 805
Rushing, Able 835, 950, 951
  Alfred 837
  Alfred, Lieut. 842
  Bobbie H. 920
  B. W. 920
  Calvin, Lieut. 842
  Crawford 837
  Dennis 833, 834, 950(2)
  Dora 937, 951
  Eliza 950
  Etta 951
  Finis 951
  H. 950+
  Holden 951
  Horace 950
  Ida 951
  Jemimah M. 943
  J. M. 920+
  John 951
  John D. 834
  J. Oscar 920
  Lee 951
  Lillie 920, 950
  Lizzie 950
  Lucy 950
  Mary 951
  Mary L. 945
  Nannie M. 920
  Nat 951
  Rachel 951
  Robert 834, 920, 950(2), 951
  Robert W. 951
  Sophia 951(2)
  Thomas, Mrs. 945
  W. 844
  Walter 951

Rushing, Cont.
  W. C. 951+
  Willis 833, 835, 950, 951
Rushing & McCullough 827
Russell, Austin 842
  A. W. 839
  E. M. 918
  George S. 821
  James H. 804
  James T. 820
Russell, ___ 915(2)
Rust, Jeremiah T. 802
Rye, T. C. 841
  Wayne 836, 838
Sanders, Elias C. 881
  F. C. 802
  Furman A. 881
  Furman C. 881+
  James 881
  James B. 881
  Lavisa V. 881
  Lutie L. 881
  Martha W. 881
  Nancy O. 881
  Ollie P. 881
Scales, James 844
Scalloin, W. H. 810
Scantlin, James M., Capt. 906
Scarbrorough, Alex 822
  Sarah 954
Scott, Bettie 858
  Gen. 848
  Thomas, Lieut. 843
Sears, H. M. Rev. 812
Sellars, Nancy 858
Sessams, Sarah 855
Sessum, Arabella 896
Sevier, George 800
  Valentine 803
Sewell, Mary 919
Sexton, Addie 898
Seymour, Horatio 886, 906, 918, 920, 925, 934, 935
Sharp, W., Lieut. 843
Shearon, Thomas R. 821
Shell, Lida L. 921
  Rebecca P. 921
  William 921
Shelley, Elizabeth 864
Shelton, George 838
Shepard, Belle 899
  C. R. 899
  L. 899
Sherman, ___ 917
Sherrill, W. B. 812
Shields, James 798
Shilling, Amanda 945
  Jacob 945
Shoffner, E. D. 807
Shoffner, ___ 807
Simmons, George 801
  John 801
Sims, J. G., Mrs. 845
  Jincy Ann 869
  Jordan G. 844
Skelt (Negro) 823
Skelton, James 825
Sloan, James F. 881+
  Minnie 881
  Oliver Cromwell 881
  William 881
Smalley, E. C. 836
  Mary Ann 909
Smallwood, W. P. 821
Smith, Alexander H., M. D. 950
  Cloann 934
  Elizabeth 924
  Joel R. 801, 803(2), 806
  Johanan 814
  John A. 950
  Obediah 822
  Thomas 832(2)
  Thomas, Rev. 846

Smith, Cont.
  William M. 824
  W. P. 853
Smith & Carnal 853
Smithers, A. C., Rev. 828
Snell, Eliza 852
  Roger 852
Synder, W. F., Mrs. 945
Somers, John 806, 824
Soule, Joshua, Bishop 832
Southerland, J. E. &
  Johnson, J. R. 857
Speight, Barney 920+
  Harris Lovelace 921
  John M., Rev. 921
  Willie Wain 921
Spencer, Frederick 952
  James M. 952+
Springer, H. K. 839
Stanford, William 838
Stark, Helen 922
  Homer 922
  James G., Dr. 921+
  Thomas 922
  Thomas C. 921
Stayton, Margaret 942
Steele, John M. 831
  W. A. 836(2), 844(2)
  Sallie 935
Stephens, J. B., Dr. 873
Stewart, Charles 827
  Sandal 901
  William, Maj. 827
Stigall, Henry G. 838
Stockard, John 798, 800, 801, 804, 805
Stockdale, B. F., Mrs. 954
  Christia 949
  Dennis 949
  D. W., Mrs. 947
  Nancy J. 949
Stocks, J. G., Capt, 826
Stoddart, John 814, 818, 821
  Will 804
Stofle, John Thomas 882
  Robert 882
  Robert M. 881+
  Thomas 881
  William 882
Stone, Polly 850, 851
  Susanah 850
Stovall, B. L. 821
Strange, Henry 806, 876
  Lucinda 876
  Mary H. 876
Street, Betty 921
  Howard 921
Strickland, N. T. 838
Sullivan, Nathan 832
Suratt, Charles 834
Swan, E. B. 903
Swanson, John, Mrs. 892
Swar, P. G., Capt. 842(2)
Swearengen, Samuel 822
Sweatt, America Florentine 922
  F. V. 922
  G. H. 922
  J. J. 922+
  Martha T. 922
  Mary 922
  Virtue 922
Sweeney, Bomar 923
  James 922
  John 923
  John C. 825, 828, 922+
  Samuel 923
Swiggart, W. H. 824, 842
Swinney, Joseph 881
  Rebecca 881
  Sarah 881
Swisher, James G. 818, 820

Tarrant, Edward H. 820
  E. H. 825
Tayloe, T. H. 826
Raylor, Artie 953
  Gen. 890
  J. M., M. C. 841
  John M. 821
  Kate L. 923
  N. C., Dr. 923
  S. J. 825
  Stacker J. 923+
  Stacker J., Jr. 923
  Thomas 804
Taylor, ___ 893
Teachout, Alva 883
  Charles 882
  Clara 882
  E. B. 882+
  Frank 882
  Olla 882
  S. M. 882
  Stanley 883
Terrell, Louisa H. 908
Tharp, Jane B. 917
  Thomas, Abner, Rev. 846
  Dorsey 891
  Haywood B. 883+
  Luke 883
  Rufus, Capt. 807
  Samuel T., Rev. 846
Thomason, Andrew M. 924
  Charles H. 924
  James, Mrs. 890
  James R. 924
  Jasper N. 924+
  J. N. 821, 824, 828
  John B. 924
  Richard L. 924
  Sarah E. 924
Thompson, Emily J. 952
  Jeremiah 952+
  Mary R. 896
  Thomas A. 800, 801, 802
  T. M. 825
  W. C. 836
  William 833, 834, 952
  William A. 797
  William H. 896
Thornton, Clementine 919
  DeWitt 919
  Nellie 919
Threadgill, John, Dr. 808
Tilden, S. J. 883, 903, 921, 922
Tiner, J. A. 857
  Mary J. 857
  Mattie J. 857
Tinin, Eliza 894
Todd, Alby 925
  Birtie 925
  James M. 924+
  Jane 870
  Jimmie 925
  Mary 925
  Moses 924
  Moses #2 925
  Virgie 925
  William Grace 925
  Zorena Penelope 925
Tolerson, Nancy 850
Tosh, Jane 858
Totten, Benjamin C. 841, 861/2
  Judge 841
Totton, B. C., Capt. 806
  Benjamin C. 806
  James L. 803
Totty, J. E. 838
  T. B. 838
Townes, Charlie M. 884
  Cora 884
  Eva 884
  H. C. 806
  Henry C. 883+

Townes, Cont.
  Herbert C. 884
  James, Col. 883
  J. F. 806, 807
  Lida 884
  Mary 875
Trainer, Rev. 830
Travis, Charles N. 853
  C. N. 838(3)
  Col. 891
  Edward A., Dr. 925+
  E. M. 839, 953
  Eugene E. 953
  Frank 872
  James V. 953
  J. H., Dr. 910
  J. L. S. 825, 839
  Ludson W. 925
  M. L., Dr. 837
  R. B. 839
  R. B., Dr. 837, 838, 948
  Robert B., M. D. 953+
  S. A. 910
  Silas 953
  Viola F. 953
  W. E. 821(3)
Travis & Crockett 839
Travis & McGee 839
Trevathan, A. G. 894
  Albert G. 925+
  G. H. 827, 926+
  Harry A. 926
  Henry 925
  Jesse 926
  Jessie 894
  Martha F. 894
  Mattie Clyde 926
  M. F. 894
  Miss 894
Trice, Rittie Moore 857
Tucker, Alexander C. 884+
  Emma L. 884
  Joseph 884
  L. M. 884
  Marietta 884
  Minnie Bell 884
  Nancy E. 884
  Percy Alexander 884
  S. E. 811
  S. Y. 884
  William Albert 884
Turner, George 845
  J. L., Mrs. 922
  Louise M. 859
Tyler, Edwin H. 927
  Hattie W. 927
  Horace M. 927
  James A. 927
  John 927
  M. E. 927
  Miles F. 927+
  Reuben 927
  Willie Lee 927
Underwood, C. 821
Upchurch, F. H. 828
  M. D. 917
Ury, Ennis 808
Utley, B. L., Lieut. 842
  Burrell L. 836
  Elizabeth 856
  Green 856
  John W. 836
  Martha J. 856
VanBuren, Martin 895, 929
Vandiver, W. D., Ph.D. 812
VanHorn, George 827, 828
VanHuss, D. H. 836
Veazey, Fielding 928
  Mary Jane 928
  Robert L. 928
  Robert L., Rev. 927+
Venable, Calvin C. 821
Vester, Berry 844

Vickers, Dollie 892
  Martha 892
  William R. 892
Vincent, John A. 832
Vise, Isabel 952
Vondyke, John M. 827
Wade, Isadora 929
  Molinda Alabama 929
  Pleasant A. 929
  Pleasant C. 928+
  Robert A. 928
  Robert J. 929
  Thomas R. 929
Wakeland, Lucy 893
  Milton 893
Walker, Alexander C. 929
  B. H. 894
  Elizabeth 929
  Isabella 908
  James 908, 929
  Jarratt 929
  Jesse 805
  Joe 929
  John S. 929
  Kate 929
  Lola P. 929
  Malinda 908
  Robert J. 929
  V. B. 929+
Wall, Henry 814, 818(2), 821, 822, 823
  H. W. 828
Wallace, L. A. 913
Walters, J. W. 802(2)
Walton, Josiah 901
  Sarah 901
Ward, Howell 805
  R. K. 825
  T. J. 836
  William 822
Warmack, T. J. 839
  W. 839
Warren, John H. 820
  Stephen 804
  W. T. 808
Waterfield, A. P., Dr. 812
Waters, Abraham 814
  Elizabeth 927
  William 814, 817
Watkins, Charles, Maj. 900
  Eliza 900
  Rosalinda A. 878
Watson, David 833
  Joel A. 865
  Mary Ellen 925
  Stewart 925
  William 830
  Z. C., nee Wilson 924
  Zorena 925
Weake, Susan, Mrs. 881
Wear, Parson 812
Webb, Julius 805
  Lovely 950
  Sarah 899
  William 815
Welch, S. H., Mrs. 828
Weldon, A. J., Dr. 914, 930+
  Ida 930
  John D. 930
  Laura 914, 930
  Louisa 931
  Mary 930
  Robley D. 930
  Sallie 931
  Stella 930
  Thomas J. 930
  W. B. 930
  W. E. 940+
  W. E., Mrs. 899
Wheat, Ellen 952
Wheatley, Charles 834
  Charles J., Lieut. 843(2)
  Charles W. 834

Wheatley, Cont.
  J. K., Lieut. 843
  Thomas 834
  William 833
Wheeler, Gen. 887
Wheelis, Elijah 805
White, A. 810
  Abram 804
  A. C. 865
  Elizabeth 897
  Jacob, Dr. 808
  L. B. 810
  Littleberry 802
  Littleton W. 800
  Martha 946
  Mary 945
  Sarah 872
  W. L., Detective 897
Whitfield, F. C. 838
  F. C., Dr. 838
Whitten, Thomas G. 832
Wilburn, Sarah 848
Wilcox, John 925
  Lillie 925
  Margaret 925
Wilder, China 803
Wilder & Dalton 808
Wiley, Jesse 806
  Thomas K. 808
Williams, Benjamin J. 886
  Bertha Mabel 886
  B. T. 885
  E. J., Rev. 846
  Elizabeth J. 885
  Ella Alpine 885
  E. N. 840
  Ephraim 807
  E. R., A. M. 812
  E. W. 802, 885+
  Fitzgerald 931+
  George W. 886
  Isaac B. 824(3), 862, 931
  James 814
  James N. 885
  James T. 818
  J. L., Dr. 837
  John E. 885
  John H. 820, 834, 836(3)
    886
  Judge 888
  J. W., Lieut 842
  J. W., Capt. 843
  L. A. 802
  Lizzie Frances 886
  Lorenzo F. 886+
  Lorenzo P. 886
  Loruza [sic] M. 885
  Marietta 886
  Martha 879
  Mary 952
  Mary P. 855
  Matthew 833, 834
  Nathan 802
  Rowland 885
  Sanford N. 885+
  Sarah A. 885
  Sidney H. 886
  S. M. 808
  Thomas 886
  Thomas H. 886
  Thomas N. 886
  Washington H. 885
  William A. 885
  W. C. 827
Williams & Hudson 828
Williams, Clark & Co. 827
Williamson, Caroline 847
  Mary 847
  Samuel 847
  Willis G. 822
Wilson, A. B. 844
  Alex. 895, 932+
  Alfred Bluford 933

Wilson, Cont.
  A. N., Col. 925
  A. P., Capt. 842
  A. R., Dr. 933
  Cardwell 826
  Cyrus 802
  Elizabeth D. 933
  Ella 932
  Emma I. 932
  Etta 932
  James A. 932
  James P. 803
  J. E. & Son 839
  John R. 932
  J. P. 802, 806
  J. W. 803
  Mary Eliza 933
  Mary S. 932
  Minnie 932
  Nellie 933
  Quitman L. 932
  Robert Howard 933
  Sammie 932
  Sarah 847
  Susan 908
  Thomas 822
  Thomas R., Dr. 932+
  Victoria 871
  William 932
Winfree, John T., Capt. 842
Winfrey, Jack, Capt. 826
  J. T., Capt. 842
  Mary 855
Wingo, J. J., Mrs. 854
Winn, Samuel 811, 821
  John H. 832(2)
Wood, Cordelia 941
  Margaret C. 950
  Peter 810
Woodcock, Alice 902
Woodfin, John 820
Woods, Elijah 844
  Levi 805
  Samuel 804, 805
  William 833
Wormack, Hawkings 804
Worthen, James 821
Worthen & Cardwell 827
Wrather, William B. 983
  William T. 933+
  W. T. 827
Wright, Charles Hanna 888
  C. N., Dr. 934+
  Dr. 934
  Ebenezer, Dr. 887
  Jamie McNeill 888
  Moses H., Col. 887
  Nellie 889
  Pleasant G. 803
  Thomas McNeill 888
  Thornton 889
  William 836
  William Eben 888
  W. M., M. D. 887+
Wright Bros. 827
Wright & Son 827
Wrinkle, Estella D. 934
  Eurah Ann 934
  Iva Josephine 934
  Iverson M. 934+
  Morgan 934
  Ola Jane 934
Wyatt, Elizabeth 936
  Mary 939
  Parlee 954
  William 814, 822
Wyguf, Isaac 842
Wygul, Elbert 942
  Elizabeth 942
  Mary M. 907
Wyly, Carrie C. 954
  Christopher K. 953+
  C. K. 837(3), 838(2)

Wyly, Cont.
  Eva G. 954
  Harris K. 953, 954
  James 834, 836
  Mary 948
  Mary (Barfield) Mrs. 943
  T. K. 837
  T. R. 837
Wynns, Ed., Mrs. 929
  William G. 935+
  William G., Sr. 935
Yarbrough, I. C. 838, 839
Young, Elbert 954
  David E. 954
  Elisha 954
  Flora 954
  Gilbert 920, 954
  John 815, 827
  J. R., Dr. 954+
  Mary Jane 954
  Rebecca 920
  R. H. 940/41
  Sallie 954
  Vibella 954
  Walter 954
  William W. 954
Yowell, H. A. 926
  J. M. 926
  Martha F. 926
Zollicoffer, Felix H., Gen. 828

___, A. J. 839

www.ingramcontent.com/pod-product-compliance
Lightning Source LLC
Chambersburg PA
CBHW020652300426
44112CB00007B/348